willow in a storm

a memoir

james peter taylor & kathleen murphy-taylor

SCARLETTA PRESS
MINNEAPOLIS

SCARLETTA PRESS
10 South Fifth Street, Suite 1105, Minneapolis, MN 55402, U.S.A.

Visit our website at www.scarlettapress.com

Lyrics from "September Song" by Kurt Weill and Maxwell Anderson reprinted with permission from Hal Leonard.

Library of Congress Cataloging-in-Publication Data

Taylor, James Peter, 1925–

 Willow in a storm : a memoir / James Peter Taylor & Kathleen Murphy-Taylor. -- 1st ed.

 p. cm.

 Includes bibliographical references and index.

ISBN 13: 978-0-9765201-5-3
ISBN 10: 0-9765201-5-X (alk. paper)

 1. Taylor, James Peter, 1925– 2. Ex-convicts--United States--Biography. I. Murphy-Taylor, Kathleen. II. Title.

HV9468.T39A3 2007

365'.6092--dc22

 2007029506

Book design by Mighty Media Inc., Minneapolis, MN
Cover: Anders Hanson Interior: Chris Long

First edition

10 9 8 7 6 5 4 3 2 1

Manufactured in the United States of America

contents

Introduction » 1

Prologue: The Myth of Tiresias » 5

1 The Slippery Slope » 9

2 The Getaway » 27

3 Life or Death » 33

4 The Medical Center » 39

5 The Magnificent Obsession » 59

6 Leavenworth » 75

7 Lewisburg » 93

8 Early Angels » 101

9 Seeking Sanity in Hell » 113

10 Warning Signs » 125

11 A Loose Cannon » 143

12 An Unusual Journey to Manhood » 169

13 The 1980s » 181

14 The Last Mile » 203

15 Willow in a Storm » 209

16 Moving On » 221

17 Love Story » 239

18 Reunion » 255

19 A New Self » 263

Epilogue: Termination of Parole » 275

Appendix One: Timeline » 279

Appendix Two: The Confession » 283

Acknowledgments » 313

to the lindberg family

K ENNETH, who lost his life at his prime; his wife who became a widow at such a young age and yet did not call out for revenge; and his children who grew up without a father to guide and support them—all who suffered more than I can know, at my hands. I offer them my most profound apology, my decades in penal confinement, my self-reformation—and this written work. May it answer some of their questions and soothe any troubles of their souls.

introduction

"Hellllp!", his scream slices, like a hot knife through butter, into my deepest sleep. I am instantly awake and in a sitting position.

I wrap my arms around him and speak softly, "It's alright, Jim. You're here with me. You're safe." He is awake now and finds himself gripping my arms. He relaxes, saying, "I'm sorry. Thank you for waking me."

Incidents like this occurred several times a week in 1996 when Jim and I were first married. In the years since, the frequency of his night terrors has decreased as he becomes more confident in the safety of our home and his own security in the world. But it still happens about once a month.

I note that Jim does not have the nightmare of impending death-by-violence when he naps during the daytime, nor even in the hours just before rising. The nightmares only come in the couple of hours after he falls asleep, that period of slumber when we are said to be in touch with the deep subconscious parts of our minds. During the decades Jim was incarcerated, he could not show any vulnerability. It was vital that his fears be stuffed so far down that there would be no possibility of their escape during sleep. Through the years, as he releases his night terrors in our bed, fewer of them remain within him. I anticipate a time when

the only disruptions he causes our sleep are the jerks and grunts produced by dreaming of his own stellar performance in one of the numerous sports he excelled in as a young man.

My relationship with Jim Taylor began in April 1995. In March of that year, I saw the movie *The Shawshank Redemption* and was impressed by its depiction of spirit, creativity, and hope within the darkness of a fortress-prison. That story—originally written by Stephen King—is of a young white man, Andy, wrongfully convicted of murder and serving a life sentence, and his friendship with an older black inmate, Red, also serving life.

A week or two after I saw the movie, I was assigned within my capacity as a social worker to assist a sixty-nine year old man in finding accommodations in Minneapolis. His dossier described him as living in a halfway house, having just been granted parole after spending over forty years in the federal prison system. In addition to this difficulty, he carried disabilities from being the victim of an unprovoked prison assault in 1987 that left his sight seriously impaired, and his hearing and sense of taste ruined. He could only swallow soft foods. I took the case with interest, saying to myself, "I guess I'll be meeting Red," since I imagined that James Taylor would be African-American. He was not. After our first meeting, I began to describe Jim as having the appearance of an aging tennis pro.

Over the next few months I helped Jim find appropriate housing and furnishings. He arrived in Minneapolis without any money, with no friends or family anywhere within a thousand miles, and with no parole plan other than the maximum four-month, basic-expenses-paid stay at the halfway house. His parole officer offered scant assistance, acting more like someone whose job it was to watch Jim fail and then to react.

After Jim encountered several landlords unwilling to take a chance on renting him a place, for obvious reasons, I asked the parole officer what he would recommend if Jim could not find housing by the time his halfway house placement was to end. The officer shrugged and suggested a shelter for the homeless. I increased my efforts, and Jim had a home of his own within the established deadline.

Over those same months, I came to know Jim Taylor as a remarkable man. In a well-worn spiral notebook, he kept track

of his contacts with a multitude of community resources from which he might benefit. He demonstrated consistent good nature and optimism despite frustrations and obstacles. After a while, he told me he wanted more from me than help finding housing; he wanted a personal relationship.

But I am no innocent. The last thing in the world I want is to be duped by a sociopath. On the other hand, in my line of work I have learned that people can change for the better. Further, I take pleasure in helping other people in their journeys to the good. So I checked out everything I could about Jim's story of his life. I explored old newspapers and consulted with people who lived in Minnesota at the time Jim's crime was a hot item in the local press. I talked with others interacting with him in the present. I grilled him to fill in some of the blanks in his story and I challenged small discrepancies.

I concluded that Jim had been honest with me. Although some mysteries remained, I became more comfortable with allowing a friendship. We spent more and more time together. But all along I prayed like crazy. I prayed for wisdom to know the truth, and for the courage to act on it. I ultimately came to know Jim as the kindest, bravest, gentlest, and most generous person I had ever met.

But how had this man I saw before me in 1995 come to commit a bank robbery and homicide forty years earlier, an offense that brought such a lengthy prison term? Why, in spite of glowingly positive prison staff reports to the parole authorities, was he repeatedly denied parole while others who committed far worse crimes were given better deals? How had he been injured so severely? Had he truly not provoked that assault in any way? And how, in the face of ongoing and potentially crushing adversity, had he not only survived but also maintained his humor and intelligence, and flourished into this faith-filled, loving person?

What follows is that story. It is written as he told it to me. Jim wants to share his life as a possible guide to others who face extreme misfortune or challenge. He tells his story so those others might find a way to move beyond their own helplessness and despair, to live in the present with peace, and to look to the future with hope.

Kathleen Murphy-Taylor

the myth of tiresias

IN 1955 I KILLED AN INNOCENT MAN. I had grown up a short-sighted fool, engaged in increasingly risky, immoral, and then criminal behavior, but I was never violent. At an age when maturity should have set in, I vainly aspired to commit the perfect crime. When I walked into the Northern State Bank in Thief River Falls, Minnesota, I intended to rob and then frame the banker. In fact, I carried no weapon. My plans went awry and I killed Kenneth Lindberg, husband and father of four.

I received a life sentence, the punishment I deserved.

At the time, I preferred death.

To be incarcerated for an extremely long time, as I was for over forty years, is to live a life radically different from others. Most men do not survive four decades of incarceration. Many prisoners with long sentences meet their deaths due to a violent altercation in the prison. Or they suffer an illness coupled with poor medical attention, and die prematurely. Some simply lose all hope and die of a broken spirit.

In my later years of confinement, inmates I knew decades earlier, released but now back inside, threw their arms around me. They exclaimed with great surprise that I was still locked up and yet apparently in decent shape. My survival is indeed a miracle for which I daily thank God.

My own peculiar life's journey, amazingly, corresponds to that of a mythological character created by the ancient Greeks. Tiresias, known as the Blind Seer, has endured through the centuries up to the present in all genres of art and literature, as a symbol of wisdom. He evolved into a wise man through two startling life experiences. First, the goddess Hera turned Tiresias into a woman as a punishment for his attack on a female snake, though he was later returned to the male gender after killing a male snake. By being the only creature experienced in living for a time in each gender, he authoritatively settled an argument between Hera and the god Zeus. Tiresias sided with Zeus by affirming that females gain far more pleasure in the sexual act than do males.

Furious that Tiresias divulged this secret, Hera acted again and blinded him. Zeus had sympathy for Tiresias and compensated him by endowing inner sight. The Greeks came to regard Tiresias as a wise man, a visionary who could see the light of truth despite his useless eyes.

I took on the female persona within the penitentiary environment as a strategy to survive. Integrating the female role into my personality placed me in a different physical, mental and emotional space from where I learned much about humanity. Direct confrontation with prison officials or inmates, a typical male approach, is very dangerous. Having at my disposal the acquired feminine skills of circular reasoning, flexibility, subtlety, along with a bit of deviousness, I was at an advantage in tense or risky situations.

As a youth I did not fully appreciate my physical and intellectual capabilities, nor the bit of goodness within my own character. I came to dwell in the darkness of ignorance, immaturity, and finally criminality. Then I was thrust more deeply into imprisonment, and later, literally, blindness. But a light always shone in the darkness and sometimes I chose to embrace it. As the years passed, I chose the light more and more often, thus transforming myself into a better person. I gained inner vision and wisdom, enough to redirect my life into respectability and to secure an eventual release from prison.

I vigorously discourage others from taking the steps that can lead to the horrors of incarceration. The path I stumbled along, devoid of romance or beauty, required me to use all the mental

and spiritual power I possessed as I traveled for over forty years through the depravity of this country's federal penal system. In my particular places of torment, including the penitentiaries at Springfield, Leavenworth, Lewisburg and Atlanta, I encountered the twisted minds and souls, as well as the dead bodies, of other travelers. In the treacherous corridors, I needed to be on constant guard because I never knew what might be skulking around the next corner. It might be another inmate running for his life. It could be a knife aimed at my chest, or a garrote intended for my neck. In my cellblock, a gang of rapists might be setting a trap for its next victim. In my locked cell, a splash of gasoline followed by a thrown match could lead to agonizing incineration. I learned to turn the corners wide, to sit with my back to the wall, and to scrutinize the other diners as we ate, rather than ever relax. I learned to sleep with my head away from the open bars of the cell and to counter the dangers lurking in the shower room. I tried to conduct this perpetual surveillance casually so that no one could detect my apprehension.

This memoir is too late a warning for some people who find themselves in the same places that confined me. Many more will experience some other kind of danger and crisis, as every life encounters challenges, some extreme. Facing a serious threat should leave a person wiser, as lessons always wait within the crisis. Even I learned that eventually. I cannot know all the unique details of another person's situation nor tell others how to live their lives or meet their challenges. Furthermore, my ways may not be effective for everyone. What I can do is share what I did to survive in the hope that others may find little lights of wisdom in my story—some they might use in their own times of trial and suffering.

My process of finding peace with the world and myself involved two serious undertakings, each of which required many years, much emotional turmoil, and relentless perseverance. First, I needed to understand and come to terms with my past, how I became the person who robbed a bank and killed an innocent man. Second, I needed to take that person and forge a new man, worthy of respect. It has been many years since I completed the first project, or virtually all of it. The second is an ongoing endeavor.

the slippery slope

M Y INVOLVEMENT in criminal activity all occurred within a five-year period, from 1950 to 1955, when I was between twenty-five and thirty. At twenty-five, I was an extremely confused and unhappy young man, full of emotion I did not understand. I say this not to disclaim any responsibility for my behavior (which by this point had become very anti-social, but not yet criminal), but to acknowledge that my accumulated life experiences to date had nurtured into young adulthood a person who was neither mature nor governed by reason.

I walked away from my immediate family—my parents and younger sister—in a rage directed at my father. In the process, I lost contact with all of my extended family, whom I loved. I felt deeply frustrated that despite my promising talent, an athletic career had not developed, due to the many injuries I had incurred. I left a trail of women, probably a few children, and many jobs in my wake. I recall feeling extreme resentment that the society of the 1950s expected me to settle down to a career, marry, raise a family, and be satisfied with this.

In the summer of 1950, I was newly married to my second wife, Mary Lou, and selling insurance for a living. I traveled on my job and met another young man whose name I do not recall. This young man knew about a couple of sisters, young women about

our age, whom he suggested we could double date. He described the sisters as party girls, but they lived with their rather strict grandparents who insisted on their return home before midnight. He proposed that we suggest to the sisters that they gain some extended freedom by telling their grandparents that we were FBI agents who needed their assistance in an ongoing investigation in the area. I thought this was a pretty good story, and the sisters agreed to tell their grandparents this tale. So on a few occasions in and around Elizabeth City, North Carolina, the young man and I dated these two young women, keeping them out until the wee hours of the morning.

Unfortunately, the grandparents became suspicious after we brought the sisters home one night much later than agreed. They contacted the FBI office in Raleigh, and the game was up, so to speak. The sisters led the grandparents to believe that they were not in on the scam and had also been deluded by us. The grandparents were extremely angry and urged the authorities to apprehend us. This resulted in my first arrest on September 9, 1950. I was charged with impersonation of an FBI agent, a federal crime, and released on bond the next day, after which I never saw or heard from my co-conspirator again.

Five months later, in February 1951, the matter of the impersonation charge was not yet resolved. I earned a promotion in my work as an insurance salesman, which required a move to Lynchburg, Virginia. That month, my wife Mary Lou gave birth to our child and I went to the hospital to see the newborn. Shown a baby daughter, I suddenly decided to desert. I did not have a good reason to do so.

Because I managed the insurance office, I could leave my work for a short period without much hassle. I contacted Charlotte, a woman I had been dating on the side, and proposed that we take a little vacation to Florida. Charlotte agreed, so we made some quick arrangements and left Lynchburg. While driving through South Carolina, we made the impulsive decision to marry. I was aware, but not concerned, that I committed another criminal offense—bigamy.

Charlotte and I drove on to St. Petersburg and stayed in a cottage on the beach. After only a couple of days, a loud knock awakened us very early on the morning of February 21. I went to the

door and was confronted by local law enforcement officers, acting on behalf of authorities in the State of Virginia. They presented me with a warrant for my arrest on charges that I had written several checks in Virginia without having sufficient funds in my account. I explained that the post-dated checks were issued to people who had agreed to hold them until a later date. I further explained to the Florida authorities that the value of the checks did not total more than about one hundred dollars, and I had several thousand dollars in cash on hand to more than cover this figure. Despite my explanations, I was brought to the St. Petersburg jail and held until Virginia authorities came to transport me. They put me in handcuffs and leg chains, like a hardened criminal, for the trip back to Lynchburg where I was jailed and formally charged.

Even though I immediately made good on all the post-dated checks, the charges were not dropped, and I remained in jail until June, when I was sentenced to over six months in a state prison, plus a $250 fine. All the personal property I had with me in St. Petersburg—my car, jewelry, clothing and cash—disappeared in the course of my arrest, with no explanation from the arresting authorities. At the time of sentencing I thus had no assets to pay the fine. So they ordered me to serve more time, which added months to my sentence, with no credit given for the time I had already served. I was sent to the State Farm of Virginia in Goochland to serve my entire sentence at hard labor.

This served as my introduction to a whole new world, that of penal confinement in the United States in the 1950s. I had not thought much about prison life before that time, since I never figured it would be part of my reality. Goochland then consisted of several old wooden buildings, a couple of which housed the inmates in large dormitories. All prisoners worked either on the institutional farm, in the brickyard, or at some form of institutional maintenance. At harvest time, farm workers were issued machetes for cutting the crops. Armed guards on horseback patrolled the gangs of inmate-workers, and armed trustees assisted the guards by monitoring the perimeter of the fields. On occasion, inmates' tempers flared and the machetes were used to settle disputes before a guard or trustee could stop the violence. I heard, but do not know from my own experience, that if a trustee

shot an escaping inmate, thus disabling or killing him, the trustee was rewarded with an early parole. If so, trustees certainly had incentive to prevent any escapes. Trustees lived and slept in separate quarters for their own protection.

I soon learned that at Goochland non-violent first offenders were incarcerated alongside a few older, hardened felons serving their final years of long, sometimes life, sentences. Most of the older prisoners had served many years in the high-security prison at Richmond and brought their violent, predatory ways with them. Some of these men were considered too dangerous to live in the dormitories, which were virtually unsupervised. These inmates were housed in cells, in the same building with the trustees, but separated. I became one of many sexual victims of these men on the work site. I served this miserable time at Goochland for about nine months, with no visitors from the outside.

On February 26, 1952, I completed my first period of incarceration, only to be immediately handed over to the U.S. Marshals for transportation to Raleigh, North Carolina, for trial on the impersonation charge. An acquaintance suggested that I hire a particular attorney previously employed by the Federal Bureau of Investigation. The idea was that this attorney would be best suited to advise me how to proceed, since he had knowledge about how the Government might regard my action. I still viewed it as nothing more than a prank. My attorney agreed with my perception regarding the lack of severity of the charge, and he advised me to plead "nolo contendere" (no defense). He told me this plea would likely lead to, at most, a sentence of probation.

I took his advice, pled "nolo contendere," and when I heard the judge sentence me to eighteen months in the Federal Reformatory for Men in Petersburg, Virginia, I felt sick. The time I did at Petersburg was certainly less stressful than that at Goochland, but still my anger and frustration grew due to my strong feeling that the severity of the punishment did not match my purported criminal behavior. From the comments of lawyers and authority figures, I intuited that the parents of the many women of whom I had taken advantage were outraged at my treatment of their daughters. Once these families knew of my early crimes, they probably influenced the criminal justice system to impose the harshest sentences possible. Even then I could understand

their feelings, as I knew that I had hurt many people with my behavior.

I felt confused and depressed; I had nothing upon which to build—no family, no friends, no educational or vocational accomplishments, no employment prospects, no financial assets—and now, a prison record. While still in Petersburg, another inmate offered me a "solution" to my problems. He suggested that upon release I could work within an organized crime ring engaged in stealing and transporting cars across state lines. My role would involve no actual theft or driving of the cars. I was simply to ensure that the cars were delivered to the assigned places. I jumped at this opportunity, and made immediate contact with the leaders of the stolen car ring upon my release from Petersburg in April 1953.

I was not on the job very long before things fell apart. Within a couple of months, I realized that law enforcement had knowledge of both the car ring and my involvement. Most of the ring's operations kept me in the southern U.S., so I got away from the heat by fleeing to Michigan. They found me in the little town of East Tawas, by the shores of Lake Huron, on July 31, 1953, and I was charged under the Dyer Act, for feloniously engaging in the transportation of stolen automobiles across state lines. In August I posted bail. When I returned to federal court in Saginaw, Michigan, in April 1954, to my surprise and embarrassment I discovered the prosecutor was a childhood friend, Bill Lambert. He lived in Birmingham, Michigan, for a few years as a boy, and we had played football together on the Quarton School playground. Bill treated me well. I pled guilty, Bill did not argue for the maximum five years, and the judge handed out a sentence of two years, to be served at the U.S. Penitentiary in Terre Haute, Indiana.

Although called a penitentiary, Terre Haute was less confining an environment than what I would later find in the high-security penitentiaries at Leavenworth, Atlanta, and Lewisburg, and less of a jungle than the Goochland State Farm. But still, Terre Haute was no reformatory and it was there that seeds were planted in me to engage in a more serious crime. Yet the records show that many times during my incarceration at Terre Haute, I asked for psychiatric treatment. I even waived a parole hearing and wrote on the waiver form "I should not be released without spiritual and

mental help." I knew that my decisions and my judgments were terribly faulty, and I wanted some relief from the daily mental and emotional pain I experienced. The only response I received from my keepers at Terre Haute was that this facility had no psychiatric personnel. I know now that I could have been transferred to the U.S. Medical Center for Federal Prisoners in Springfield, Missouri, for psychiatric care, if those in charge had initiated such a transfer on my behalf. But this was not offered.

I mostly kept to myself and again thought about my future, which by now seemed even bleaker than when I was in Petersburg. I thought about my father, my anger still roiling, and I considered how I might still impress him. Financial wealth would do it, and would give me great satisfaction if I could flash it in his face. Sometimes I listened to groups of inmates talking about their future plans, which usually involved continuing a life of crime and violence. There were also discussions of "the perfect crime" and what would constitute that. The concept of "the perfect crime" intrigued me and I began to think how I might execute this and impress my father at the same time.

An inmate quite a bit older than me, Ben Bakken, had been a bank examiner in northern Minnesota before entering Terre Haute for embezzlement. He had some thoughts about how a bank might be robbed without violence or a way of tracing the robber. I approached Bakken and asked more questions, telling him that I was very interested in executing "the perfect crime," whereby I would carry no weapon, do no violence and gain substantial funds. He told me he would think further about it. When he contacted me with his fleshed-out plan, he appeared truly excited about the prospect. For him, the discussion had gone from mere theory to the actual possibility that he could obtain the revenge he sought against a particular banker. His plan called for the man to be found responsible for the robbery of his own bank. Bakken's only request, in exchange for the information he would provide that would let me walk off well-compensated, was to receive a couple thousand dollars—and the revenge.

Ben Bakken then told me a story that I wanted to believe. Probably because I rather liked Ben, I was easily influenced into sympathy for his desire for revenge. I have no proof that what he told me was the truth.

Bakken's story began a couple of years previously, when he attended a convention for bankers at which he performed his usual role as the rare bachelor in the group of male officials. Bankers attending the conventions often asked Bakken to line them up with a date as they were away from their homes and families and wanted a little fun in the big city. One of these bankers was Kenneth Lindberg, employed by the Northern State Bank in Thief River Falls, Minnesota. Bakken said that he found a young woman for Lindberg to "recreate" with during his free time away from the convention.

A few months later, the young girl contacted Lindberg to report that she was pregnant as a result of their encounter, and she wanted to know what he would do to help her. Bakken claimed that Lindberg called him in a panic, very afraid that his community, employers and family might learn of his indiscretion, and he pleaded with Bakken for help. At first, Bakken responded that he held no responsibility for a problem that Lindberg had created. But after some thought, Bakken offered a proposal by which both men might benefit. He suggested that, as a bachelor, he could marry the young woman and thereby take "the problem" off Lindberg's hands. But there would be a price. Lindberg would pay Bakken five thousand dollars to initiate the plan, and then another five thousand dollars after the marriage was legalized. Bakken intended to divorce the young woman soon after the child was born.

According to Bakken, Lindberg accepted and gave him the first five thousand dollars. Bakken then married the girl. He returned to Lindberg and asked for the next installment. Lindberg laughed in his face, saying that he had no intention of forking over any more money, and that Bakken would just have to deal with the marriage and divorce without any more compensation from him. Bakken was outraged at the betrayal. After all, he said, he had saved Lindberg's reputation at considerable inconvenience to himself, and to be denied the agreed-on price was a gross insult. Ever since, Bakken had mulled over how he might achieve revenge.

And here I was, willing and able to do Bakken's dirty work for my own benefit. Bakken knew the bankers in northwestern Minnesota very well, and he knew Lindberg. He suggested that Lind-

berg would be vulnerable to a scam that included the likelihood that he would gain further status in his community. This is how the idea came about for me to present myself to Kenneth Lindberg as Herbert F. Johnson, owner of the Johnson Wax Company of Racine, Wisconsin, interested in bringing a Johnson plant to Thief River Falls.

I was released from Terre Haute on October 29, 1955; Ben Bakken was still in custody. By mid-November of that year, I had committed the offenses for which I was later sentenced to ten years, plus ten years, plus life, each to be served consecutively, with a recommendation from the judge that I never again be permitted my freedom outside prison walls. I had killed Kenneth Lindberg, although that had never been my intent. The confession I gave to the FBI in April 1956 is reprinted in full in Appendix Two. It contains some errors of fact that are explained in the footnotes. But here I will set forth what actually occurred as best I can recall, about fifty years later.

Two other Terre Haute inmates, Lloyd Kern and Roy Moore, agreed to participate in the caper at the Thief River Falls bank. Kern and Moore were released from prison before me, but Moore almost immediately eliminated himself by proving unreliable on some task I assigned him. Upon my release, I contacted Lloyd Kern in Louisville, Kentucky, where he lived with his wife, and he indicated a willingness to proceed.

Lloyd and his wife were in bad shape financially, so I sent funds to repair his wife's car for our use. I went to Louisville to complete the final plans with Lloyd. We decided that we would meet at a Chicago hotel, where he would arrive by car. We planned for Lloyd to steal a car in Chicago to use in Thief River Falls. Afterwards we would return the stolen car to Chicago and then escape using his car. Before I headed out of Louisville, I telephoned Lloyd's home to be sure that he was underway as planned, and another man, not Lloyd, answered the phone. I learned that Lloyd had indeed left, but the man who answered was very hostile to my questions and I ascertained that he was the boyfriend Mrs. Kern had enjoyed while Lloyd was in prison.

I arrived in Chicago first, checked in at the hotel and went to bed. I had given Lloyd almost all my money before he left Louisville so that he would be prepared if his car broke down on the

way to Chicago. When he finally arrived at the hotel, I made a fateful mistake. I mentioned in passing that another man had answered the phone when I called his home. Lloyd did not seem in the least surprised or disturbed by this comment, but a very short time later he left our hotel room saying he had to attend to an errand and would return in thirty minutes. It was about eight o'clock in the morning.

I waited for hours and Lloyd did not return. I searched the hotel lobby and parking lot, and then returned to the room to count my money. I calculated how I might proceed without Lloyd, his car or the stolen car. I checked airfares from Chicago to Minneapolis, and charter flights from Minneapolis to Thief River Falls, and discovered that if I purchased those fares I would arrive in Thief River Falls with less than five dollars in my pocket. The original plan called for Lloyd and me to obtain disguises. There was certainly no money for that if I was to buy the airline tickets. I should have realized then that there was little likelihood I could successfully complete the original plan. However, I felt somehow compelled to proceed and to attempt to implement the scheme. I purchased airfare to Minneapolis.

When I arrived, a young lady at a cigar counter in the airport recommended the Nicollet Hotel to me. I went there and registered as Herbert F. Johnson of Racine, Wisconsin. After registering at the Nicollet, I went to the Jolly Miller Bar and Grill, located on the street level of the hotel, where I downed several Scotch and sodas before going to my room. It was Saturday, November 12, about 1 A.M. In my hotel room I again questioned myself. What should I do? Should I continue on? I seriously considered forgetting the whole thing. However, for some reason I could not even begin to understand at the time, I pushed on. I had a bottle of Scotch in my suitcase. I removed it and made myself several more stiff drinks before I went to sleep.

The next morning, I fortified myself again with a couple shots of Scotch. I then went to another hotel, the Leamington, also in downtown Minneapolis but many blocks away from the Nicollet, entered a telephone booth, and made a call to the Northern State Bank in Thief River Falls. I asked for Kenneth Lindberg. I introduced myself as Herbert F. Johnson, president of the Johnson Wax Company of Racine, Wisconsin. I advised Mr. Lindberg

that I planned to arrive by charter plane in Thief River Falls at about 3 P.M. that day, and that I had significant business to transact there. I informed him that my company was seriously considering the construction of a new plant in the Thief River Falls area, and though I realized that my timing might inconvenience him, I would nevertheless greatly appreciate his assistance that afternoon and evening. I would arrive in his town with considerable cash and I asked him if I might be able to deposit this in the bank's vault that afternoon, even though normally the bank would be closed by the time I arrived. I also invited Kenneth Lindberg to have dinner with me that night so that we might discuss the various characteristics of Thief River Falls that might have impact on my company's decision to build the plant there.

Mr. Lindberg was very interested in all that I told him. He replied that he would keep the bank open for me. He said he had planned to attend one of his children's school events with his wife that evening, but he would be glad to make other arrangements with his family so as to accommodate me. Just after hanging up the phone, I realized I had neglected a couple matters in my conversation with Mr. Lindberg. I called him again and this time told him that I needed him to keep everything in the strictest confidence. He assured me that he would. I also asked Lindberg to make a reservation for two rooms at a local hotel, as I said I would be traveling to Thief River Falls with my executive secretary, Miss Hadley.

I left the Leamington Hotel telephone booth and went directly to the Minneapolis airport where I chartered a small plane to fly me the approximately three hundred miles to Thief River Falls. As I flew north, I reflected on what lay ahead. My challenge at this point—with virtually no money, no accomplice, no car, and no weapon—was to persuade Kenneth Lindberg to participate in taking the money from his bank and to also provide me with the means of escape. We would leave town together with the money and travel in some fashion to my Minneapolis hotel room, where I would drug him with the Nembutals I had secured for this purpose. I would then abscond with the money, and he would be found in Minneapolis days later, a suspect in the robbery of his own bank. This was the crucial part of the plan from Ben Bakken's viewpoint, and though Kern and Moore had complicated things by dropping out, that portion of Bakken's plan remained intact.

I arrived at the Thief River Falls airport at approximately 3:15 P.M., went into the airport restaurant, and ordered a sandwich and a cup of coffee. I discovered there were no taxis at the airport, but even if there had been, I did not have the money to pay the fare. By this time I had less than one dollar in my pocket. Fortunately, a man offered to give me a lift into town. I gratefully accepted, and he dropped me off at the hotel he supposed had my reservation. I entered the hotel and said I was Herbert F. Johnson. After checking his roster, the desk clerk indicated he had no reservation in that name, and suggested that I check with the other nearby hotel. I walked to that hotel and found there the reservation for Herbert F. Johnson and Miss Hadley.

I felt exceedingly nervous at this point, and once again almost called the whole thing off. Yet I continued on. I advised the hotel desk clerk that I would return later to register and asked him for directions to the Northern State Bank. Empty suitcases in hand, I walked to the bank and knocked on the front door. A man several years older than me opened it, extended his hand in a friendly manner, and introduced himself as Kenneth Lindberg. I told him I was Herbert Johnson, we shook hands, and I noted the firm grip of a confident man.

We walked into the bank together and I was confronted by further complications. Ben Bakken had all but promised me that if I arrived after-hours as I had arranged with Lindberg, all other employees of the bank would be absent. But first I noted that a janitor was there, sweeping the floors. Then, upon our entering his office, Lindberg called out for Mr. Werstlein, the bank president, to come out of the adjoining office and meet me. I wanted to fall right through the floor—what else could go wrong?

Mr. Werstlein, after some introductions, retreated to his office. I knew I could not chance revealing the true nature of my business to Lindberg while Werstlein and the janitor were in the bank. So for a substantial period of time—for several hours, in fact—I engaged Lindberg in a dialogue about the Johnson Wax Company and its plans in Thief River Falls, Minnesota. I had to improvise quite a bit, as I had not intended to continue the ruse much beyond the first minutes of our meeting. I came up with conversation points about the number of local high school graduates looking for employment each year, promising Lindberg that my company intended to employ as many local people as possible.

I went into great detail about our plan to purchase a large tract of land in the area, and I said that these matters were extremely confidential, as we were only in the preliminary planning stages of this new enterprise. Lindberg, as Bakken predicted, was eager to present Thief River Falls in a most favorable light. Finally, Mr. Werstlein came to Lindberg's office to say he was headed for home unless there was any matter with which he could help us. Lindberg turned to Werstlein, "Go ahead, we're doing fine. There's no need for you to stay."

I did not know if the janitor was still there, so I next engaged Lindberg at length on topics of hunting, fishing, and athletics. During this time, the phone in Lindberg's office rang, and Lindberg again spoke to Mr. Werstlein, assuring an apparently uneasy bank president that everything was all right. We continued to talk while I pondered how I might back out of the whole thing. But instead, I decided to find out whether the janitor was in the bank. I remarked on what a modern-looking bank it was and asked Lindberg for a tour of his operation. Lindberg seemed truly proud of his bank as he guided me through it and explained the various systems and equipment in the place. In the process, I learned that the janitor had left for the evening. Lindberg and I were finally alone.

All this time I hoped that Lindberg would not prematurely press me about the $35,000 I had told him I wanted to deposit. I started to talk again about hunting and fishing, but Lindberg could not be put off any longer, and he asked me whether I wanted to deposit the money. While I danced around this question, an alarm sounded loudly, and Lindberg said he needed to turn it off. He left hurriedly. As I sat there wondering if I was about to be arrested, the alarm ceased and Lindberg returned. He asked again about my deposit. By this point, I fervently wished I could remove myself from the entire situation. As a last desperate ploy to avoid going forward, I asked Lindberg if we could just place the two suitcases containing the supposed money into the bank vault or safe. But he insisted that he needed to count the money first.

The time for hesitation or delay had passed. I said, "Prepare yourself for a shock. Are you aware of what a syndicate is?" Lindberg looked puzzled as he verbally defined what he believed a business syndicate was. Then I looked at him, smiled, and told

him the following: "I am associated with a large criminal syndicate and your bank, at this moment, is in the process of being robbed." Kenneth Lindberg very nearly passed out. I said, "Please stay calm and you won't be hurt as long as you cooperate." Lindberg went white; his jowls trembled. I thought he might have a heart attack right there, but then he asked me if he could get a drink of water. I replied, "Most certainly," and I accompanied him in leaving his office while he got a cup of water and drank it. He seemed to recover somewhat and we returned to his office. It was then about 9:30 or 10:00 P.M.

Lindberg asked me several times why his bank was being robbed. I did not answer these questions, but told him that other members of the syndicate were stationed near his home and that his family would suffer if he did not cooperate fully. He then blurted out, "Well, you might as well get on with it." He also remarked that he had just that day said to his wife what a funny thing it was that the bank had never been robbed.

At this point, I picked up my suitcases and told Mr. Lindberg to take me to the main vault. He replied that the main vault, where the bulk of the bank's money was kept, had been locked when the bank closed, and could not be opened until Monday morning. I have since felt that Lindberg locked the vault when he went to shut off the alarm, or that Mr. Werstlein locked it before he left the bank, as either man may have been suspicious about the true nature of "Herbert F. Johnson's" business.

However, Mr. Lindberg took me to another safe, which he opened and which contained some bills, coins including silver dollars, and travelers' checks. I held first one, then the other, suitcase open, while Lindberg transferred the contents of the safe into them. Lindberg spilled a box of silver as he started trembling again. I asked him if he was sure that he could not open the main vault, as I had in mind paper currency, not all these coins and travelers' checks. He manipulated the dials on the vault, as if trying to open it, but maintained that it was impossible to do so at this time.

Much of what I encountered in the bank up to this point substantially contradicted the detailed information I had received from Ben Bakken. But Lindberg did convince me there was no more money available to me in the bank, so I had no reason to

stay there any longer. Just before we left, I wiped off the areas where I thought my fingerprints might be. As we put on our coats and hats, I told Lindberg that we should put the suitcases into his car and that we would drive together to Minneapolis, where he and his car would be left unharmed. I concocted most of these details about leaving Thief River Falls as the day had progressed, since I had not clearly thought them through before I left Minneapolis earlier in the day. I do not know what I would have done if Lindberg had refused to comply with any of my requests. My only weapon was the false threat I had made that his family's well-being was in jeopardy. No doubt this is why Lindberg gave me no argument. This is also the reason I later wrote a letter to Mrs. Lindberg before my sentencing, to tell her that her husband died a hero, as he did so trying to protect his family and the bank's assets.

We walked out of the bank together, carrying the extremely heavy suitcases that contained about three thousand silver dollars. After loading these into the trunk of Lindberg's car, which was parked at the rear of the bank, I told him I wanted us to walk toward the front of the bank and stand on the sidewalk conversing casually. My thought was this would allow passersby to see Lindberg around the bank at this hour, and he would thus be implicated in the offense. I neglected to consider that these people would also see me and be able to provide authorities with my description. Lindberg did as I asked, and we had a little amiable conversation on the sidewalk in front of the bank, and in fact, several people did walk by and greet him.

We returned to his car, and I opened the passenger door, expecting Lindberg would drive. However, Lindberg asked me to drive, as he said he was too nervous. I agreed, but told him he needed to provide directions, as I was unfamiliar with the highways in northern Minnesota. We drove out of Thief River Falls and proceeded south toward the town of Detroit Lakes. As we drove, Lindberg turned on the car radio to a music station. We began to talk about fishing and hunting again. Lindberg asked me several times during the drive to please leave his car in good condition, at a location he could find it, since he had taken exceptionally good care of it and would hate to see it damaged in any way. His concern about the car seemed misplaced considering his cir-

cumstances, but I assured him that I had no interest in taking or damaging his automobile. I told him that I wanted to get out of Minneapolis as fast as possible, and that he and his car would not be hurt.

Thinking about my intended escape, I began to realize the problem I faced. I did not have suitcases full of paper bills, easy to carry and negotiate, but instead had suitcases far too heavy to carry onto an airplane. I had not resolved this problem in my mind as we approached Detroit Lakes. We needed gas, and Lindberg used his money to pay for it when we stopped at a gas station south of town. As we began to drive south again, Lindberg asked if he could make a telephone call to his wife. He said he would tell her that he was on his way to Minneapolis with Mr. Johnson in order to do necessary business there on Monday, and that he would not return home until later that day. I agreed the call should be made, and decided the quickest way to do that was to return to Detroit Lakes to find a telephone. I turned the car around and Lindberg directed me to the Greystone Hotel.

We went into the hotel, where first we used the lavatory. Then he made the call to his wife while I stood a few feet away. We started to leave, but Lindberg said he needed cigarettes. I told him that I would buy some. I left him sitting in the lobby and went to a counter to make the purchase. He might have attempted a getaway while my back was turned, but he did not. We walked out of the Greystone Hotel together, got back into the car and resumed our travel.

Lindberg smoked nervously. I continued to think about the weight of the silver dollars and how we needed to make good time on the highway in order for me to catch the flight to Detroit. I decided to ditch the silver dollars, preferably in a spot where no one but Lindberg would know where to find them. I asked Lindberg if he knew the area we drove through, and he indicated he was quite familiar with it as he hunted and fished there. I told him I wanted to find a suitable place to dump the bulk of the silver and he said he thought he could help.

As we traveled south on U.S. Highway 10, a snowstorm developed. Shortly thereafter Lindberg called my attention to a narrow asphalt country road to our right, and suggested I turn there. He then directed me to what appeared to be a rough road through a

farmer's field, where he told me to turn left. We entered a grassy, bumpy stretch and I noted some old tire tracks that the heavily falling snow had not yet completely obscured. Lindberg said he had used this road in the past while hunting. He suggested we stop and look for a place to bury the silver.

So, heavily garbed in our winter overcoats and hats, we got out of the car. First, I found a flashlight in the glove compartment. I opened the trunk and Lindberg took a box of silver dollars in each hand. As I recall, each of those boxes contained two hundred coins. I saw a World War II foxhole digger in the trunk. I quickly snatched it up in my free hand. I thought it would be very useful in our effort to conceal the silver under snow or soil.

I closed the trunk door and we proceeded, Lindberg with the two boxes of silver and I with the foxhole digger and flashlight. We soon came to a barbed-wire fence where I held the wires apart so that Lindberg could climb through. Then, without putting the boxes down, Lindberg used his arms to hold the fence wires apart to allow me to get through. We walked down a slight incline toward a thicket of small trees, with me in the lead, shining the flashlight. I learned later that we were in Clear Lake Township and that at the bottom of the slope sat Crescent Lake, which I could not see due to darkness and the snowfall. When we were almost at the bottom of the incline, we agreed we had found no place to bury the silver, and so we reversed our course, working our way back up the incline.

Lindberg led and I shone the flashlight out in front of him. Halfway up the incline we noticed a very narrow path cut into the side of the hill, where we decided to turn left. At first I was in the lead as we walked northward on the path, a deer trail, I believe. After searching for a while I told Lindberg to turn around so we could search in the other direction. Lindberg was ahead of me as I shone the light out ahead. Suddenly my left foot slipped off the outer, downhill side of the slick path, and instinctively, I grabbed the back of his coat to avoid sliding down the slope.

Probably Lindberg thought this was an attack, for instantly he swung around, and with one of the heavy boxes of silver dollars, smashed me on the side of my head and knocked me down the slope. Lindberg would have had ample time to run back to the car, where I had left the key in the ignition, although he may not have

known that. Instead, he came down the slope after me. Against a night sky, I saw the silhouette of his large shape barreling down that slope and I heard the thick underbrush being trampled as he lunged downward toward me. Then commenced a violent struggle, the details of which I remember very little today, except that I believed then, as I believe now, it was life-or-death. Most likely Lindberg also felt this was a fight for his life. He rushed at me with his head lowered and tackled me around the knees. As he made contact with my lower body, I struck him with the foxhole digger in the back of his head. We tumbled further down the slope together and I hit him over and over with the foxhole digger, as he struck me many times with the heavy boxes of silver.

Finally, Lindberg lay on ground, no longer moving. I had fallen close by. I got up and tried to find the flashlight, which had flown out of my grasp when I made the quick grab for Lindberg's coat. I could not find the flashlight in the dark so I dug in my pockets for some matches. I bent over Lindberg and lit several matches to ascertain his condition as he continued to breathe heavily and groan. What I saw in that dim match light—a bloody, dying man— has been imprinted on my mind ever since, and I have occasional nightmares of the scene to this day. My first conscious thought upon viewing the fallen Lindberg was what a horrible thing I had just done. I had never intended to use any form of physical violence, and yet I had just taken the life of Kenneth Lindberg, a man I had come to like as a person, certainly much more than I liked Ben Bakken. I never before, nor have I ever since, felt such immense sorrow.

the getaway

I STOOD OVER THE MAN I had killed. In the next instant, my panicked mind began to make decisions. I tried to find my hat, which had fallen off my head into the darkness. At first I found Lindberg's hat, then searched on my hands and knees for mine. I finally found it, put it on, and then did my best to pick up as many silver dollars as I could find. I climbed back up the slope, maneuvered myself through the barbed wire, and put the coins, along with the foxhole digger, onto some newspapers in the trunk of the car. When I got into Lindberg's car, I drove the next sixty miles south on Highway 10 toward Minneapolis at a hazardous speed.

Because of the emotional distress I did not notice the bruises and lacerations I had incurred in the struggle at Crescent Lake. My thoughts raced as to what I should do next. When I reached the outskirts of Minneapolis, the highway crossed a river that I later learned was the Mississippi. At the far side of the bridge, I stopped the car and waited until there were no other vehicles in sight. Only then did I open the trunk, remove the foxhole digger and the newspapers, and hurl them into the river. Somewhat relieved, but still shaken, I resumed my drive into the city.

I asked someone on the street for directions to the Nicollet Hotel and parked the car about a half-block away. Carrying the suitcase containing the travelers' checks, I walked into the hotel.

I must have been in shock for I cannot recall being even the least bit apprehensive at that moment, though I was bloodied, disheveled, and some of my clothing was torn. I went directly to my room, took a shower, and changed my clothes. I called for room service, and had ice brought to the room so I could try to reduce the swelling on my face and head, as well as make myself several stiff drinks.

After cleaning up and fortifying myself again with Scotch, I walked out of the hotel in the still, early-morning hours, intent on moving Lindberg's car to a location where it would not be quickly found and identified. I drove to a fairly quiet neighborhood not too far from downtown. Later I learned that I had parked about one block from a Minneapolis police station. I removed the automobile registration card and the car keys, which later that day I dropped into a trash receptacle in Chicago. I walked a short distance to an all-night diner where a number of milk deliverymen were having a coffee break. I had coffee and doughnuts before I called a cab and returned to the Nicollet Hotel.

I figured I had to check out of the hotel and pay my bill. My only choice was to use the stolen travelers' checks for payment. I cashed four $50 checks, paid the bill and pocketed the balance. The desk clerk never requested any identification as I signed the name of Herbert F. Johnson. I had no identification whatsoever at this time, much less any specific identification as Mr. Johnson. I took a cab to the Minneapolis airport, flew to Chicago and immediately checked into a hotel there. I went out into the city streets and cashed many more of the travelers' checks at stores and shops while purchasing small items. I returned to the hotel, checked out, not having spent even one overnight there, and cashed more checks in the process. On this same Sunday evening, I boarded a flight to Willow Run Airport near Detroit. At the airport I rented a car and drove to the Detroit home of my boyhood friend, Bill Keller, and stayed with Bill and his wife, Patty, for the next several days. I do not recall when I called Bill to ask if I could stay, but I do not believe I just showed up on his doorstep that Sunday night.

On Monday morning I drove into downtown Detroit and bought a new topcoat. I had cleaned up the coat I had been wearing in order not to attract attention. Now I put it in a shopping

bag and later burned it in a deserted field north of Detroit along with other soiled and torn clothing I had worn on the night of the deadly struggle. I checked into a downtown hotel for the purpose of using some of the travelers' checks there, as well as at the bank across the street. I went there next and told a banker that I wanted to open a new account with a number of the checks. He put me to work countersigning the checks, and reminded me that I would need to provide identification in order to withdraw from the new account.

I told the banker that I had inadvertently left my wallet in the hotel but that I would go get it. Needless to say, I never returned to the bank and so lost all the potential cash related to those numerous checks. I checked out of the hotel in the early afternoon and in the process cashed the remaining travelers' checks. I felt the need to leave Detroit quickly because when I did not go back to the bank as promised, I had probably aroused the banker's suspicion. So I thought I would return the rental car and head out of Michigan right away.

Much to my surprise, as I cleaned out my property from the rental car, I shifted the back seat and discovered a stash of American Express travelers' checks. These had apparently slipped down into the space behind the seat sometime earlier. Every check I had cashed, or attempted to cash thus far, had been a Bank of America check. To celebrate my American Express bonanza, I went directly to the J.L. Hudson department store in downtown Detroit, and purchased some expensive luggage. I also cancelled my plan to leave town quickly, as having found a whole new cache of travelers' checks, I wanted to negotiate them in a familiar city. So I stayed with the Kellers a few more days, during which time I cashed some of the American Express checks, always using phony names and providing no identification.

I began to think about Lloyd Kern and his lack of an explanation when he left me in that Chicago hotel room. I rented another car and drove to Louisville, arriving at Kerns' home in the middle of the night. I awoke Lloyd out of a deep sleep and brought him up to date on what had occurred in Minnesota. I told him how angry his disappearance in Chicago had left me. He admitted he owed me something. We agreed he could now assist me in cashing the remainder of the travelers' checks.

Lloyd and I traveled to a number of states adjacent to Kentucky and we succeeded in cashing many checks with several different scams. In one, I indicated I was an eminent surgeon who had come to that city for the purpose of performing a serious and delicate surgical procedure. Lloyd played the role of the very grateful husband of the woman whom I had miraculously spared from a painful death as a result of my surgical expertise. He greeted me as I attempted to cash the travelers' checks. This ploy always worked. I don't remember if I gave Lloyd any of the proceeds.

For some reason, I wanted Lloyd to drive the rental car back to Detroit while I took a plane. I met Lloyd at the Detroit airport after he returned the car and I saw him off on a flight back to his home in Louisville. I never saw Lloyd Kern again.

On November 18, 1955, soon after Lloyd had left, I met another flight bringing Margaret Richards into Detroit from Joplin, Missouri. I had met this woman weeks earlier in Joplin while there in a fruitless attempt to find some money stashed years earlier in an abandoned mineshaft near that city. A fellow inmate at Terre Haute, an old bank robber serving a very long sentence, had told me I could find and keep this money he supposedly had hidden in the mineshaft. The only condition he set was that I use a small portion of the hidden money to secure an attorney for him in his efforts to be transferred to a federal prison medical facility. I never found the money but I did meet Margaret and her family, who all seemed to like me.

That weekend, Margaret Richards and I stayed at a Detroit hotel, and we spent a lot of time with the Kellers, including attending a University of Michigan football game in Ann Arbor on Saturday. Margaret returned to Joplin on a flight out of Willow Run later on Sunday and she invited me to come to Joplin to visit her again soon.

A number of days later, I flew to Miami with plans to visit my parents in nearby Fort Lauderdale. It was not a typical son-visiting-parents experience. I wanted to fulfill my burning desire to display myself to my father as a well-to-do person. He did not give me the opportunity. I had not seen my parents in at least five years and I do not remember how much they knew about where I had been during that time. I do remember my father as immediately very cold toward me, and I am sure I responded in kind. My mother proved more approachable. She drove me to the storage

facility where my parents had put all my possessions. She made this decision despite the objections of my father, which endeared her to me more than ever. I bought a steamer trunk, packed what I needed in it and had the trunk shipped to Joplin, Missouri. I watched my father lock the house while my mother and I conversed outside. I am sure he did this to show me that he did not want me in his home. Greatly angered, I kissed my mother good-bye, and bid a cool farewell to my father. My attempt to impress him had proven futile. I never saw my parents again.

I returned to Detroit by air and contacted Bill Keller. Again I rented a car, this time a Cadillac. I told Bill I would drive to Joplin and stay there through the Christmas holidays since the Richards family had invited me. He suggested that I drive his brand-new Pontiac while he used the rental Cadillac in my absence. He thought the Pontiac could use some highway driving to break it in, and I would save many miles on the rental car. Plus, he would have the opportunity to drive a Cadillac for a few weeks.

I drove Bill's Pontiac to Joplin and spent a few days in the Richards family home. One night I decided to call Bill and Patty. I talked with Bill, and clearly discerned that something inhibited his natural conversation. I sensed that he wanted to say or ask more, but was unable to do so. I could have fled but I did not. Tired of being a fugitive, I wanted to resolve the situation somehow.

I hung up the phone and prepared for bed in the guest room of the Richards' home. I had purchased a 30.06 semi-automatic rifle and a .22 caliber revolver sometime earlier in order to hunt and target-shoot with the Kellers, who were avid hunters. I took those weapons out of my trunks, assembled and loaded them, then set them within my reach from the bed. I slept like a log, but was awakened in the early-morning hours by a loud crash as federal agents simultaneously smashed through the two bedroom doors. Blazing lights blinded me, and before I could reach for my guns, I heard a voice order me to bring my hands out from under the covers, "Slower! Slower! Slower!" Armed FBI agents filled the room, and more agents, weapons and lights surrounded the house. The date was December 8, 1955.

Only after I was arrested and transported back to Minnesota did I learn for certain what I knew in my heart: that Kenneth Lindberg's body had been found and that I would be held respon-

sible not only for the bank's missing assets, but also for Lindberg's death. In the latter part of November, two young boys, hunting rabbits near Crescent Lake, had stumbled over something they thought was a snow-covered log. On second glance, as the snow fell away, they were shocked to see a man's body. Soon, Kenneth Lindberg was identified and the newspapers screamed that the "missing banker" was now the "slain banker."

CHAPTER THREE

life or death

I WAS HELD IN CUSTODY at the Hennepin County Jail from December 1955 until my sentencing in July 1956. As time elapsed and many procedural court hearings occurred, I began to fully comprehend that my life dangled in serious jeopardy. Would I be sentenced to death, or would I be sentenced to spend the rest of my life in a federal prison? The State of Minnesota had abolished the death penalty in 1911, but mine was a federal offense and the federal law permitted the death penalty if imposed by a jury. The U.S. Attorney prosecuting my case, George MacKinnon, made a supreme effort to persuade the judge to impanel a jury for consideration of the death penalty. My attorneys vigorously fought the prosecution, as they did not want their client to be the first person in decades to be executed in Minnesota.

I was as depressed as a human being could be while these legal maneuverings swirled around me. My earlier experiences of being victimized at Goochland State Farm in Virginia were so horrendous that I could not reconcile myself to a lifetime of similar or even worse punishment in a federal maximum-security prison. Given a choice between the death penalty and a life sentence, I began to prefer death. But the choice of sentence was not mine. I finally decided that I would commit suicide if the Government did not execute me. I shared these thoughts with a fellow inmate

who participated in a work-release program. He left the jail daily to go to his job in the community, and he offered to smuggle some drugs into the jail in sufficient quantity that I could fatally overdose.

I observed during the several times I had been in the presence of my prosecutor that he did not seem to be held in high esteem by his fellow legal professionals. A political appointee, word had it that his skills lay more in administering his office than in actually trying cases. But MacKinnon specifically had chosen to prosecute my case himself, hoping to gain from the attendant publicity that swirled around it. I took an instant dislike to the man, not just because he worked hard to attain my conviction and harsh sentence, but also because of his arrogance. On a day I was scheduled for some procedural hearing, I waited in the jailhouse day room to be brought to court, dressed in a suit and tie. I started to peruse a *Life* magazine and came upon a ridiculous full-page photo of a baboon standing in a puddle of water with one finger up his nose and another finger pointed at his rear.

An idea struck me. I ripped the page from the magazine and found a pencil, then scrawled "George MacKinnon" on the picture of the baboon. I folded the page several times and tucked it under my white shirt near my chest. A while later, the deputies escorted me to the courtroom and I sat at the defendant's table. The attorneys and court personnel engaged in small talk and the judge sat on his bench waiting for the right time for the hearing to formally begin. When I thought the moment was perfect, I put my hand to the knot in my tie and slowly started to loosen it. Then I started with the top button of my shirt and began unbuttoning. Soon one pair of eyes, then another, stopped what they were doing and began to watch me nervously. The court deputies moved in closer, ready to pounce.

With enough buttons unfastened, I moved my right hand ever so slowly inside my shirt, then quickly whipped out the paper and plopped it baboon-side up on the table. Attorneys, court personnel, and even the judge burst into laughter, then quickly stifled themselves. But not MacKinnon. He saw my stunt and the reaction it obtained from his fellow professionals, and his face turned beet red. The hearing proceeded. I felt smug then, embarrassing my prosecutor, but I believe I set him on a course of personal

hatred and vindictiveness that would have a negative impact on me for decades.

In April 1956 I confessed to being responsible for the death of Kenneth Lindberg under Title 18 of the U.S. Criminal Code, Section 2113 (bank robbery and incidental crimes), subsection e: "Whoever, in committing any offense defined in this section, or in avoiding or attempting to avoid apprehension for the commission of such offense, or in freeing himself or attempting to free himself from arrest or confinement for such offense, kills any person, or forces any person to accompany him without the consent of such person, shall be imprisoned not less than ten years, or punished by death if the verdict of the jury shall so direct."

The Court accepted my guilty plea, and sentenced me under the provisions of this statute. Yet all through the years, my official documents stated that I was convicted of murder. I believe that the word "murder" with its implications of premeditation served to keep me confined for much longer than others convicted of similar crimes.

On July 5, 1956, when I received the longer-than-life sentence, I was ready to put my suicide plan into action. My friend on work-release brought into the jail, in the inner lining of his belt, a stash of about fifteen sleeping tablets, "yellow jackets," which I then hid. Just before leaving the jail with the U.S. Marshals for transport to the U.S. Penitentiary at Leavenworth, Kansas, I swallowed all the tablets. I got into the transport vehicle, in handcuffs and ankle shackles, and the trip began. Soon I said, "I guess I'll take a nap," and went soundly to sleep. I do not know how far we drove before the marshals attempted to wake me, but when it happened they were unable to rouse me. They rushed me to the nearest hospital where my stomach was pumped. The trip to Leavenworth resumed immediately, and I recall watching the passing scenery and thinking, "I'll never again see cities and countryside and people freely going about their business." We arrived at Leavenworth the same day we began the trip, July 12. My suicide plan had been thwarted, and I felt angry and disappointed.

My depression centered not only on the idea of spending my whole life in a federal prison, but also on the weight of the crime that I had perpetrated. In my daily thoughts and night-

time dreams, I saw the face of the dying Lindberg and relived the horror of the moment I realized he would die. I became determined to kill myself. Within a few days of my arrival at Leavenworth, I asked another inmate, a trustee as I recall, if he would get me a single-edge razor blade. He agreed, and soon I had the means for suicide again. I was not housed among the regular inmate population, but rather in some form of segregated housing used for new arrivals needing close supervision. The authorities knew I had attempted suicide on my trip to Leavenworth, and no doubt they were charged with keeping a close watch on me. But they never guessed I would be able to get that razor blade.

I observed the routine of the guards monitoring me and ascertained there were intervals of approximately fifteen minutes between their checks. On about the third day at Leavenworth, I cut open the arteries in my left arm and wrist with the razor blade. On the guard's next round he discovered me bleeding profusely, and rushed to perform first aid, thus thwarting my suicide again. Two days later, I was transferred to the U.S. Medical Center for Federal Prisoners in Springfield, Missouri, and placed in a psychiatric section. In Minnesota, my defense attorneys and I attempted for months to convince the Federal Court that my history of traumatic brain injuries and irrational behavior were indicative of a mentally ill person, but our efforts failed. Now, within two weeks of sentencing, the prison authorities themselves diagnosed serious mental problems requiring specialized psychiatric treatment.

I felt satisfied that finally I would be provided treatment that might help. In fact, much of the "treatment" I received at Springfield proved to be punitive and counter-therapeutic. Treatment at first consisted only of the popular new psychiatric medication of the time, Thorazine, which I came to believe was used in my case more for control than for treatment. My hopes for psychiatric assistance quickly evaporated and I reverted to suicidal thoughts. I started anew to plot suicide. At the time, I lived in a single room. I began to study the routines of the guards, especially on their nighttime rounds. I waited for several months until I made another attempt. This time, after a guard checked on me one night, I took a sheet off my bed, tied it to an overhead vent, and hung myself. One might wonder how it feels to hang by the neck. I apologize for being unable to provide much description,

because I retain only some vague recollection that I felt satisfaction at beating the system. But I do know what happened next.

A guard rushed into my room, and cut me down. Other guards were summoned and they placed me in a strip cell. I learned later, from the guard who first rushed in to help me, that after he checked on me that night, he proceeded on his rounds down the hall. When he reached the end of the hall, he experienced an overwhelming feeling of something amiss in the area he had just passed. He decided to return and recheck, and when he looked into my room, he found me hanging. He told me that he had never had a premonition like this before, but when it happened that night, his sense of unease was exceptionally strong.

In the strip cell, I lived naked and alone in a room eight-foot-square, without a toilet, toilet paper, bed or bedding, furniture of any kind, playing cards or reading material. All social interaction ceased. The food tray arrived through a small trapdoor without a word from the server. The floor of a strip cell was unfinished concrete. A red light bulb glowed twenty-four hours a day and I lost all concept of time. No one can stand and do nothing all day and all night, so I would sit and lie on the floor. On this occasion, and during the many subsequent periods I spent in strip cells, I developed sores all over my body that would not heal. I endured months of this form of existence as a result of my attempt to hang myself.

Months later, housed in more normal living quarters, I again felt hopeless to the point of desiring death. This time I took additional precautions so that I would not be discovered until after I died. I obtained a razor blade and several blankets, and then waited until the guard made one of his nighttime checks. After that, I placed a few blankets around my bed on the floor and sliced gaping wounds into my left wrist and arm. I let my arm hang over the side of the bed near the wall and covered all but my head with a blanket. I drifted into unconsciousness. Suddenly, I was shaken into reality by a guard who summoned help, and again I escaped death. This guard, not the same man who prevented my hanging, also told me later that when he reached the end of the hallway after checking on me, he had a powerful inclination to retrace his steps. When he returned to my room, he noted the blankets on the floor, and this change in the scene alerted him. He unlocked

my door, kicked aside the blankets, and the dammed-up blood poured out across the floor.

After stitching me up they sent me back to segregation. With ample time to consider my situation, I concluded that my lack of success in killing myself must mean that I should give up the idea. I decided to live day by day the best way I could. I never attempted suicide again.

the medical center

U NLESS PEOPLE EXPERIENCE the iron bars of incarceration slam shut behind them, they have absolutely no concept of what prison is. Prison staff have some idea, but these people walk out of the place at the end of their workday to be with family and friends, to take vacations, and even to decide to seek other employment. Researchers may study prisons for years and become familiar with their very odor, yet still not truly comprehend. Prisoners alone know what prison really is.

The institutions where I served most of my time were huge facilities, some incarcerating thousands of men. When I entered the federal prison system in the 1950s, about ninety percent of the inmates were Caucasian, as was virtually all of the staff. By the time I left the system in 1995, I estimate that eighty percent of the inmates were people of color, along with at least half the staff members. The racial mix in the inmate population changed, in part, due to a huge increase in drug offenses, which had over the years become federal crimes.

Inmates were segregated by race in their living quarters during my early years of confinement. In the 1950s, the government increasingly applied pressure on the authorities to integrate inmate living quarters. Of course, many inmates and staff resisted.

But the authorities conceived of a brilliant plan. They emptied a dormitory building and put televisions, then a growing commodity, only in that building. They offered that living space to inmates of all races who volunteered, knowing they were choosing integrated living quarters. The plan worked because so many inmates wanted to watch TV. Slowly, through this and similar methods, the entire federal prison system became integrated.

The choices that inmates make about with whom to associate, and to what extent, have enormous and grave consequences. Racial, religious, and sexual-preference groups, in addition to gang affiliations, are prevalent in prison and extreme pressure is often applied to join them. Many prisoners join groups because they expect protection and safety in the company of others. But the groups and gangs are cauldrons of emotion, containing feelings of anger, jealousy, frustration, resentment, anxiety and hate, which are often fanned into white-hot intensity. This happens easily in an environment where there are not enough positive outlets for inmates' attention, and because most inmates are full of rage. Ruthlessly violent actions often explode from these cauldrons, yet paradoxically, gracious attitudes and generous acts also occur.

A novice inmate coming into a major federal prison walks into a jungle he does not initially recognize. He needs to quickly determine the exact nature of his environment and his role therein if he is to survive. For example, a new inmate may be pleased to find a candy bar or tube of shaving cream on his bed. But the minute he accepts such an item for his own use, he is indebted far beyond the real value of the candy or shaving cream. Most likely the "gift" was offered as payment for future sexual favors that he is expected to provide upon demand. Another almost-certainty occurs for any new and young inmate who goes on his first trip to the commissary with notions of indulging in a little pleasure such as snacks or a personal hygiene item. On his way back to his living quarters with his small sack of goodies, one or more armed inmates often confront him. At this point, the novice must make a major decision: to relinquish his purchases, or not. If he chooses the former, he is known immediately as weak, and as a result, from that point on, he will be pressured for favors, usually sexual in nature. If he refuses to give up his commissary items, he may be beaten up or killed on the spot. If he survives, he is still viewed as weak because

he was not able to defend himself from injury. Even if he does not immediately realize the full implications of his choice, every novice loses.

I was incarcerated at the U.S. Medical Center for Federal Prisoners in Springfield, Missouri, for two periods, the first from 1956 to 1968 for my mental condition following the suicide attempts, and the second nineteen years later for rehabilitation for physical disabilities. The Medical Center was organized so that prisoners were initially domiciled in separate units according to their medical needs, regardless of their custody designation. If a prisoner in a unit for physical or psychiatric treatment proved himself to be too unmanageable or dangerous, he was transferred to a more secure unit within Springfield. In general, inmates viewed the Medical Center as a more desirable place to be incarcerated than a high-security facility, because the overall conditions such as food, living quarters, medical care and even safety were better. Many sought to affect their transfer there by any means, even to the extent of maiming themselves. At one time, the authorities decided that all known homosexuals throughout the federal penal system would be incarcerated at the Medical Center. This influenced many hardened criminals to pretend they were homosexual, thus resulting in their transfers to Springfield. Why not put ribbons in your hair and feign a limp wrist if you have 250 years to serve and your living conditions could stand improvement?

When I first arrived at the Medical Center in 1956, I was not the picture of mental health. In fact, I was soon diagnosed as schizophrenic—a diagnosis I questioned. I do believe my history of multiple head injuries, childhood abuse, and unresolved emotional problems left me emotionally disturbed, but I never suffered the breaks of reality that characterize schizophrenia. In Springfield there lived many inmates who outwardly exhibited extremely serious psychiatric problems, far more pronounced than any of mine. My introduction to these individuals came while I sat in an admissions area to wait for assignment to living quarters. There was a Ping-Pong table in the room, and another man began to hit a Ping-Pong ball against a wall, over and over again. Irritated by the sound, I went to the man and asked him if he would like to play a game of table tennis. He agreed, and

we played a couple of games before I was called into the office for my interview. The next day, another inmate told me how fortunate I had been the previous day because a group of inmates had prevented a crazed inmate from killing me. The crazy guy, housed near the admissions unit, had the notion that use of the Ping-Pong table was his to dictate. When I played Ping-Pong, I encroached on his turf, and he fully intended to kill me for it. I profusely thanked my new prison mates, and became extremely vigilant when in his vicinity.

While placed in segregation, as I repeatedly was for "treatment," I often witnessed the abuse of a mentally ill inmate locked up in a room across from mine. He had acquired the nickname "Pennies" because he could not bear to hear that word. While I watched from a little window in my strip cell, some of the guards assigned to the unit brought guards from other units to Pennies' door in the evenings, after the medical staff had left for the day. The guards called out the word "pennies" over and over, and the poor sonofagun inside his strip cell would go wild, frothing at the mouth and trying to climb the walls. The guards found this hilarious. Pennies provided a freak show for those guards who were supposedly trained to work with psychiatric patients. I often wondered who really were the sickest human beings, the kept or the keepers. I asked medical staff and others about Pennies, and learned that he was a highly educated person who conversed with full rationality about any subject unless the word "pennies" came into the discussion. I greatly doubt that Pennies received adequate treatment at the Medical Center, so I hope that somehow he later found himself in a true treatment facility.

Leroy was another fellow inmate-patient who could have acquired a nickname for all the weird manifestations of his mental illness, but I do not think that ever happened. When Leroy had the opportunity to go out in the yard, he invariably gathered feathers deposited by the flocks of pigeons that also frequented the yard. Leroy liked to put these feathers in his nappy hair where they would remain until a staff member insisted on their removal.

There was a recreation yard for 10-South, less than half the size of a football field, the perimeter formed by walls of buildings and fences. If a 10-South inmate was a "good boy," the staff allotted him an hour in the yard five days a week. The yard contained

an oval-shaped sidewalk on which the men usually walked. Inside the oval, some inmates played catch with a football or softball. Inmates from other units sometimes threw knives into the yard from their second-story windows in the surrounding buildings, so 10-South inmates had frequent access to weapons in the yard. Usually only one guard supervised the yard, and violence occurred with some regularity. Because a solitary guard could not control a group of violent inmates, he usually waited until the violence subsided, then blew a whistle to indicate the end of the yard-period for the day. At that point, other guards were called in to help, and they retrieved the wounded or the dead and tried to locate the weapons involved. Despite my fear of becoming a victim in the yard, I did use my allocated time there because it was an opportunity to breathe fresh air and to socialize.

One day in the 10-South yard, I sat on the end of a little bench, in the shade of a big tree, engrossed in my own Thorazine-induced thoughts. Though in a stupor, I knew that someone took a seat at the other end of the bench. I continued to stare out in front of me. Then the sound of something hitting the sidewalk caught my attention. Into my field of vision from the far left crawled a large iridescent beetle. I watched as the beautiful bug ever so slowly made its way advancing in front of me and to my right. Suddenly, I saw a long, black human arm reach out and snatch the beetle. Hearing a crunching noise, I slowly turned my head and saw Leroy, feathers in his hair, chewing and smiling as if he had in his mouth a fine culinary delicacy. A strong feeling of revulsion catapulted me out of my stupor.

Another day, in a special treatment area taking a hot tub bath, one of the techniques of the time, I looked out of my tub to view my surroundings. There, nearby, I saw Leroy bedecked with his usual pigeon feathers, in his own hot tub, again chewing and smiling. I wondered what he could be eating, apparently happy as a bug in a tub. I eventually discerned that he had defecated into the hot water and was eating his excrement. I could not believe my eyes and was only too happy to complete my treatment and be brought back to my own secluded room. Life in these surroundings frequently resembled a nightmare, and I continue to be aghast when I remember poor Leroy who ate live beetles and his own feces.

More than once, authorities threw me into an end-of-the-

line unit for dealing with psychiatric patients who presented serious behavior-management problems. Though isolated in our individual rooms most of the time, occasionally a group of patient-inmates was granted time to socialize. One such occasion occurred on a Thanksgiving Day, and those of us who gathered eagerly awaited the annual Detroit Lions vs. Green Bay Packers football game on TV. We settled into the huge, solid oak chairs and began to watch the game, like any group of typical American men. After the action and the tempo of the game increased, the receiver snatched a long pass out of the air and started to run toward the goal line. Suddenly a patient jumped up and switched the TV channel to "Wally Gator," a cartoon show featuring alligator characters.

Immediately, another inmate turned the TV channel back to the game, while shoving the original channel-switcher in the chest and warning him, "Leave this TV alone." Before this inmate-enforcer got back to his chair, the Wally Gator fan again switched the channel to his cartoon. The enraged enforcer stood up, turned the channel back to the game, and this time, more forcibly, yanked the cartoon fan away and yelled into his face, "I've told you once already, don't mess around with this TV." The enforcer then settled down to watch the game. The other guy flipped channels once more, and again, we found ourselves gazing at Wally Gator. Whereupon the enforcer leapt up, grabbed one of the oak chairs, which must have weighed a hundred pounds, brought it up over his own head and smashed it down on the head of the Wally Gator fan, killing him instantly.

The rest of us retreated into our rooms and I never saw the killer again. I was stunned that someone had died for a cartoon and someone else had killed for Green Bay football. I wondered if anyone ever considered putting the epitaph "I died for Wally Gator" on the victim's tombstone.

Also at Springfield, a fellow inmate, Uckle, worked a long time in the strip cell adjoining mine with a mainspring from a wristwatch, managing to cut through the bars. He asked me to join him, which involved some plan for me to cut the bars in my window. I declined the suggestion. As I heard it later, Uckle made it over the fence undetected, and went to a nearby airport, intending to steal a plane. Bright but eccentric, Uckle then realized he did not want to leave the Medical Center without saying good-bye

to his friends. He came back, scaled the fence again, and was shot in the knee by a guard as he stood outside the window of a strip cell bidding farewell to a friend. As long as I knew him afterwards, Uckle walked with a slight limp.

Don was one of the first inmates with whom I became friendly when I got a job in the prison's accounting office. Don already worked there and my desk sat behind his. A light-skinned African-American, Don came from Washington, D.C., where he had attended Howard University. We talked about our comparative histories playing college sports. He had been involved primarily in track. I found Don to be intelligent and very personable. If he suffered from mental illness, he hid it well. But I believe he certainly must have been mentally ill at the time of his crime.

Don may have told me that he killed his lover, but I only heard some of the more graphic details of the crime from the gossip of other inmates who came from D.C. According to these reports, Don came to the attention of others, including law enforcement, when he smelled extremely foul. Police discovered that he carried in his pockets decaying body parts of a woman, specifically the genitalia. From this horrible discovery, Don was convicted of killing his girlfriend, and appropriately, sent to the U.S. Medical Center for Federal Prisoners. After learning this, I had a hard time not thinking about it when Don and I interacted. But I did not want to let this knowledge preclude our friendship because the Don I knew was a pleasant person, and one with whom I enjoyed sharing work and free time.

Across from my room in 3-2-WEST lived a strange fellow. The doors of our rooms lined up directly so I could not help seeing his morning routine. Every day he took out of his locker a centerfold picture from a girlie magazine, unfolded it carefully, and placed it gently on his bed. Then, as he muttered something I could not hear, he stroked the picture of the scantily clad woman. After peeping out of his room and looking in both directions, he would cautiously tiptoe down the hall. When he reached an intersection he would check again in both directions. If the halls remained empty, he proceeded down the hall to an elevator. I could hear the elevator ascend and stop at our floor, and then the sounds of the elevator door opening and closing, which might lead one to assume that the man had left our floor. But, no, this fellow would sneak back to our hallway and start checking all over again. I feel

certain that all this secretive behavior was to "protect his woman." Anyone who entered the room to look at the centerfold likely would have been strangled or beaten to death.

Another man, whose name I should remember but do not, regularly participated in the evening bull sessions that often took place in my three-man room. On the outside, he was a musician, a cornet player with a well-known big band of the time. His instrument was not allowed in the Medical Center, but the authorities did permit him to wear the cornet mouthpiece on a cord around his neck as a symbol of his musicianship.

One summer evening, several of us gathered in my room while it grew dark outdoors and in the room. The hallway lights remained on. Six or eight of us lounged on the three beds and the few chairs, just chatting. Although I had previously decided not to commit suicide, in view of my dismal existence the idea periodically returned to me. This was one of those periods, and for some time I had been saving the liquid phenobarbital prescribed to help me sleep. I would put the liquid in my mouth at medication times, pretend to swallow, wave at the staff dispensing the medications, and proceed to my room to spit the sedative into a bottle. In this fashion, I collected quite a large amount. The cornet player somehow knew about my bottle, because that evening in the darkened room where we gathered, he asked me if I would give him a shot of my phenobarbital. Without much thought other than a willingness to share, I reached into my locker and handed him the bottle, figuring he would take a swig and return it. Meanwhile, I continued my conversation with the others, never looking back at the cornet player. Then, one of our group members directed a question to him and received no answer. Someone gave the cornet player a little shove, to wake him up, but he did not. Someone else tried harder, and still he was unresponsive. "The man's really out—call a guard." At that point, we snapped on the overhead light and I saw my empty bottle. Though I must have realized what the empty bottle meant, I poked the man with increasing force. Another man slapped his cheeks. His body rolled back and forth limply and we all realized that the cornet player was dead. I felt sick. I never considered that he would try to harm himself and I felt guilty for inadvertently providing the means for his suicide. I experienced particular regret because I regarded this man as a fine person and a friend.

Conditions within any prison are highly variable, depending upon which administrators are in charge at the time. In my early days at the Medical Center, a psychiatrist served as the warden, and medical personnel held authority over the custodial forces. While I remained an inmate at the Medical Center over that period of twelve years, there was palpable tension in the power struggle between the two disciplines since the custodial authorities had lost their previous dominance and wanted it back. Prisoners often got caught in the middle of the power struggle. When I returned to the Medical Center in 1987 after a nineteen-year absence, the custodial forces ruled.

For the first several of my years at the Medical Center, the warden strictly enforced a "no touching" rule. This was one of the hardest rules to remember and observe, especially in athletic situations when slapping a fellow player's back or hands to commend his performance is commonplace in mainstream culture. Also, because touching is such a basic need of humans, the yearning for it never left me. Perhaps the prison officials came to appreciate this basic need because the rule did relax considerably, but then was partially reinstated when problematic homosexual activity occurred.

There are philosophical differences among wardens, which lead to variations in policy and procedure among institutions. A prime example of this, from my experience, is the way staff dealt with homosexual activity among inmates. I did not consider myself homosexual, but was nonetheless engaging in sexual activity with other inmates. Sometimes, all such activity was forbidden, and when it occurred and was discovered, punishment came severely and swiftly. Other times, staff tried to turn their heads the other way. Once a warden at Springfield decided there would be more harmony and order in the institution if homosexual activity was permitted by policy. The warden told the inmate population he would allow overt homosexual relationships on the condition that the intended couple inform him which person dominated. The warden then allowed the couple to share a private room as long as the dominant partner fulfilled the expectation that no problems related to the relationship occurred. If a problem arose, usually because of infidelity, the partner designated as dominant was held responsible. This policy required a cooperative captain of the institution, and for a while, this went smoothly.

But the policy ended when either a new warden or a new captain did not approve of the license given to homosexuals.

Whether homosexuals were acknowledged as couples or not, they lived within the general population. But there came a time when the authorities decided things had gotten out of hand. Basketball games were sometimes scheduled between inmates and groups from the communities in the area. A few community people attended these games, but mostly the audience consisted of inmates. One basketball season, the authorities agreed that an inmate band could play at halftime. The first occasion of this innovation left the inmates in a jubilant mood. A few of the homosexual inmates, brave men or fools, decided to dance with each other on the basketball floor. Other inmates appeared amused and the few staff supervising did nothing but observe, probably not knowing what they should do. At the next game, more inmates danced with each other, and the number of dancers increased from game to game. Then, some guys, effeminate yet aggressive types, took it beyond bounds. They went into the bleachers and dragged community men onto the dance floor. The outsiders looked obviously uncomfortable, uncertain how to react. The officials knew what to do this time—they ruled that there would be no more dancing at halftime and they decided to make a major change in homosexuals' housing. All the known homosexuals in the facility found themselves transferred into one living area, 10-North. The band played on at halftime, but henceforth, the new 10-North residents were escorted as a group to the gymnasium, where they sat in a balcony under close supervision.

Many homosexuals were not happy in the segregated unit. I have thought about what is fair for both heterosexual and homosexual inmates, but I can offer no satisfactory answers. Allowing homosexuals the freedom to express themselves sexually with their partners may relieve tensions for those inmates, but then results in feelings of jealousy and perceptions of unfairness within the heterosexual population. However, to contain the expression of homosexuality in an environment where homosexuals live in such close contact with their preferred potential sexual partners is impossible. And for inmates of any persuasion to contain all expression of sexuality is unlikely, at best, especially if they are serving long sentences, or have no significant loving partner on the outside who remains in close contact. Every option I can

think of for managing this issue is fraught with grave difficulties and injustices.

A white inmate, Steve, who looked every bit the part of a young professional football player, hooked up with John, a light-skinned black man slight of stature and effeminate in demeanor. Everyone, even staff, knew that Steve and John not only had an intimate relationship, but a partnership in an enormous amount of wheeling and dealing within the prison setting. They were involved with drugs and other contraband, so they served as the "go-to guys" for many whites and blacks. They involved themselves in many arts-and-crafts programs at the Medical Center, and they found ways to ship their own and others' projects outside for very profitable compensation. They lived the high life as much as is possible in such surroundings.

I knew these guys at first by reputation, and later became better acquainted with them when I frequented the craft shop. I came to fully appreciate Steve on an occasion when most of the inmates were placed in lock-up during a disturbance and both of us found ourselves in a security cell meant for about four men, but crammed with close to ten. I looked around at my companions and noted that Steve and I were the only whites among a large group of blacks. Soon I overheard a few of the black men plotting to rape me. Steve also heard these rumblings. He immediately said that he considered their intent to be cowardly and they would need to whip us both because he would stand beside me. Although outnumbered, Steve's assertion added considerable weight to our side, so much so that the would-be rapists thought better of their plan.

The fact that white Steve had a black "old lady," or shemale, was unusual in the prison system, where most mixed-race homosexual partnerships fell along the lines of black man/white sissy. Steve often defended John, as he had me, and though John was small, he used a knife or other weapon to defend Steve when the situation required. Such an occasion occurred at the Atlanta penitentiary where I lived for a few months in 1978, and discovered that Steve and John were incarcerated there at the time as well. Since I rarely watched movies or television in a group of prisoners because of the risks of violence in such a setting, I did not witness this incident but only heard about it. Steve and John watched TV wearing the necessary headphones for sound. Someone with a

grievance against Steve came up behind them, lifted a heavy oak chair, and brought it down on Steve's head and shoulders. Steve fell to the floor, gravely injured. The assailant attempted to continue beating Steve with the chair, but could not because John picked up another oak chair and warded off the assailant until others rallied to protect Steve and custodial officers arrived.

As a result of this incident the authorities decided it was time to split up the Steve-John partnership. One of them, probably John since Steve required extensive medical care after the assault, was transferred to another penitentiary. The transfer happened not only because of this incident, I surmise, but also because Steve and John had continued to deal extensively in contraband of all sorts throughout their years together, including during the time they were at Atlanta. Some of the property they dealt in came from inmates dead or suddenly transferred, because Steve and John made a point of scavenging the possessions of incapacitated or absent inmates before custodial officers could clear out a room properly. Such was the source of a very high-quality tennis racket that Steve gave me at Atlanta. Steve knew I played tennis regularly and he apparently did not want or need the racket himself when it came into his possession. Using the racket made me nervous, however, because I did not know who else might have known that it came from a dead man's estate.

I first met Robert Stroud, the so-called Birdman of Alcatraz, at the Medical Center sometime in the early 1960s. I came to know Birdman through our common practice of spending many hours each day in the prison library. We talked, and I soon realized that every conversation gravitated, not through my contribution, toward a discussion of birds. I knew Stroud had acquired the Birdman nickname because he developed a passionate interest in birds while confined at Alcatraz Island Federal Prison in San Francisco Bay. But I did not know that he had written at least one book on the subjects of bird life and bird diseases. My first impression was that of a very strange, if not mentally ill, man, as evidenced by his fixation on birds. I did not want to spend much time with him because I felt we had little in common. The only connection Birdman and I did have was our extremely long sentences that left us with little hope of ever again returning to outside society. Life

sentences in the federal prison system during those times tended to create a certain bond among those serving them.

Alcatraz was once regarded as the most secure of the maximum-security penitentiaries of the Federal Bureau of Prisons. Stroud was transferred to Alcatraz after he killed a guard at the U.S. Penitentiary at Leavenworth, the prison he landed in after he was sentenced for a manslaughter he committed in Alaska. While at Leavenworth, the story goes, Stroud was in the mess hall one day and a guard called him a "jailhouse punk" within hearing range of other inmates. To be called such a name in that setting is an insult needing response because the term "punk" meant "male whore." A "punk" in that sense was bait for the many sexually aggressive prisoners. Stroud reacted instantly, and in a rage, killed the offending guard. Almost as quickly the judge issued a life sentence to be served completely, incredibly, in solitary confinement. Alcatraz was the place for such punishment.

Stroud lived in solitary for many years, enough time to drive anyone crazy. During those dreary decades of solitary confinement, without any form of human companionship, he first acquired his interest in birds when a wounded bird flew into his cell. The interest in the one bird grew into an avid interest in all bird life. Famously, Robert Stroud became a cause célèbre, and a movie was made about his life, with Burt Lancaster playing the title character.

In the early 1960s, the Bureau of Prisons deemed Alcatraz Island Penitentiary too expensive to maintain and that it should be closed. This old facility required all prisoners, staff and supplies be transported to and from the island by boat. Alcatraz already had a low inmate population when the decision to close it came. Most Alcatraz inmates were sent to other high-security prisons in the system, but a few, including Birdman, were transferred to the Medical Center due to their physical or mental disorders, or the frailties of age.

I attributed the obvious mental problems of Birdman to the extraordinarily long time he had spent in solitary. He also suffered from a skin condition, which left large scaly patches on his arms and head. He was fairly elderly when I met him, but he was certainly not feeble. I learned Birdman had a heart condition that required him to carry nitroglycerine in his pocket in case of imme-

diate need. Despite the previous court order that he remain in solitary confinement for life, the Medical Center authorities soon decided to place him on an open medical ward. Stroud could now mingle with all other non-segregated inmates and move about within the institution as he pleased.

It is my belief that such freedom suddenly thrust upon Birdman was more than he could handle. After so many years in isolation he did not know how to socialize successfully with other human beings, as I first experienced during our awkward conversational encounters in the library. Soon Birdman threatened other patient-inmates with a knife, demanding sexual acts. One can only imagine his desperation. Birdman's first victims were primarily unsophisticated young men—easy prey—and initially Birdman experienced no serious repercussions.

Birdman's family, plus a woman who worked with him on his avicultural interests, a great number of movie stars, politicians and penal reform groups whose advocacy was inspired by the movie, made great efforts to gain his release from prison. While these efforts continued in earnest on the outside, Birdman laid the seeds for his downfall on the inside.

Birdman's sexual aggressiveness increased and his behavior escalated to a new level of provocation. He began to approach the warden of the Medical Center when the warden escorted tour groups of prominent people around the complex. On these occasions, Birdman loudly proclaimed, "Warden, I'm not a homosexual, but you are. In fact, you're known by everyone here as a promiscuous fag!" Birdman turned up in the hallways and tunnels of the institution, confronting the warden, frequently enough that a decision was finally made that he needed to be locked up every time the warden led a tour.

About this same time, Birdman sexually assaulted at knifepoint another young inmate, but this time he picked the wrong victim. The young man happened to be from a prestigious family and they created waves of public protest. This resulted in an abrupt decision by the authorities to further restrict Birdman's freedom within the institution, although they still did not place him in solitary confinement. A more far-reaching result of all this sexual aggressiveness and his other inappropriate behavior was that many of his advocates became disillusioned and faded away.

Birdman's behavior also did not endear him to the staff members of the Medical Center. He lived then in 8 Building, and my friends there occasionally passed along Birdman stories. One day I heard a distressing tale. Birdman fell to the floor in his building, in full view of some staff members. His nitroglycerine pills rolled out of his shirt pocket, just out of his reach. He knew he was having a heart attack and needed the nitroglycerine. According to what I was told, as he groped vainly for the pills, the officers stood by—legs spread, arms crossed—merely observing. Those officers were fully trained in the emergency medical procedures that this situation required. But they did not move to help this unlikable man in distress, and Birdman died right there on the floor. The year was 1963.

The famous rock-and-roll musician, Chuck Berry, also served time at the Medical Center. I never detected any physical or mental disorders in Berry, nor did he need the protection of the Medical Center due to any frailty. Nonetheless, he was there, along with other famous people who seemed perfectly healthy. I guess the authorities wanted to offer a degree of protection to their more-famous inmates and so did not always send them to penitentiaries. I know that Chuck had been convicted of trafficking young women across state borders.

Unlike my friend the cornet player, Chuck was allowed a guitar. He spent the majority of the day with his music, often positioning himself in the yard, just outside my room. My Saturday and Sunday morning attempts to sleep a little later than usual were frequently thwarted by the thumping of Berry's guitar. But I liked Chuck. He was a sociable fellow, always willing to play and sing with other aspiring musicians. Chuck liked to compose on the spot, and seemed never to repeat a song in the same day. Highly risqué lyrics peppered his songs.

"The Madman of Biscayne Bay" was the nickname of Huntley Dean. Huntley, who had been a professor at the University of Miami, loved to challenge the elements by jumping into his small sailboat and heading out into Miami's Biscayne Bay every time a hurricane brewed, just at the time everyone else headed for shore.

I got to know Huntley when he was sent to 2-1-EAST, one of

the worst places at the Medical Center. In this unit federal prisoners served as guinea pigs to learn how large dosages of the antipsychotic medications Thorazine, Stelazine and Prolixin affected them. Despite both of us being heavily sedated during that time, I still got to know Huntley Dean socially and I liked him immensely. He was intelligent, had a great sense of humor, and told a good story.

Huntley told us that he inherited a substantial sum of money and decided to have the time of his life. He took a leave from his professorship and bought an ocean-going yacht. He packed up his wife and children, and away they went, around the world.

With most of his funds exhausted, Huntley resisted a return to life as usual. So when he came back to Miami, he simply went out and cashed a half-million dollars of worthless checks. Then he quickly scooped up his family and they took off again in his boat. This time the trip proved disastrous. A storm came up off the coast of some South American country and the boat smashed onto a reef and was demolished. With great effort Huntley managed to deliver himself and his family to the perceived safety of a small island just beyond the reef.

Unfortunately, they landed on an island-retreat of one of the Latin American dictators of that time, a secret place where the dictator could withdraw from the stress of ruling or from revolutionaries intent on killing him. The dictator's guards arrested Huntley and his family, sent his wife and children back to the United States, but kept Huntley in a dungeon-like cell. The cell walls were made of huge coral rocks and water dripped between the rocks continually. The coral reef inflicted many cuts and bruises on Huntley, and these became infected. He also lost a couple of fingers and toes and these areas did not heal well in the dungeon environment.

Finally, Huntley devised a plan. There were other prisoners on the island, close to but separate from him in the dungeon. He communicated with these guys by tapping Morse code on the walls. He learned that one of the prisoners was near release. He asked this guy to contact the FBI and tell them his exact location so he might be brought back to the United States as a fugitive before he died. The plan worked. The FBI retrieved Huntley and then convicted him of passing the worthless checks. He was sent to the U.S. Medical Center to receive mental health treatment.

He, too, became an experimental subject, placed on mega-doses of tranquilizers. One day Huntley and I sat at the same table for a meal and we were each given a small serving of ice cream, a rare treat. Before I could savor my little cup of ice cream, I became very dizzy. I thought, "I'm going to pass out." I wanted to get to my room. I grabbed my ice cream, rose from the table, but stumbled and collapsed before I could exit the mess hall. The last thing I remember seeing was Huntley rushing toward me and I thought, "Good old Huntley," as I passed out.

I woke up later that day in my own bed and there was Huntley sitting at my bedside. I said, "You know, that was really decent of you to try to help me in the mess hall." Huntley laughed and said, "Jim, I wasn't coming to help you, I was coming to get your ice cream before someone else could grab it!" And that was the truth.

In federal prisons, delivery of healthcare is unpredictable—the importance authorities attach to offering high-quality care to inmates is not necessarily related to the custody level of inmates, i.e., the less troublesome inmates do not always receive better medical care. And yet, when the health care provided is really inferior, this may very well impact the mood of the penal population and be the cause of considerable unrest, and even rebellion. I experienced a range of quality of medical care in the prisons. Occasionally I received high-quality care, especially when I had permission to see a practitioner in the community. More often than not, medical personnel inside the prisons were not well educated nor positively inclined toward meeting inmates' medical needs. The system included relatively few M.D.s, some osteopaths and physician-assistants, and nurses of various levels—but taken all together, there were never enough medical personnel to meet the often-serious medical needs of the inmates. Many of the doctors had trained in foreign medical schools and likely could not qualify for state licenses to practice elsewhere.

Particularly at the Medical Center, but also in some of the other facilities, many of my fellow inmates were ordinary con men and ne'er-do-wells, but some came from the ranks of attorneys, bankers, sheriffs, and senators. One in particular I remember from Springfield was General Vaughn, presumably of the U.S. Army. The General was one of many people during that era

convicted of "five-percenting." This crime involved kickbacks received by a person, usually a government employee, who made decisions regarding the award of government contracts. Millions of dollars cycled through and kickbacks could be significant. The sentences received by these people convicted of five-percenting tended towards the lenient.

In one of my periods of confinement at the U.S. Penitentiary at Terre Haute, Indiana, the Assistant Postmaster General of the United States served a sentence. Later, at one of the Federal Correctional Institutions, there was a judge housed next to me on one side, and a sheriff on the other. Obviously, these officials were, by then, former officials.

While I remained an inmate at the Medical Center, sometime before they transferred me to Leavenworth in 1968, the infamous organized-crime figure, Mickey Cohen, was brought in from the U.S. Penitentiary in Atlanta, Georgia. Mickey sorely needed the facilities of the Medical Center since he had been brutally assaulted by another inmate at Atlanta. His shaved head resembled a sewn-together patchwork of skin and it soon became clear to anyone who interacted with him that he no longer possessed his full mental capacity.

Despite being a man of only diminutive physical stature, Mickey Cohen became a figure in the California underworld through his bookmaking operations. He was convicted of income tax evasion and sent to Atlanta on a ten-year sentence. The story goes that Mickey Cohen replicated in prison some of the luxuries to which he was accustomed in Los Angeles. He soon attracted a gaggle of sycophants among the inmate population, eager to serve him in any way. In no time, wannabe-mobsters manicured his nails, shined his shoes, and provided him each day with freshly laundered and pressed pants and bed linens.

Apparently this did not sit well with many of his fellow inmates, particularly not with one named MacDonald. This man was housed in a disciplinary section but regularly permitted to take some fresh air and exercise in a small yard surrounded by high metal fences topped with barbed wire. From this yard, MacDonald daily viewed the bowing-and-scraping rituals accorded Cohen, and he seethed with anger. One day, MacDonald somehow got through or over that fence, despite a guard tower over-

looking the area, and with a metal instrument he beat Mickey Cohen to a pulp.

At the Medical Center, Cohen reestablished the ability to arrange special luxuries for himself. Fancy foods began to flow into the institution and onto the plate of Mickey Cohen. Aside from the food, cash, drugs, lingerie, cosmetics, liquor and other contraband came into Mickey's possession for his own use or disbursement to his friends.

One day, a young lieutenant who happened to be on the ward observed what Cohen was eating, and asked, "Where did you get that food?"

Cohen replied, "From the inmate mess."

The lieutenant quickly went to check it out, taking the suspect tray with him. He soon learned that no such food came from the inmate kitchen or from any other place within the institution. Other authorities became involved at this point and went back to Cohen to find out how the contraband had made its way into the Medical Center. Eventually, enough pressure made Mickey Cohen squeal his guts out, giving up all the people involved in contraband scams.

The next day, the feds waited as a new shift of workers came on duty. Those employees named by Cohen all got busted in the parking lot as abundant evidence of the staff's involvement in the contraband operation was found on persons and in vehicles.

When word filtered out among other staff and inmates, Mickey Cohen became one of the most-hated individuals I ever encountered in the federal prison system. He certainly would have been killed were it not that he was personally escorted from his living quarters in the Medical Center by U.S. Marshals to official vehicles and then to an unknown destination. Possibly the authorities placed him in the witness protection program where he would have received another identity and been assigned to a special prison facility to serve out his sentence.

While at the U.S. Medical Center, I witnessed an incident of overwhelmingly violent proportions. While eating a meal in the inmate mess hall, I observed two black inmates approaching the cafeteria line. They did not fall into line, but rather walked along the line and stopped just behind two white inmates who

did not notice them. The two black men suddenly stabbed the two whites, who fell to the floor. Then the attackers moved along the line, indiscriminately stabbing others. I sat mesmerized and motionless at seeing the first two victims fall, but after that, I left my seat and the mess hall as fast as I could. I later was told the assailants had learned that their own sexual partners, the first victims, had become sexually involved with each other, and the assailants could not accept this. Apparently after the killers disposed of their primary victims, they decided to take out a few more people while they were at it. About ten men were stabbed, I heard, but I asked for no more details, because to know too much is to be vulnerable.

I was only two and a half years into serving my longer-than-life sentence when Medical Center staff informed me that my father, James Walter Taylor, had died. My relationship with my father was highly conflicted and mostly hostile, yet when I received this news, I experienced deep grief, in part because I realized there was no longer a possibility of any reconciliation with him. As the many years went by, and I matured and gained some perspective, I often thought that had I the opportunity of being with my father again, I would put my arms around his shoulders and say, "Dad, let's put all the past behind us and go forward with love for each other."

In 1964, a few years after my dad died, I received word that my mother had passed away. As was the case with news of my dad's passing, the information of my mother's death was relayed many weeks after the event, and long beyond the time when I might have tried to gain permission to attend her funeral. Though angry when this occurred at my father's death, it now hit me especially hard because my feelings for my mother were entirely loving and without conflict. I felt sorrow that, over the years, she had endured verbal and physical abuse from my dad as she tried to take my side in our conflicts. When my mother died, I felt even more alone in a harsh world.

the magnificent obsession

THERE WERE NO guiding lights for me, at least none that I noticed, from my late teenage years until I crash-landed into the Hennepin County Jail in December 1955 at age thirty. The time most critical for me was my first incarceration at Goochland State Farm in Virginia, directly afterwards at Petersburg Federal Reformatory and then at the U.S. Penitentiary in Terre Haute, Indiana, all between 1951 and 1955. During that time, I had no contact with any family member or friend. I became hardened by these experiences, viewing everyone with suspicion. It took a great deal of personal interaction and concern, as well as a long period of time, to soften me up.

At the Hennepin County Jail in Minneapolis in 1956, Al Hitchcock was the head jailer. I developed an amiable relationship with Mr. Hitchcock. He often put prisoners who needed assistance or protection in my cellblock, and said, "Try to look out for this guy, Jim. He might need your help. Call one of the guards if you need to." Mr. Hitchcock treated me like a human being, even an equal. His kindness extended to all the inmates, as far as I could tell. During my prior incarcerations, I was subjected to contempt, revulsion and brutality. He provided me with another view of law enforcement.

Al Hitchcock asked me to watch over John Hewitt, an obvi-

ous homosexual. John seemed very apprehensive in the jailhouse setting. He created some problems for himself with his feminine style of speech and demeanor. I befriended John because I felt sorry for him and did not want to see him abused. On occasions when I witnessed other inmates ridiculing John, or when it looked as if someone wanted to take sexual advantage of him, I would persuade the aggressors to back off and leave the man alone.

John appreciated my efforts on his behalf and wanted to help me in some way. He decided that the best thing he could do was to stay in touch over the years. He came to visit me once at the Medical Center during my first years there. He continued his contact with me into the early 1970s when I presented my first argument to the U.S. Parole Board for release. During the time leading up to that hearing, John suggested that I could base my parole around some of his contacts. He had moved to San Diego and he offered his own residence for my first home. He developed a plan for me to attend San Diego State University and become involved in a vocational rehabilitation program in San Diego.

The Parole Board turned me down flat in 1971 as they stated simply: "Too close to the border." Sometime after that, I lost contact with John Hewitt. I continue to remember John as an intelligent, generous and kind friend at a time when I had few friends.

I was first in the Hennepin County Jail from December 1955 to July 1956. Fairly early on, Reverend Leo Vetvick, the Protestant chaplain, came to meet me. Leo spent hours and hours trying to understand me, why I committed the crime. This was an introduction to the introspection I desperately needed to develop. Leo came to believe I had serious mental problems that originated in my youth. He enlisted another pastor, Reverend John Oman from the Wesley Methodist Church in Minneapolis, to visit and evaluate me. These two clergymen agreed about the seriousness of my mental condition. They tried to advocate a mental illness defense for me, but were not successful.

With the issue of my mental health raised by my attorneys, the Court directed that three psychiatrists should examine me. The psychiatrists assigned were reputedly held in high esteem within their profession. The three came together to my single cell. Each man, in turn, entered and the other two doctors observed the evaluation through the bars. Each doctor tapped my knees with a

rubber mallet, held my testicles and asked me to cough, checked my orientation to person, place and time, and concluded his assessment. Each doctor then submitted a "Psychiatric Report" in writing to the Court. The judge relied on these questionable examinations.

Leo learned about these "psychiatric evaluations," and became outraged with the chicanery. Leo also saw, as the proceedings unfolded, how my case became the means some people in the criminal justice system used to advance their own careers and political agendas. Leo maintained a long-term interest in me. We corresponded for years after 1956 while I moved around to various penal institutions. He also interrupted his studies at Yale, in the summer of 1961, I believe, to return to Minneapolis in order to testify on my behalf as I sought relief from my sentence on mental grounds.

I want to highlight one more person I met before I began to serve my life-plus sentence in July 1956. U.S. Marshal Bob Allie was assigned to transport me to the penitentiary in Leavenworth. As such, he dealt with the crisis I caused by my suicide attempt on that first trip. He also drove me to and from Minneapolis for post-conviction hearings so we had a lot of time to chat alone. Bob loved fine dining, and he had excellent intuition about his charges. On the more than one occasion when Bob transported me, he said, "Jim, I believe I can trust you. What do you say I unlock those chains and shackles and we go to a really nice restaurant for dinner?" I so appreciated being treated like a decent human being, as I was by Al Hitchcock and Leo Vetvick, that I did not think about escape or harming this man's professional reputation in any way. Bob took me to those elegant restaurants, let me order whatever I wanted, and I ate like a free man.

In the years of my first imprisonment at the U.S. Medical Center at Springfield, Missouri, from 1956 to 1968, the warden was a psychiatrist, Dr. Russell Settle. The person in charge of one of the units I lived in for several years was Dr. Ernest Bergel, also a psychiatrist. Even though some highly questionable psychiatric treatments were used during those years, he employed some positive practices. For one, Dr. Bergel met with inmates for individual therapy sessions, and as one of his patients, I became of interest

to him. I liked the doctor but cannot say that I really trusted him until the day that he stood up to a custodial officer on my behalf.

One day I returned to my room and found it totally trashed by someone with apparent particular intent on destroying everything of mine that I held dear. The only pictures I had of my parents and my sister, along with the rare letters I had received from them, were all torn into shreds. All the belongings from my locker were scattered around the room and anything breakable was broken. The sheets and blankets were ripped off the bed, thrown on the floor and covered with dirty shoeprints. Enraged, I soon determined that Lieutenant John Blatchford was responsible for this outrageous invasion. Blatchford was a big, burly man who had earlier introduced himself by warning that he intended to personally harass me as he had heard about my defiant attitude toward custodial authority. I went directly to my work site, an office in the Education Department, where I intended to retrieve the knife I concealed there and return to deal with Blatchford. My boss, Larry Nelson, calmed me down.

Probably Dr. Bergel heard from Larry about the incident that had occurred on his unit. Bergel was no physical match for the burly Blatchford; the doctor was of slight stature and build, and he wore eyeglasses. However, in front of me, Dr. Bergel confronted Blatchford, "Get off this ward and don't come back. You've undone in five minutes what took me five years to accomplish with this man." After this, I had much greater trust in Dr. Ernest Bergel, which may have allowed me to develop trust in others as time went on.

Without doubt, the most trustworthy person in my life at that time was Larry. For reasons unknown to me, Larry took unusual interest in me during the depths of my existence. I had spent an enormous amount of time in solitary strip cells mostly because I would not bend to staff demands. One day, after I had gone a couple years without speaking, a lanky, six-foot-eight stranger with a disarming smile came into my strip cell. He introduced himself as Larry Nelson, Supervisor of Education, and he got down on his haunches to look me in the eye while I sat in a corner of the room, totally naked and embarrassed. He spoke only about small, unimportant things. He did not demand that I respond as the other authorities had done for so long. Larry came to visit me in the

strip cell weekly for a long time—probably for more than a year. I learned, among other things, that Larry had played varsity basketball at the University of Nebraska. I looked forward to these visits and appreciated the time this gentleman gave me.

After many, many visits during which I spoke not a word, one day Larry said to me, "Jim, I've looked over your records. I know that you've been an excellent athlete and that you're an intelligent guy. I need someone like you to help me. I could have you out of here in fifteen minutes if you'd agree to come work for me in my office."

I broke my silence. "If you get me out of here in fifteen minutes, I'll come to work for you. But I have one stipulation. I can't deal with your assistant, Montgomery. I don't want him in my face or even talking to me." I had met Assistant Supervisor Bert Montgomery during an orientation to the institution and his smart-mouth attitude rubbed me the wrong way. I asked for distance from Montgomery not just because I knew he could set me off, but also I think I set the bar rather high for Larry as a way of testing him. He assured me he would keep Montgomery out of my way. Then he left my cell and I wondered if he would return. He did. In fifteen minutes or so, Larry appeared with a custodial officer who provided me with clothing and permission to leave with Mr. Nelson.

It was an incredible situation. I rejoined the real world, where people wear clothes, eat meals with other people, use a bathroom, walk around in adequate space, and talk socially. And no one made me promise to be a "good boy" or reform my ways. This man saw in my eyes something good and he invited me into his domain as a potential contributor. None of my attempts to thank him truly expressed the gratitude I felt.

I worked for Larry Nelson for a year or two, basically running his office since he was frequently in other parts of the institution or traveling. I never had to deal with Mr. Montgomery. After I became well acquainted with the routines of the office, which included oversight of the education and recreation departments, the inmate library, and the craft shop, Larry asked me to take on a special project. He wanted me to design a five-year plan for all the departments under his supervision. I felt sure I could do what he asked and extremely pleased that he put his confidence in me. I

already had ideas about improvement, since I had the experience of being a recipient of the departments' services. I had observed how often the staff of these supposedly rehabilitative programs took on a custodial demeanor. The staff was not fully involved with inmates in their rehabilitation, but rather provided equipment and supplies and then stood back. I felt the staff needed to become involved as helping professionals, people who would be friendly and supportive in their respective programs. The plan I designed in my mind, and then in writing, reflected those ideas.

I lay my written plan on Mr. Nelson's desk one day. I figured that might be the last I heard of it, thinking perhaps he only intended to give me a meaningless exercise to enhance my feeling of self-worth. Or perhaps a good five-year plan would get lost in such a large bureaucracy. I went on to other activities. A few months later, Larry and I were both in the office when Warden Settle came in. The warden threw his arms around Larry, saying, "Larry, I didn't know you had it in you. That five-year plan you submitted has been well received by the Bureau. It's going to be adopted and funded for implementation throughout the whole system."

Larry disengaged himself from the warden's bear hug, and turned to include me in the conversation. "Warden, my inmate clerk here, Jim Taylor, deserves the credit. He's the person who did all the design and writing of the plan. I merely approved it and forwarded it to Washington."

Later I received both monetary and written commendations for my work. But I received much more: a reason to believe there are good people in the world, even among the staff of a federal prison. I think that most people, were they in Larry's position when a warden came with praise, would have grabbed the credit for themselves. Larry's generosity, honesty and humility made a huge impression on me.

So when I learned that Lieutenant Blatchford had ruthlessly violated my living quarters some time afterwards, I went to my work site in the Education office in a rage. I had concealed a large blade there in case I ever needed it. I felt this was the occasion for using that knife and I intended to go after Blatchford with it. Larry was in the office and saw the knife. Somehow he already knew about my trashed room and belongings and he knew that

Blatchford did it. Larry stepped between the door and me and said, "Jim, you've every cause to go after Blatchford. If you head out this door with the blade, I won't call anyone and I'll never say a word about it. But, I beg you, as your friend, don't do it. This is just what Blatchford and the rest of the custodial force want you to do. Don't play into their hands." I shook all over. I stood for a few moments and let the words of my friend sink in. Then I walked over to my desk and hid the knife again. I went back to my unit and felt some satisfaction that I did not respond as custody would have expected. I felt additional pride when Dr. Bergel confronted the Lieutenant.

I gained respect from the other custodial officers and from inmates for my self-control regarding Lieutenant Blatchford. I did not see Blatchford for quite some time since he no longer worked in my unit. Much later, he approached me one day on the yard. He told me that he also appreciated that I did not retaliate with violence to his serious provocation earlier. He seemed to have mellowed considerably and he never again gave me any grief.

In 1997, I tried to locate Larry Nelson. Through telephone information services, I found a number for a Lawrence Nelson in Springfield, Missouri. I called and spoke with this Larry, who identified himself as the grandson of the man I knew forty years earlier. My friend had passed away fairly recently, the grandson told me. I let him know what a giant of a man his grandfather had been.

In those early years of my sentence I was still very depressed and angry about my life situation. In 1957 the Medical Center held a psychiatric seminar entitled the "Sixth Seminar in Forensic Psychiatry." It attracted psychiatrists from around the country. The Menninger Foundation of Topeka, Kansas, sponsored this seminar, and I was one of three inmates chosen for study by these respected members of the psychiatric profession. I cooperated because I strongly believed that the Judge had not adequately considered my mental condition in the sentencing. In preparation for the seminar a doctor administered a battery of intelligence and psychological tests. I learned that all my records maintained by the Bureau of Prisons were duplicated and sent to the psychiatrists in advance of their assembly.

In the prison auditorium I sat on a stage with a microphone in front of me and looked out on a large group of psychiatrists. The doctors took turns with direct questions and I responded as best I could. Then I was dismissed so the doctors could discuss my case privately. I am sure the authorities never wanted me to know the precise results of that discussion but I obtained those records through another inmate who worked in the office where the report of the seminar proceedings was typed and printed.

The inmate told me the office only made enough copies so that each professional participant of the seminar could be given one. I persuaded this inmate friend to give me a copy; I assume a doctor was shorted. From these written records I learned that many of the psychiatrists felt that the sentence given to me was grossly inappropriate and did not properly consider my mental condition. I typed excerpts of the various psychiatrists' statements and then disposed of the full copy of the proceedings. I used those excerpted statements at several legal proceedings in subsequent years as I sought a reduction of my sentence on mental grounds. It greatly angered the federal authorities that I had my own copy of their records, but the psychiatrists' recommendations for a lesser sentence never persuaded any court to provide me relief.

One happy result of my participation in the seminar was that Dr. Karl Menninger, the director of The Menninger Clinic, took an interest in me. Dr. Menninger studied criminal behavior and its psychological roots. He wrote several books on the subject, including *The Crime of Punishment*, which title indicates his opinion of this country's criminal justice system. Dr. Menninger reviewed the results of my testing and verified what the authorities questioned from the tests, that my IQ was in the superior category. I later learned that on the Beta IQ Test, one of the standard tests of the times, I attained the highest score possible. This surprised me because I had concluded earlier, from my multiple academic failures and my father's repeated disparagement, that I was rather stupid. Dr. Menninger and then others helped me accept a new image of myself as a person gifted with high intelligence. Dr. Menninger enrolled me and paid my first year's dues to Mensa, the high-IQ society. Ever since, I have maintained my own membership in Mensa.

Dr. Menninger and I corresponded over many years during my incarceration, and when he visited the Medical Center he made

a point of seeing me. He sent me a copy of *The Crime of Punishment* with a personal inscription to me on the inner front page. In 1981, while on my brief parole in Indiana, I decided to contact him. I made an appointment to see him in Topeka and I intended to drive there in early May 1981 for that significant event. Much to my disappointment, I did not keep that appointment because I was arrested on April 25, 1981, and held in jail much beyond the date of our intended meeting. The signed book he gave me remained with my ex-wife Patsy. I learned that Karl Menninger died in 1990 at the age of ninety-seven.

Until the late 1950s, most of my interactions with other people were predicated on what I might gain in the process. While confined at the Hennepin County Jail during 1956, I became acutely aware how gloomy my future was likely to be. The death sentence was a distinct possibility. I interacted daily with needy men; some lacked money, others protection. Some needed the companionship and comfort of a friend. I began to respond to them, mostly because I had nothing else to do. I had already decided my own life was of no consequence.

A few years later, around 1960, I came into possession of a book entitled *The Magnificent Obsession*, written by Lloyd C. Douglas and first published in 1927. What I perceived in my initial reading and subsequent re-readings of this book radically changed my life. The main character in *The Magnificent Obsession*, a well-to-do young man who pursued only his own pleasures, inadvertently causes the death of an older man, a doctor widely loved for his kindness and generosity. The young man, Bobby Merrick, comes to terms with himself in the process of realizing how irresponsible he had become. By modeling himself after the other man, Bobby sets out to change. He adopts the doctor's vocation and secret philosophy of life: to give to others in need with no thought of reward. Over time, Bobby develops into the same kind of highly respected man of inner peace that the older doctor had been. I began to wonder if the philosophy described could have meaning for me, and might possibly provide some direction to my life, which seemed at this point to be without purpose. The basic premise I derived from my reading was that a satisfying life could result from reaching out to and helping other people with no thought of a reward.

Reading *The Magnificent Obsession* changed my motivation for helping others. I became obsessed about whether I could model my own life after that of Bobby Merrick. By this time, I no longer considered suicide an option but I still felt desperate with the realization that I faced decades, and perhaps my entire life, in prison. I had no idea how I could endure. I possessed no insight nor could I perceive a future that afforded me any peace of mind. I decided to experiment with the methods of Bobby Merrick to see if this might direct me to a purposeful life.

Though it was not easy for me to understand my own gross deficiencies, I had no problem seeing and understanding the same inadequacies in others. Still today, I am often struck with the observation of the poet popular in my youth, Robert Burns: "O wad some Power the giftie gie us, To see oursels as ithers see us!" However, by observing and then involving myself with others, I started to see myself. Certainly, at that time, it was not a pretty sight. But it was not entirely negative, either. No longer did I give to others as a random act to fill my time, nor a tentative experimental action. Generosity became a tangible roadmap towards a sense of self-worth for me, just as it had for the Merrick character—a philosophy and a way of life.

Over the years, I developed legal skills through long hours of study, and these I offered to my fellow inmates in their efforts to gain privileges or freedom. I devoted a substantial amount of time to these legal efforts and asked nothing in return. When the American Red Cross conducted drives in the prisons, I gave blood and always encouraged others to do the same. I also started to donate a large percentage of my meager prison earnings. My donations usually went to individuals, rather than to large charitable organizations, because I have an aversion to the bad management and corruption that I believe can creep into these organizations. I also developed a decided preference for giving to a person over a long period of time, years sometimes, in order to give that person real hope of permanently changing the conditions of an unhappy life. Providing a holiday dinner to a poor family makes no sense to me. I tend to think that a gift such as this can be more destructive than helpful because it gives people only a taste of something better before they have to return immediately to live in the miserable reality of their everyday lives. I prefer to give over a long

period, not to create any dependency, but rather because I believe that this kind of giving can lead to the permanent independence of the recipients, and create in them the idea that they need to "pass it on."

Giving anonymously was the precept described in *The Magnificent Obsession*. I strove for this ideal, but when I gave time, knowledge or money to a fellow inmate, he would know. I started practicing my new behaviors within the prison, but I soon wanted to give monetary assistance to others on the outside. I had to fight with the federal officials for permission to do this, obviously destroying any ability for me to give without others knowing. In the beginning, the authorities granting permission for my donations set conditions of anonymity, which suited me fine. I could not know the last name of the recipient, so I sent a donation through an intermediary, like a social worker. The recipient would also not be allowed to know my name.

One of the first people on whom I tried to practice the philosophy of *The Magnificent Obsession* was an inmate at Springfield, Edward Holzhauser. I met him while we were held in separate isolation cells but both assigned the same hour each day for exercise on the yard. Later we lived on the same unit in the general population. I liked Eddie for his gregarious personality and great sense of humor. He could do card tricks for days, without repetition. He obviously had a wonderful memory and high intelligence.

One day I noticed Eddie holding a book upside down. I said, "Eddie, if you want to read that book, you'd better get it right side up." Embarrassed, he reversed the book to the proper position, and then put it down. The room was empty, so he decided to trust me with his secrets. Not only was he illiterate, he said, but also he came from a very impoverished family background.

Eddie grew up in Harlan County, Kentucky, one of the poorest counties in the United States. He was born and raised in a one-room shack, which afforded the family members meager privacy by way of a blanket hanging from a wire strung across the middle of the room. The shack had a dirt floor, chinks between the exterior log walls, a ramshackle door, and glassless window frames. Eddie's father was an unemployed coal miner with black lung disease complicated by alcoholism. Eddie's mother also suffered from alcoholism. To support the family, she frequented the local

taverns in order to meet men interested in her sexual services. Eddie's mother performed her services in the family home, on a crude homemade table on one side of the blanket barrier. The father stayed on the other side of the barrier, but Eddie and his eight siblings often stood around the table to watch their mother earn the money. Needless to say, after alcohol was purchased the remaining money failed to provide enough food or other basic necessities for the family members. Eddie did not own shoes until the state reform school provided him a pair.

Eddie told me he never attended school while living at home, so I gingerly approached the subject of the benefit of an education. I gained his attention by pointing out how the parole commission would look more favorably on him if he would show that he was trying to better himself. I offered to tutor him privately, since I knew he never wanted to attend classes in prison where others would learn of his educational inadequacies. At first he seemed incredulous, suspicious that there must be a catch to my offer. But ultimately, he came to believe I would help him without expecting any form of payment. With my experience in teaching high school courses combined with his innate intelligence and motivation, I effectively tutored Eddie for about a year until he acquired a high school equivalency diploma.

Eddie treasured the diploma. I decided to take away a little of his pride by pointing out that a high school diploma was nothing unique. I then encouraged Eddie to take advantage of his education and proceed further in a field with good prospects for the future. I directed him to several programs offered in the prison whereby he could be trained as a laboratory technician, a dental technician and as a maker of prosthetic devices. I thought Eddie had the best chance of going straight on the outside if he could become employed in a field where professionals would surround him. Too many ex-convicts gravitate toward employment where they are in contact regularly with people prone to risky behavior.

Eddie thought about my advice and decided to accept it. He took and passed all three courses, but he found the greatest success and enjoyment in making prostheses, a skill he used in the orthopedic section of the Medical Center. I represented Eddie when he came before the parole board and we were successful. Eddie went out, secured employment in the prosthetic business,

and married. Later, the owners of the prosthesis business, an older couple who came to love Eddie like a son, offered to sell the business to him for a pittance before they retired. But by then, Eddie had acquired such high self-esteem, he declined in order to pursue another career idea, the insurance business. Again, he succeeded.

In December 1965, I read an article in the local Springfield newspaper entitled "Share Your Christmas." The local welfare department supplied "cases" to the newspaper, describing individuals or families in the local area whose Christmas was likely to be quite bleak considering the circumstances under which they lived. Case 18 particularly drew my attention. Alice, age fifteen, had asked the county welfare authorities to remove her from her family home as her father had deserted the family and her mother was a serious alcoholic. The article told how Alice worked for her room and board and for necessary school expenses. She aspired to complete high school and go on to college. Though a good student and a hard worker, she had very little money to pay for clothing and the normal necessities of a teenager. The article asked for a donor to provide her with resources for some clothing.

I perceived a young girl with a lot of courage. I wanted to support her in her own efforts to make a good life for herself despite the inadequate family resources. She needed to know someone cared about her for the long term, someone whom she could depend on for support as she proceeded through her adolescence toward adulthood. I did not want to send her money only for the few items of clothing she needed, but enough so she could purchase some things that most other girls had and thus be able to really enjoy Christmas. My goal was that she would have some funds left over for the months afterwards.

I knew there was only a short time available to respond to the newspaper appeal for Alice to receive the assistance I wanted to give her before Christmas. I also knew that institutional regulations would interfere with accomplishing my goal; to employ the usual routes for obtaining permission to send a donation would greatly delay the process. So I approached a chaplain and asked him to be an intermediary for me. As I recall, the chaplain agreed to arrange for my $250 donation to go directly to the local wel-

fare authorities. I also sent a letter asking Alice to use the money on her needs and wants. I dealt with the prison authorities only after the money arrived at its destination in December. They did not want me reaching out of the prison, and made many excuses. I fought off each of these by appealing decisions to higher authorities. Finally, I received approval to send money to individuals in the community, but only through an intermediary.

I communicated with Alice's caseworker over the next few years, sending money and good wishes to Alice as she went through high school without a normal family's involvement. I earned thirty-five cents per hour in the prison industry program during those years. In 1967, Alice, through her caseworker, wrote me a letter of appreciation. It began, "Dear Sir," since she never knew my name.

I responded with a long letter to Alice in which I told her that I, though a stranger, had been trying to become a person in her life who made a real and positive difference. Also, I said that someday, when she was older and had attained some of her life's goals, I hoped she would reach out to help some other person who needed assistance. Alice graduated from high school in June 1969, and, her caseworker wrote me, she left Missouri soon after to seek a better life for herself.

From May 1968 until November 1969, I was in the Hennepin County Jail, awaiting disposition of one of my appeals. Being in Minnesota led me to think that I owed something to the people of this state, since my actions caused the death of one of its citizens and the untold suffering of his family and friends. I also wanted to be sure that whomever received the money had no way of repaying me. These thoughts came to a focus, again around Christmas, this time in 1968. I read in a Minneapolis newspaper about a volunteer project for providing Christmas gifts to the patients at the Faribault State School and Hospital. The project was named the Cedric Adams Memorial Gift Center, after a famous Minneapolis newspaper columnist who established the fund to provide some joy to the mentally retarded residents at Faribault State School. I wrote a letter to the Director of Volunteers at Faribault, enclosing all the money I had at that time—one dollar—and asked that a child at the institution who had little or no family support receive it.

This began a long affiliation between the Fairbault State School and Hospital and me. In 1969, I wrote to Mrs. Helen Stabbert, the Director of Volunteers, and asked if she could assign two residents to me. I asked that one be a child, and one be an older adult, both people who had no other means of meeting their wishes for treats and other little items that might provide some pleasure. She quickly responded that the hospital social workers selected two residents for me to "adopt." I was thus introduced, on paper, to Rene Heggedahl, then age fourteen, and Manon Walls, age fifty-eight. The last names had been provided because I was not in a federal prison at the time and the previous restrictions did not apply. Rene was a profoundly retarded, multiply handicapped child, unable to walk and confined to a wheelchair. The social worker thought Rene might be brighter than her testing indicated and described her as alert and certainly able to enjoy sweets from the institution canteen. Manon was ambulatory, yet not a physically active person; one of his few pleasures was a good cigar.

Over the next ten years, I sent greeting cards many times each year to Rene and Manon, along with notes of encouragement and small amounts of money for treats. I tried to be sure that they both had a little money in their personal accounts at all times. After a while, the hospital social workers sent me photos of my two new friends.

During those years I engaged in a favorite handiwork of inmates—the art of crocheting. I never became a fine craftsman in it as some of my fellow inmates did. But I crocheted a pair of mittens, a hat, and finally a sweater for Rene, which I thought she could use because she liked to spend time on the open-air porch of her residence.

Eventually I heard that Manon's relatives, upon learning of my involvement with their family member, decided to offer Manon more assistance themselves. Some family member took Manon into his or her home and he died about a year later.

It is my understanding that the 1970s saw the beginning of the big move to de-institutionalize the mentally retarded. I know that the population at the Fairbault institution fell from over three thousand to just over one thousand, and efforts continued to find more community placements for even the more severely retarded people. I lost track, but I assume that Rene became part of this great social movement and that she, too, found her way to living

in a smaller, community-based home. Today, if she still lives, Rene would be over fifty years old.

Certainly my life did not become perfectly happy and comfortable as I put into practice the philosophy I learned from the Bobby Merrick character. Legal struggles and disappointments, along with physical assaults, still occurred. Yet life evolved into something increasingly bearable. After many years of following the precepts outlined in *The Magnificent Obsession* as closely as I could, I felt increasing peace of mind, a tranquility of soul, and purpose in my life. For this I am forever grateful to the author, Lloyd C. Douglas.

leavenworth

BEFORE FURTHER DESCRIBING my life as a federal prisoner, I want to delineate the types of federal penal facilities. I was sent first to the U.S. Penitentiary at Leavenworth, Kansas, a maximum-security institution. Other high-security facilities are located at Lewisburg, Pennsylvania, where I spent about nine years, and Atlanta, Georgia, where I served only about three months. There are several other federal high-security institutions, a few of which I encountered briefly en route from one place to another. The high-security institutions house the greatest number of inmates and the offenders who have committed the most serious crimes. They are the most volatile and dangerous institutions.

Inmates regarded as requiring lesser security than those housed in the high-security prisons populate Federal Correctional Institutions, FCIs. Toward the end of my sentence, when I was considered relatively harmless because of blindness and other disabilities, the authorities incarcerated me at FCIs in Phoenix, Arizona; Ashland, Kentucky; and Fort Worth, Texas. In the FCIs with which I am familiar, most inmates are assigned to live in single or double rooms, or wards with up to ten inmates, rather than cells. There may be slightly more rehabilitative and recreational programming available at FCIs than at high-security prisons, but the

primary benefit is that they provide a more relaxed atmosphere, since there is less violence among the inmates and not the same level of escape-prevention as in the penitentiaries.

The least-restrictive type of federal penal facility is the federal camp, where some inmates work in staff houses and drive institutional vehicles into surrounding communities. I was never assigned to a camp.

In 1968, the staff at the Medical Center determined I no longer needed psychiatric treatment, and they therefore arranged my transfer to the U.S. Penitentiary at Leavenworth, Kansas. I had sought a review of my case by the sentencing court in Minnesota, which authorities finally granted. So before I was at Leavenworth more than a week or two, they sent me to the Hennepin County Jail in Minneapolis to await my review hearing.

One day a young inmate approached me. He said that others told him something about my prior dealings with investigative authorities. This young man had been arrested in California for his involvement in a Minnesota bank robbery. Only he was apprehended while his partners remained free. The authorities investigating the matter, as well as his family, were pressuring him to reveal the identity and whereabouts of the others. The choice he faced troubled him, and he came to me for advice when he heard that I had faced a similar dilemma when the investigators wanted me to snitch on Ben Bakken. I told the young man I would not tell him what he should do, only what I had done and why. He could then decide his own best course of action.

I told the young advice-seeker the following: When I was arrested for Lindberg's death and placed in the Hennepin County Jail, FBI investigators questioned me repeatedly, day and night, in order to gain a confession. I am sure the FBI already knew about Ben Bakken's involvement, as I believe Bakken gave me up in a deal whereby he would not be prosecuted for his part in my crime. But they did not know all the details of my offense and so they pressured me to tell the whole story from beginning to end, including the involvement of other people. They implied that I would receive considerable leniency if I revealed everything. But I remained unwilling, at first, to provide any information.

They increased their pressure by involving my family. One day,

my two maternal uncles, Joe and George Norton, both doctors living in Florida, visited me in jail. I was shocked to see them. George, "Curly," did most of the talking. They begged me to consider the offers of the authorities, telling me the investigators had informed them that if I revealed the identity of my co-participants, I would be released. They said my father would set me up financially in a sporting goods business in Florida. I wanted to believe them, but I cannot really say that I did. I highly suspected the FBI offers were traps, and that my revealing anything would lead to worse outcomes for me, not better. But still, confused about my present and future, I definitely felt tempted to believe that there might be a way out of the morass. I thought long and hard about coming clean to the law. My uncles stayed in Minneapolis for several days, waiting for me to make a decision.

After much reflection, I concluded that I could not look myself in the mirror every day if I knew I had snitched. When I told my uncles of my decision to keep my mouth shut, they were devastated that their rescue mission had failed. I felt sad that I had caused them this distress, as I had no beef with Uncle Joe or Uncle Curly; in fact, they had always been good to me. In this situation, I felt they had my best interests at heart, as well as the reputation of the family, but I believed them to be misguided in trusting the authorities. Some months later, I gave the FBI a confession, which—though not totally accurate—named the others involved and provided enough evidence for my conviction. I told the identity of the others involved only after I was absolutely convinced that the authorities already knew of them through other avenues.

After hearing my story, the young man went off to be alone to think about the decision he would make. I went about my routines of jail life until an interruption a day or two later. A group of federal officers awakened me in my cell in the middle of the night and brusquely ordered me to get dressed. Then they whisked me out of the jail, down the elevator, and into a basement garage. Before shoving me into a car, they cuffed and shackled my ankles and wrists, attaching these to a waist chain by means of more chains. Officers sat on each side of me in the back seat with two more in the front. We drove out of the garage onto the dark city streets of Minneapolis, where I noted an official car ahead and another car

behind, each one containing several officers. I thought I might be the object of a lynching party, because I had no idea what else to believe. We headed out of the city and drove silently for a couple hours. Finally, we approached a town named Sandstone, where there was a Federal Correctional Institution. They put me in solitary confinement. There I waited in a sort of daze; I do not know how long.

One day they told me to get ready, that today was my long-awaited review hearing before the sentencing court. Again, I was in the custody of many federal officers for the transportation back to Minneapolis, and I anticipated with great hope my day in court. I would finally be able to articulate the reasons why my longer-than-life sentence should be reduced, based on the mental health factors associated with my offense. I walked into the courtroom, in shackles and handcuffs as usual, and waited for the judge. He entered the room to the tune of the court deputy's chant, "Hear ye, hear ye, all rise. Judge so-and-so presiding." I noted a scowl on the judge's face.

Before anyone else could speak, the judge glared at me and said, "Mr. Taylor, I understand that you are pretty free with giving advice. I understand that you gave some advice to a young man in your cellblock in the jail. Now, Mr. Taylor, I'm going to give you a little advice. I advise you to give less advice, and I now advise the federal marshals here to take you back immediately to the U.S. Penitentiary at Leavenworth, Kansas. This will conclude today's hearing." They pushed me out of that courtroom, and without any review of the merits of my writ, I found myself headed back to Leavenworth. Plunged into the darkness of despair again, it took a long time before I regained some hope.

I now faced the prospect of learning how to survive in a high-security prison where violence was an everyday occurrence. The Medical Center certainly had violent inmates, but they represented a much smaller percentage of the inmate population, and they generally were segregated in their own units with a higher level of custodial supervision and some provision of psychiatric attention. Leavenworth housed many violent inmates whom the authorities believed would not benefit from mental health treatment. Inmates lived in huge cellblocks, often in ten-man cells with iron bars as the front wall. In each five-story cellblock, there were

hundreds, perhaps more than a thousand inmates, with only one or two guards providing supervision. During the daytime, many inmates worked at jobs in the institution, so they were not actually present in the cellblocks during those hours. In the evenings and during other free periods, inmates could leave the cellblocks to spend time in the yard, the gym, the music area, educational classes, or the law library. Opportunity abounded for inmates to engage not only in positive activity but also in all manner of foul play, which could occur without the custodial staff's knowledge or control. New inmates were commonly advised by other inmates to carry a knife, a "shank" in prison vernacular, as in, "You can get five years for carrying, but you'll die if you don't." I decided to reject the advice because I did not want to take the chance of damaging my slim hope for parole.

Food served in any institution is likely to be inferior to home or restaurant fare. But in a prison, the meals are generally tasteless, starchy, tough, and repetitive. Once, when assigned kitchen duty, I observed maggots crawling in the meat. I asked the civilian cook, "What about that stuff?" He blithely answered, "Just grind it up with some other meat and we'll serve it." As quickly as I could, I found another job far from the kitchen. From that time onward, I never trusted any food that was ground or mixed out of my sight, which eliminates a lot of food choices. If I had depended solely on what I could eat in the mess hall, I would often have gone hungry. But like many others, I found ways to secure some decent food for myself. A large underground traffic in food existed. Guys who worked in Food Service smuggled enormous quantities of fresh and raw food out of the huge kitchens and acquired significant pocket money marketing it among the inmates. Smuggling is possible because in any prison kitchen there are fifty times as many inmate workers as civilian supervisors. In the evenings, the smells of cooking eggs and meat wafted from the cells as inmates prepared their snacks on makeshift heating elements.

During the last five years of my incarceration, I spent time in three Federal Correctional Institutions. It might be expected that the food in these settings would be of better quality than in the penitentiaries. But in fact, I noted the situation to be quite the reverse. When I remarked about the abysmally low quality of the

meals, I was told that in an FCI where men can see the end of their sentence, it is unlikely they will revolt if served terrible food. But in the penitentiaries, food must be edible enough to function as a form of insurance against riots or work strikes, as these are places where men have almost nothing to look forward to except, perhaps, their next meal.

I remember another conversation with a civilian cook. I asked him how he obtained his job and how he advanced. He told me that he had received several commendations and promotions because he made it his practice to always under-spend his budget.

In my opinion, the prison and parole authorities misused religion in the earlier years of my confinement. During those years, prison staff advised inmates to attend religious services regularly since the parole board looked favorably on those who did. Naturally, inmates wanted such consideration; therefore, many complied with the advice and signed the attendance cards provided at the chapel entrance. I rejected this practice because I objected to the force and pressure, and this was one thing they could not compel me to do. Eventually, as I became more spiritually inclined, I vowed that, though I did not want to attend religious services to gain parole, I would attend a church service weekly if ever I gained my freedom. I heard that the parole board later abolished its practice of granting favorable consideration to regular churchgoers. But I still did not attend these services until a Catholic priest at FCI Ashland responded positively and generously to my request for his advocacy, and thereafter I chose to attend the services he led in order to express my appreciation for his support.

Each Christmas season the institution's staff attempted to provide some holiday activities for the Christian inmates. A few decorations were distributed around the facility. Sometimes groups from surrounding communities came to the prisons to perform concerts, organize gift-giving parties or lead sing-alongs. This never brought me much cheer, and in fact, I avoided these events because they reminded me so much of what I had lost. The officials usually added to my annual Christmas depression by punishing me for non-attendance at the special Christmas events by withholding privileges or even confining me.

At Leavenworth in my mid- to late-forties, I rehoned my youthful basketball skills and established my reputation as a winner. I became friendly with a couple of black guys from the Washington, D.C., area, Dodi Mite and Josephus, both in their twenties. One day Dodi Mite and Josephus approached me with the exciting news that an acquaintance of theirs was on his way to Leavenworth. They described this prospective new inmate as an excellent athlete, known in D.C. as a fierce competitor on the basketball court. They wanted to set up a basketball competition between this new guy and me, so they suggested a game of one-on-one basketball on the yard. I agreed that I would play against this competitor, and without observing the man's talents first, I placed a number of bets on myself. Dodi Mite and Josephus also bet on me, crossing racial lines to do so.

When the promised athlete finally arrived in the general population at Leavenworth, Dodi Mite and Josephus were there to hype the prospect of his going one-on-one on the basketball court with this older white guy who was a pretty good player. He jumped at the challenge, certain that he could handily take care of me and start building his reputation as a "bad ass" at Leavenworth. The time for the competition set, many bets flowed among the inmate population, generally along racial lines.

A large crowd of inmates came to watch and cheer. I thumped him, about 22–4, as I recall. In this case, "white man *can* jump!" The guy wanted to fight at the end, but several of the black men talked him down. After that, we got along all right as I did not lord it over him and he accorded me a little respect.

Privacy and safety are never present in prison. Officials do not recognize the right to such niceties for inmates; why should they, when they cannot guarantee safety for themselves? An inmate who asserts his rights might be effective in temporarily impressing other inmates with his power, but ultimately the authorities are more effective in proving that inmates have few rights. An inmate's living quarters are always subject to being torn apart by custodial staff in a justifiable, yet irritating, attempt to get to the bottom of a problem. In the high-security prisons where unreformed men live for years and decades, there are many occasions when rooms and private property are trashed. If an inmate finds

his property violated, he should think clearly before acting on his outrage. The perpetrator could be staff or inmate. Motivations and responsibility are often difficult to ascertain in a prison, and the quest for who is responsible can be hazardous.

Often, penal authorities use some form of segregation for punishment. Sometimes inmates seek segregation for protection, and the authorities agree that protection is warranted. In either case, a segregated inmate is supposed to be kept safe by the authorities. But there is no such thing as certain safety in segregation. I know of an instance where a man in protective segregation was shot and killed by an inmate acting from a window in another building. Another inmate was burned to death while locked in segregation.

At one time, a fellow inmate was punished for furtively writing, duplicating and distributing a scandal sheet to inmate areas and staff offices. In this regular publication, he revealed as much negative personal information about staff members as he could gather by listening to, conversing with, and cajoling others. At first many staff members found it amusing, but as the scandal sheet continued to arrive under office doors with accurate and embarrassing revelations about more of them, they became annoyed and, finally, irate. Discovering the responsible party became an obsession for the authorities. When they succeeded in finding him, they placed him in the cell across from mine. One day, from the window of my own strip cell, I saw three or four guards unlock and enter his cell, carrying with them a bed sheet. After a few minutes of silence, I watched them leave the cell without the sheet and lock the door behind them. Soon after, another officer making his rounds discovered the inmate hanging in the strip cell. If caught watching this activity, I may well have met the same fate. To this day, I become outraged when recalling this incident; at the time it happened, I experienced great fear for my own safety and extreme anger toward custodial staff who perpetrated such abuse and then expected me to respect their authority.

The penitentiaries I knew all had factories within them where many inmates worked and earned a pittance, while the private corporation contracted by the federal government, Unicor, Federal Prison Industries, Inc., made huge profits. Because of the

factories, inmates had access to raw materials and the tools for making many forms of weaponry. Supervision was not adequate to prevent inmates from using these opportunities. Hence, weapons abounded in the penitentiaries. A shakedown of a major cellblock one day might net a bushel-basket full of weapons, mostly knives, while on the following day, if repeated, another basketful would be discovered. Weapons were replaced almost as quickly as the authorities could confiscate them. Inmates seldom obtained guns and ammunition, but it did happen. A civilian employee once told me that a crate of 30.06 rifles, which had been delivered to the prison for use by custodial officers, seemed lost for a day before it was found, unguarded, on a loading dock where inmates worked. This particular lapse of security was caught and corrected, but hours of opportunity for disaster existed in the interim.

An atmosphere of fear and tension pervades all high security institutions due to drug trafficking, presence of weapons, and rivalries based on race, religion, and sex. Some inmates decide to survive in this situation by instilling fear in others, and they usually achieve this by inflicting violence. They let others know how "bad" they are by mouthing off about their violent exploits. Some accumulate a count of "bodies," meaning the number of people they killed, or have had killed, within the prison.

In this environment, life is cheap. It can easily be lost through a simple wrong move, particularly by someone viewed as weak, or merely by being in the wrong place at the wrong time. An old man, an inmate I greeted each morning and who never bothered a soul, watched religious services on TV early Sunday mornings. Two or three young guys knew the old man was alone in the TV room one day. They went in and simply murdered him.

The difference between living and dying can be determined by something as seemingly inconsequential as whether one walks on the inside or outside position when rounding a corner. One day I walked down the hallway with another inmate on the inside of me, fairly close to the wall. Just before the corner, where we intended to turn right, I stopped to take a drink from the fountain there. While he waited for me, my companion stepped to the inside, along the wall. When I straightened up and rejoined him, I walked on his left. We rounded the corner, and instantly two people with pillowcases over their heads stabbed him. I got out of

there as quickly as I could, and later learned that my companion was dead. If I had stayed, I probably would have become a second victim, since as a witness I posed a threat to the assailants. I could not report this incident, because to do so would have made me a snitch in the eyes of the inmates, and a primary suspect to the authorities. Even though I exited the scene quickly, I did not feel safe, and for a long time thereafter I lived in fear.

Another murderous event was seared into my memory, but I cannot recall whether it occurred at Leavenworth or Lewisburg. A group of inmates, spying a man alone in his room, closed his cell door and jammed it shut before the man realized it. The perpetrators threw flammable fluid onto the man inside and onto the floor of the cell. Flaming rags were then launched through the bars. Instantly the room and the man were engulfed in fire. The victim ran to the door, gripped the bars, and screamed in torment while the killers stood boldly nearby, smiling and clapping rhythmically. These guys must have known they had time to watch and cheer, which raises a lot more questions in regards to security and custody. This shook me to the core for a long time afterwards. I cannot think of a worse way to die.

All of the terrible things that occur in a federal prison lead to intense feelings of vulnerability, anger and despair. Escape plans abound, and some are serious, but very few are potentially effective. From the early years to the later ones, I had a number of opportunities to escape my confinement. The first opportunity I recall occurred in Minnesota while I waited for a court review of my sentence. While in jail, I needed to be hospitalized for surgical removal of a large tumor that had developed in my arm. A deputy sheriff guarded not only me but my roommate, also an inmate. I do not remember why the deputy left us, but my roommate decided to split by going out the window. He urged me to come along, but I declined, primarily because I had such faith in my own legal case for relief from my life sentence that I did not want to blow that opportunity. Another thought in those early years always accompanied any ideas of escape: I felt that if I actually succeeded in escaping, I would always need to be armed so that I could kill or be killed rather than be returned to prison. To be captured and returned seemed worse to me than to remain in prison and fight for legal release.

On another occasion, some inmates invited me to use a tunnel that they dug, and then to leave via helicopter, which some inmates actually managed to arrange with outside help. The feds got wind of that one, and the would-be escapees got caught in the prison yard as the helicopter landed.

Another consequence of the horribly violent environment of a federal penitentiary is the corruption of the many civilians who work within it. Some of them become as bad as or worse than the inmates. Inmates far outnumber guards, and in general, only guards assigned to towers have permission to carry a weapon of any kind. Faced with violence while earning only a modest wage, custodial officers often find ways to feel safe and to supplement their incomes.

Some misuses of authority occur because a staff member tried to gain prestige or promotion. I spoke with one of the older guards one day. He had been a custodial officer for most of his life, yet never moved above the title of junior officer. I asked this likeable fellow why he had never advanced. He told me about an event that occurred soon after he began his career as a custodial officer. A lieutenant asked him to join a group of officers needed to respond to the psychiatric ward's urgent request for help with a situation in progress. He readily agreed, and soon after he arrived in the psychiatric ward, he and the others were told to take off their rings, watches, neckties and jackets. He complied and then went along with the lieutenant and others to the cell of the troublesome inmate. The lieutenant said that they needed to enter a man's cell to subdue him. Upon entering the cell, his fellow officers proceeded to severely beat the inmate, who offered little resistance. The young officer did not engage in this activity, and he left the cell, never again allowing himself to even accompany others in this form of discipline. In fact, he never wrote a disciplinary report on any inmate for misbehavior. He used his authority in non-violent and non-punitive ways and the inmates appreciated that. The result was that he was never promoted.

Many staff are not even above petty theft. At the Federal Reformatory in Petersburg, Virginia, in 1952, I became aware that employees in the business office sold meal tickets at unauthorized bargain prices to some of the officers. Forced to do time for what I considered a bogus offense—the impersonation charge—

I could not stand by silently and watch civilians cheat to get a cheap lunch. In my bellicose state of mind, I reported the scam to one of the managers in the business office, and was rewarded the next day with a transfer to a different job. For the rest of my sentence, I wore waders and raked raw sewage in the institution's cesspool.

A few of the officers are themselves sick individuals before they ever entered the perverse prison environment. Sadistic guards set up fights so officers can wager on the winner of an inmate brawl. Some sexual aggressors obtained sex from inmates by granting favors or, sometimes, by plain coercion. Many became involved in the drug trade. Enormous quantities of all sorts of contraband came into the institutions via the staff. The prison system as I knew it, and I have no reason to believe it has improved, served primarily as a breeding ground for corruption of every life it touched.

As much as I tried to avoid violence, it often came my way. Early one weekend morning, I decided to enjoy some exercise in the yard. I walked down the stairwell from my fourth-floor cell and started across the first-floor hallway heading toward the doorway to the yard. Just as I came to where the hall widened out into an open area, I heard the sound of running footsteps. Immediately I noticed on my right a man staggering and running, trying to stay ahead of another man carrying a bloody knife. I stood transfixed for a moment, and saw the first man fall to the floor, losing his slight lead. The pursuer caught up and plunged the knife into the fallen man. Just as I realized I had witnessed a murder, I saw the assailant look up to see if anyone had observed. Our eyes met and I knew I had to act to protect myself. I immediately turned back and walked up the stairs to my cell. I knew the killer had seen me and would wonder if I was a threat to him because I knew his identity. I let a couple of guys know what I had stumbled upon and that the killer did not have to worry about me. I watched my own back for a long time thereafter.

Since custodial officers carry no weapons in the cell houses, their lives, too, are in constant danger. I did not witness this next incident, but I may as well have, because the image of what I heard remains very vivid. A shoe factory within the penitentiary at Leavenworth employed many inmates. One of them talked a

lot with the other inmates while they worked. There was a guard who supervised the inmates, not so much for the quality of their workmanship as for management of their behavior. The guard felt that this particular inmate talked too much and worked too little. The guard approached the worker from behind, put his hand on the inmate's shoulder, and suggested, "Let's have less talk and more work."

The inmate quickly turned on the guard and retorted, "Get your hands off me."

This same interaction between inmate-worker and guard-supervisor happened again the next day, and on several more days after that. Each time the inmate became more aggravated by being touched and corrected, so that he finally yelled, "I've told you to keep your hands off me. I'm telling you for the last time, don't do it again."

The guard apparently thought he could keep pushing it, and again the next day, he put his hand on the inmate's shoulder, "More work, less talk." With that, the inmate swung around with the sharp-edged tool he used to cut leather, and came down with the blade across the guard's wrist, severing the hand completely. Blood spurted everywhere and pandemonium broke out. I heard the uproar from my work site in an office nearby, and I came to watch as the guard and his hand rushed past me for medical treatment. I do not know whatever happened to the guard in terms of recovery, or the inmate in terms of punishment. But I bet that one-handed guard never made that mistake again.

Serious violence thrust itself on me at Leavenworth in 1975. On a weekday in the early morning, before my shift as an accountant for Unicor began, I was out on the tennis courts practicing my serve. A young inmate whom I had helped on some legal matters approached me and said we needed to talk. I knew this young man as a paranoid thinker and due to his odd personality no social group would have him. Though eager to converse, he declined my suggestion that we do so right there on the tennis court. He wanted to go to the nearby bleachers so I reluctantly agreed. I became more skeptical when he walked past the bleacher seats and led me around to the rear, where there were some benches underneath. It looked like a big stadium there, with some offices

at one end and several concrete benches spaced fairly far apart in a row under the bleachers.

As we walked into this area, we saw that we needed to go down to the far end to find an empty bench. Other inmates used the benches to talk and wait until it was time to report to their jobs in the prison factories. As we walked toward the empty bench, I strongly felt that this young man was up to no good. I took a precautionary position, walking along his right-hand side. If he intended me harm, that is to stab me, he would only be able to stick me in the chest with a weak, backhanded motion rather than with the full, forehanded thrust that would be possible if I was on his left. We reached the empty bench and he out-maneuvered me so that his right hand occupied the end of the bench and I was seated to his left. I set my tennis gear down on the bench to my left.

The young man did not make his point quickly. He engaged in inane conversation, and at first I went along with it. Then I asserted some control of the conversation by telling him things to make him laugh. I noted as we talked that the other men in the vicinity began to vacate the area, heading for their jobs. Hoping to get out of there quickly, I said to the young man, "Well, I guess it's about time for me to go to work now." As I said these words, I moved to rise and leave.

As I reached over to pick up my racket and a sack full of tennis balls, I saw it coming. It happened so fast that I could not do anything defensive. All I saw was a long blade, and then I felt it plunge into my chest. I do not remember any pain, just a sudden weakness as I fell backwards. The bench had no back but there was enough of a seat under me that I did not slip off. Rather, the top half of my body stayed suspended in mid-air supported by my head that had hit the ground. Before I could pull myself upright, the guy yanked the knife out and plunged it in and out of my chest again.

In a flash it came to me that my only hope was to move out into the open yard where I might find some help. It took all my effort to pull myself back upright and I staggered to my feet. My eyes were not working properly. I could only see areas of darkness around me and the light of the open yard in the distance. I put my head down and ran as fast as I could (not fast at all), toward the

light. The attacker followed me, continuing to slash at my back but only landing superficial cuts. Large red bubbles popped out of my mouth and nose in response to my labored breathing.

I finally made it out from under the bleachers. I turned around and faced my attacker and said, "Now, do it to my face." My vision cleared somewhat, and with two hands, I grabbed the blade, which now I realized was razor-sharp on both edges. He pulled it back through and blood poured from my hands. I fell to the ground, expecting that he would now finish me off. I looked up and saw him looming over me with the knife raised above his shoulder. I had no more strength to defend myself. I could not have brushed a fly off my nose if my life depended on it. But nothing happened. I waited, and then realized that my assailant appeared frozen in place. Though his eyes were directed toward me, I realized he did not see me.

Not expecting to get away, I started to slide out from underneath the man-statue poised over me. I kept my eyes on him as I continued to edge out and still, remarkably, he did not move. I finally maneuvered myself out from under him far enough to stand, and then I tried to run. People later told me I staggered about fifty yards to a recreation building. An officer in the building had been told about a stabbing in the yard and he came running down the outside steps just as I approached. We collided, chest to chest, and I fell to the ground.

Before the officer recovered from our collision, two hefty young inmates came around the corner near us. These guys had snuck off from their job assignments and planned to do a little weightlifting in the exercise area of the yard. They saw me on the ground with the blood bubbles coming out of my face, and quickly decided to do what is almost unheard-of in a penitentiary: they came forward to help. Both of them knew me since I had helped each with legal and personal problems in the past. They hoisted me up into a firemen's carry and ran right past my assailant, who still stood motionless, looking at the ground, with the knife above his head. They carried me into the prison hospital, about two hundred yards away. I was incredibly fortunate to have such speedy transportation to emergency medical care, and also fortunate to have a surgeon known as the best knife man in the Bureau of Prisons on duty to fix me up.

Both my lungs were hit and collapsed. I had nine stab wounds. After two or three separate surgeries in the first twenty-four hours, staff hooked me up to a breathing machine and tubes were inserted into my body to carry off fluids. A big jug, placed under my bed to collect the draining blood and fluids, filled up every few hours. I existed like this for several weeks unaware if I was making progress or what the long-term future held for me. One day, the doctor came to me and explained that there was a limit on the length of time I could be hooked up to this equipment before it would kill me. That time limit was fast approaching and the doctor said that he needed to take me off the machine. He said there was a slight chance I would be able to breathe and absorb my body fluids independently. But because there was a much greater chance I would die, he inquired if there were any telephone calls I wanted to make to people on the outside before he disconnected the tubes and the breathing machine the next morning. I asked to call a friend, Jean, whom I had known for a few years purely through correspondence. Jean had become a true friend and fierce advocate, the only person I knew who really cared about me at that time. I may have called others but I cannot remember. The hospital staff also contacted several of my friends among the inmates to come visit with me that evening. This was highly unusual as general policy held that inmates did not visit other hospitalized inmates. But I guess the staff figured that since I was dying they could grant me a favor.

I slept through the night. I felt pretty philosophical about my impending death. I knew I had fought as hard as I could to live. But if I was not meant to exist anymore, I would die peacefully, without fear of what lay on the other side of life. In the morning the doctor came, said a few words to me, pulled the plug and disconnected me from the tubes. I started to breathe on my own. I did not even catch a cold, much less die. All the medical staff seemed happy that I survived. I thanked God for His many blessings.

A few weeks later, I walked out of the hospital. Waiting for me outside the hospital door were the two burly guys who had picked up my bloody body and carried me into the hospital. They heard from their inmate friends who worked in the hospital about my discharge, and they again left their jobs in order to greet me. To

my utter surprise, they asked, "What can we do for you?"—as if they had not done enough. I should have asked what I could do for them.

I went to the warden shortly after this incident and told him, "In all the years I've been locked up, I've never seen an inmate come to the aid of another injured inmate. The usual thing for us is to get as far away as possible from a scene of injury or death for fear of being somehow implicated. And here were two guys who carried me over to the hospital, covered with my blood, right past the guy who knifed me. They could have been killed by him later or could have been suspected of causing my wounds themselves. They didn't even stop to think about these things. They just moved to help me." The warden listened and I went on, "You should reward these people. Instead of punishing them for missing work, you should treat them as if they did something extraordinarily good by taking these risks. They should be made to feel proud."

The warden gave them each some time off their sentences, a month or so, and thankfully, no punishment for missing work. Though not a great deal of reward, it demonstrated that he at least recognized my entreaties as valid, and their actions as positive.

Later I read the FBI reports regarding this incident of my close encounter with death at Leavenworth. I knew my assailant as a mentally unstable fellow even before he went after me. This did not explain why he chose to attack me. Perhaps I had displeased him with some advice about his legal case. The FBI report described questioning him about why he did not kill me in the yard when he had the opportunity. The investigators said he told them that he just could not bring his arm down.

"What do you mean, you couldn't bring your arm down?"

He said, "Well, I tried to move my arm and I tried to fall onto my knees on top of Taylor, but I just couldn't move." What explanation was there other than the power of God saving me? After I recovered somewhat, the authorities transferred me, supposedly for my own safety, to the U.S. Penitentiary at Lewisburg, Pennsylvania.

lewisburg

THE U.S. PENITENTIARY in Lewisburg, Pennsylvania, is almost indistinguishable from Leavenworth in my memory. Some incidents I can recall occurred near the end of my sentence, and that is the only reason I know they happened at Lewisburg, my last maximum-security prison.

Beginning in the 1980s, as the inmate population became more heavily African-American, a radically militant faction of Islam gained in number of participants and influence. I noted this especially at Lewisburg, where many blacks from the inner city areas of the East Coast were incarcerated. The Black Muslims actively recruited these men as soon as they arrived. My observation of Islam in this setting was that its influence extended far beyond that of other religions as a cultural and political force, based primarily on race, aggressive in its anti-Caucasian and anti-Christian rhetoric and activities. At one point, the Muslims were so predominant that they executed a well-designed scheme to take control of the entire maximum-security facility. For a half-hour or so it felt as if the custodial forces had lost control. During that time, I waited in solitude and wondered how the situation would resolve; I tried to imagine what might happen if the Muslim group gained the upper hand. But because the Muslims' plan was not

perfectly executed by the small groups, where each one was to take control of a certain area of the penitentiary at a certain time, the plan failed and custody regained control.

During this same period, on several occasions, a group of Black Muslims, thirty to sixty in number, often gathered in the yard and formed a phalanx of men, two abreast, chanting in unison as they jogged, "Kill, kill, kill." There was no doubt in my mind who was the target of this intimidation. The staff apparently viewed this activity as threatening to institutional order, and likely to themselves as well, for they soon outlawed it.

One day a young black man came to me for advice. He had difficulty verbalizing his problem. Finally, he told me that an older inmate was pressuring him for sex. I suggested that he seek the protection of his fellow Muslims by going to their leader for help. He cast his eyes down and turned his head away. Then he quietly said the leader of the Muslims was the person from whom he needed protection. I had no answer for him.

Just as at Leavenworth, I had the privilege of an office job at Lewisburg, where I worked for Unicor, Federal Prison Industries. Another inmate, younger than me, was also assigned to this Unicor office. I had just become acquainted with him when one day he dropped a manila folder on my desk and suggested I look over the contents. I took the folder back to my room in the building where Unicor workers lived, and that evening read about the development of a flying saucer at some fledgling company in California—interesting stuff. In confidence, the next day he told me that he was in contact with a friend on the outside who had access to one of the prototypes of this flying saucer. The friend proposed an escape plan from Lewisburg using the device, and he asked if I wanted to come along. This guy was not a nut case. I believe that he did have access to something that might have been able to land on and take off from the prison yard. I told him I would think about it. He wanted me to decide quickly because he and his friend planned the escape soon.

Soon thereafter, I worked one evening in the law library and this fellow inmate came to find me. He ran into the library, and breathlessly asked me what I needed him for. He explained that others told him that I needed to see him right away in the law

library. I was puzzled at first, because I did not want to see him and I had not given anyone a message for him to be sent to me. I figured that some inmates had concocted this story so they might ransack his room. "You'd better get back as quickly as possible in order to protect your property," I told him. I thanked him for thinking enough of me that he ran to see me when told he was wanted.

The next day, I saw this fellow at work and asked him if everything was okay. He assured me that none of his belongings had disappeared and I mentioned that was fortunate. That evening, again in the law library, the same man came running, asking me if I had sent for him. This time I had a feeling that something was deeply amiss, but I could not articulate the problem. I told the guy that again he had been duped, that I had not sent for him and he should not fall for that message again unless it included the word "Alpha," which I would use if I indeed needed him.

The next night while I typed a brief in the law library, again, foolishly, he came running in to find me, this time with an explanation he heard that I had an emergency and required his help. He had become so emotionally involved in his future escape plan that he did not fully appreciate the signs of imminent danger around him. I felt extremely nervous for him and told him he again had been misled. The next day he did not appear at work. Instead, I learned that this new friend of mine was confronted on a stairwell in his cell house the previous evening, right after leaving me, by three guys in front of him and three more from behind, all hooded and carrying knives. Several days earlier, he had changed the TV channel in defiance of the wishes of others and so they killed him. I had decided not to accompany him in his prison break attempt, but I had not told him. Left with his written material about the flying saucer, I hid it in a folder marked "Menu," so as not to attract the attention of custodial officers.

A revealing edition of "60 Minutes" in the late 1990s covered the extent of drug dealing in the federal prisons. A drug lord incarcerated at Lewisburg was interviewed and claimed that he generated revenues of $400 million annually when he was on the streets. In this TV report, he further revealed that his business volume had increased while incarcerated to the tune of over $500 million

annually. One might think that this guy engaged in some bragga-docio for the cameras, but I believe him, because over the years I observed for myself the great increase in drug activity within the federal prison system. An inmate's ability to oversee and manage sums in the hundreds of millions of dollars relies upon trustworthy associates on the outside to make deals. The majority of the money and drug trafficking occurs on the outside, although some drugs and money exchange hands within the walls. Some of this activity is facilitated by prison staff, corrupted by the appreciable monetary rewards they can earn from the drug lords within and outside the penitentiary.

One evening, I was alone in my cell, A-404, occupying myself with my newest pastime, oil painting. Most of the other inmates from Cell House A had gone to the movie that evening. As I painted, I heard a strange noise—a low, gurgling cry—from the rear of the cell house. Next came the sound of running footsteps heading toward my cell. I stepped out and saw an inmate approaching from the area of the cry. Then I heard the sounds of many feet, that of guards probably, bounding up the stairwell near my cell at the front of the cell house. I realized that the running inmate was headed for the same stairwell, unaware that he would head right into the guards if he continued. I silently motioned for him to enter and hide himself in the toilet stall in back of my cell. He entered the stall, and lifted his legs so they could not be seen below the raised walls of the stall. I went back to my painting. The guards ran past, quickly observing that I was alone in the cell. After they passed, I shooed the inmate out. He dropped himself over the railing just outside my cell, lowered himself onto the third-floor walkway below, and made his escape. I learned later it was a guard he had stabbed at the rear of the cell house. Again, as the only witness to the crime, I was in jeopardy of this man's suspicions that I might reveal his identity. It could have been to my advantage to tell what I knew, particularly because the victim in this case was staff. I may have been able to trade information for some serious consideration of release or a sizable number of years off my sentence, as this is the type of bargain that can sometimes be negotiated in the federal prison system. But I had long ago decided not to snitch.

Violence once more came very close, a reminder yet again just how quickly a life could be snuffed out. I used Lewisburg's law

library often. A man who lived in the cell next to mine, A-402, also frequented it. Early one weekend morning I left my cell, heading for the law library. As I passed A-402, this man asked, "Hey, Jim, would you reserve me a typewriter in the library? I'll be over there in a few minutes." Happy to do so, I set some books and paper in front of a vacant typewriter and went on about my own legal research.

After some time, I noticed other men needed a typewriter and told a few of them that I had reserved the typewriter next to me for a friend. Time passed and I became uncomfortable continuing to tell others they could not use the typewriter. After an hour or so, I decided to check on my neighbor in Cell House A.

I crossed the huge rotunda from which the library and all the cell houses radiated, and headed into Cell House A. Immediately upon entering A, I sensed something was amiss. When I got to the fourth floor, I ran into another inmate who told me that my neighbor had been stabbed to death in his bed. His head lay very close to the bars that formed the front of the cell; he had apparently fallen back asleep after asking me to reserve the typewriter, and someone reached through the bars and killed him. I had just spoken with the man an hour or so earlier when he was very much alive. This was when I learned to always lie in bed with my head and chest positioned toward the inner part of the cell and my feet toward the bars.

Guards did not like my behavior in this regard because it made a head count more difficult for them. On more than one occasion they told me to turn around, but I refused. This was the kind of behavior that gained me the reputation of being resistant to authority. That I might have an interest in protecting my own life did not matter to them. Guards cared only about the rules and procedures of head counts, and whether a particular inmate lived or died did not concern them. In fact, I often heard staff talking about how easily one inmate could be replaced by another. We heard about other inmates even riding a prison bus for weeks because of the bed shortage. Is it any wonder that prisoners whose lives have been so disrespected in prison might have less than a high regard for their own lives or the lives of others?

What follows is perhaps the most ugly and gruesome act of violence that took place around me. There was a popular, gregarious inmate who loved to talk with pride about his home state

of Kentucky. For this reason, he acquired the nickname "KY." Although gambling violated prison rules inmates still managed it, and KY did so with great enthusiasm. A guard, irritated by KY's demeanor and behavior, found KY at a gambling table and ordered him to leave the game but let others continue to play. KY groused as to why he should be singled out, but he did comply for a few successive days.

One day, the guard gave him the same order, and this time KY was not about to comply. He jumped up from the card game, grabbed the guard, threw him down to the floor and sat on top of his chest, threatening to kill him with the blade he carried. The guard yelled for help and another guard, Jones, got there in time to see the incident. KY looked up at Jones and let him know that he had better "get in the wind." Jones ran, probably to get reinforcements, and KY returned his attention to the guard he straddled. The guard shouted his pleas after the retreating guard, "Jonesy, don't leave me. Please, Jonesy, don't leave me." Somehow, KY cut off the guard's head. Witnesses told me that KY even took the head by the hair and tossed it, just like a bowling ball, rolling it down the walkway outside the cell where it all happened.

In any situation such as this, no inmate would ever try to control the raging inmate assailant, for he would be the next one killed if he ever took the side of custody. Likewise, in many instances I witnessed officers who could have stopped an act of violence before an inmate was killed or severely wounded without serious risk to themselves, but they did not. They all stood aside, waited and watched until the violent deed was done, then mopped up as needed.

KY was put in "the hole" of the institution. Custody put a snitch in the hole with him, hoping that KY would acknowledge responsibility for the act. KY apparently recognized the man as such and quickly killed him. Then, he was transferred out of the institution, first to a solitary cell in the Leavenworth city jail. I have no idea where he went after that, or if he ever left that jail cell alive. Men who kill staff members often do not live long.

In the latter half of 1979, I received the tremendously good news that, after twenty-four years served, my efforts to gain release would result in parole in January 1980. At that time I lived on the

second floor of the three-story building for Unicor workers, and a strange thing began to happen. The authorities started moving inmates out of the third floor, placing them elsewhere in the institution. We asked for an explanation and they told us there were plans to renovate the building and all of us would soon be moved. Then they vacated the first floor.

When the second-floor inmates began to be moved out, no one told me to do so. I returned from work one day to find that I was the only resident left in the entire Unicor building. When I asked, they said they did not plan to move me because my parole was close (though I still had a few months to go). I felt unsafe in that building alone, without even a guard assigned. I was vulnerable in that building at all times unless locked in my room. I knew that I should not formally complain about this, so I tried to live watchfully with the extreme quiet and solitude.

One day I returned from the shower at the end of the hall to my room with only a towel wrapped around my waist. I just started to put on some clothes when suddenly the heavy metal door to my room flew open. In a flash, a big inmate was in my face, brandishing a blade about a foot long.

He said, "I want some pussy."

I answered, "Just a second, let me get some lubricant." I bent down and reached into my locker where I kept a weapon for such an occasion. I grabbed the heavy athletic sock, filled with three or four padlocks and knotted shut. I whirled around, bringing the sock up and into the head of the intended rapist with all my strength. As he fell backwards, I rushed to the door and pushed it hard. Then I realized a second man waited just outside the door, acting as a lookout. I think I caught him by surprise because he was knocked to his knees by the door. That gave me a little time to run to the stairwell.

There I encountered a third man sitting on the top step. He jumped up but I landed a moderate blow with the padlock-filled sock as I ran past. However, he recovered quickly and grabbed at my ponytail as I ran down the steps in front of him. I kept going, leaving this third guy with a handful of my hair. I made it to the safety of a cell house across the hall where I had some friends, one of whom quickly provided me with a knife. I had mayhem on my mind, and then I ran into a black man I especially liked. Since he

was one of the leaders of the Islamic group, I said, "I'm going to kill those sonsofbitches. Three of them just tried to rape me and I'm going to get them!"

The Muslim inmate quieted me, "Don't worry, I'll take care of it. You won't have any more trouble from those guys."

I did not report this incident to custody, but I believe they found out because soon thereafter I was moved out of the Unicor building. Worse yet, I was put in 10-A, a unit that housed at that time, other than myself, only inmates who had killed one or more other inmates. I had a month to go before my parole date, and I felt as if I might not make it after all this time. It scared me that I could be killed by someone who did not have much to do but add to his body count. I asked to be placed in segregation for my own protection. My request was denied with the explanation, "We put you here to be a calming influence on these guys." I told them I did not want to be "a calming influence," but no response ever came. I kept my guard up every moment, every day, until I walked out of there in January 1980. I do not believe the authorities meant for me to gain parole. There were staff members who resented the hell out of me for the litigation I continually brought against them over the years. I believe they wanted me to die in 10-A. But I cannot prove that.

early angels

A S A CHILD, I loved the summers' long hours of daylight and freedom from the confinement of school. I adored sports, especially anything to do with the water, and being a northern boy, I could only enjoy these pleasures that time of year. Summertime also meant going to Connecticut for most of June, July and August. My father dominated my world back home in Michigan. But in Quaker Hill, Connecticut, I became part of the extended Taylor family, where I felt a sense of belonging. From September to the following June each year, I looked forward to the next summer in Connecticut.

Quaker Hill is a little community about five miles up the Thames River from New London, a city located where the river empties into the Long Island Sound. When I was a boy in the 1930s, New London was a bustling city, and most enterprises involved the sea. Along the Thames stood the U.S. Coast Guard Academy, Electric Boat Company, which built all the submarines for our country's military, a U.S. Navy submarine base, and the Connecticut College for Women. The city also boasted a considerable fishing industry, an active train station and three movie theaters. One of New London's many trolley lines ran frequently from the city through Quaker Hill on its way to the next little community of Montville.

My father was one of five children born to Fanny and Peter Taylor. Four of the five Taylor children, as adults, moved to either New York or Michigan to make their living. However, the New York and Michigan Taylors, with their young families, came back to the family home almost every summer for as long as their employment and spouses permitted. The only exception was Jack Taylor, my father's younger brother, who had followed my father to Michigan and into the road construction business. Perhaps this family came to Quaker Hill less frequently because one of the Taylor brothers needed to stay close to the business.

The visiting family members all stayed in Grandma Taylor's home, a house built in 1736 by Benjamin Greene, an ancestor of my grandmother, Fanny Greene Brown Taylor. Later that century, much of the action of the Revolutionary War took place in this area. My father researched and learned that Benjamin Greene, Jr., served in the Continental Army, was taken prisoner by the British, and later escaped. The elder Benjamin Greene built the house on a large tract of land granted to one of the family ancestors by the King of England. The house was placed on the front, western edge of the property. Surrounding the property on the north, west, and south perimeters, a waist-high stone wall built of large field boulders grew thick with poison ivy vines. The land immediately behind the house was open with a creek running across it, beyond which sprawled an apple orchard. Past the orchard, rocks and caves covered the face of a heavily wooded slope that then flattened out and provided space for a rail line along the Thames River. The house and property remained in the Greene-Brown family for over two centuries.

By the time I came along on the summer visits, my grandfather, Peter Taylor, had long since passed away and left his widow as the indisputable matriarch. Grandma Taylor gave me unconditional love and I reciprocated. Grandma often sent me to the woods to pick huckleberries and blueberries so that she could make her wonderful deep-pan pies. I loved to pick the berries because she hugged me for the full pails I brought her and then served up huge portions of her berry pies to the whole family.

One Sunday when I was about six, I wore my best clothes to go to church. While waiting for the other family members to be ready, I watered flowers with a hose in the backyard. Out the back

door came Grandma, all decked out in her female finery including a long dress and a fancy hat above her freshly arranged hair. On an impulse, I turned the hose on my grandma, laughing as I did so. I let her have it and she squealed, "Oh, Jimmy Pete, stop." But she smiled as she ran toward me.

My father heard her outcry, and burst out the door to witness his mother wet and disheveled. The expression on his face became murderous as he ran toward me. My heart caught in my throat as I anticipated the walloping of a lifetime. Before he reached me, Grandma Taylor loudly directed him, "Stop! Don't you hit that child!" as she physically stepped between us. My dad halted, immobilized, briefly unsure of what to do. He turned and walked away without a word. Grandma returned to the house to dry off and change her clothes. I never again worried about my father's anger during the summers. She was the only person from whom he ever seemed to be able to take criticism. I believe he loved and respected her, proven by his generosity over the years in the great number of improvements he added to her old home.

Each Christmas and birthday I received one gold coin in the mail from Grandma Taylor in the denominations of two-and-a-half dollars, five dollars, or ten dollars. My father kept these gold pieces in a drawer of his desk and he told me not to touch them.

One day when I was about ten years old, I decided I needed one of those gold pieces to buy myself a present. I went into the forbidden drawer, took out one coin, and went to my favorite drug store, owned by my father's friend, Ralph Wilson. I asked Mr. Wilson if he would give me some common money for my coin and he readily exchanged it for a few bucks. Mr. Wilson apparently telephoned my dad to tell him about the exchange, and my father went to Wilson's Drug Store to retrieve the gold coin. He put it back in the desk, and threatened me with punishment should I ever go in that drawer again.

Over sixty years later, after I began a correspondence with my sister Sally, she sent me one of the gold coins that I had received from Grandma Taylor. I do not know what happened to all the others.

Grandma Taylor's house was the heart of my idyllic summers in Connecticut. From there I explored the world of Quaker Hill.

My first cousins, Joanne and Mary Taylor from Michigan, and Jane Semmig from New Rochelle, New York, also stayed at Grandma's, but I played mostly with other, more remotely-related cousins, Jiggy, brothers Bobby and Jimmy, and Jake. Jake was a character, even as a boy. He focused almost exclusively on animals and baseball. Every summer when I first arrived in Quaker Hill, Jake had to show me his new favorite horse or cow. Other neighborhood kids, Joan Kerr, Jerry Alexander, and even my sister Sally, also joined us. Jerry and I took on the daredevil role, Joan was a regular tomboy, Bobby calculated the risks, and Jimmy followed whatever Bobby, his older brother, decided. Sally, four years younger than most of us, had a hard time keeping up.

We intentionally provoked the bulls in the nearby pastures, and then climbed on the huge rocks to escape the maddened animals. We explored the caves and played Cowboys and Indians, using our cap guns. We found the remnants of children's play china from the years-ago tea parties that Beth Alexander and my cousin, Jane, had held. We met Johnny the Tramp, who showed us the modest secluded dwelling he made for himself among the house-sized boulders on my grandma's property. We loved to watch the frogs and turtles surrounded by scores of large water lilies in Alexander's Pond. One day when I was aggravated that my little sister tagged along again, I left her stranded on top of one of the boulders on Hempstead's farm with an enraged bull at the base, pawing the ground.

Jake lived in a big, old stone house, with a rock-strewn pasture between it and the home of an elderly relative of ours, Aunt Annie. She was hostile toward us children, because we played in the pasture and occasionally hit a ball onto her property. We quaked in fear while retrieving any ball, as Aunt Annie invariably marched out her door, large rolling pin in hand, threatening us with a beating.

Grandma Taylor's side yard was large and flat, a perfect place for croquet, and I kept it mowed. We kids played croquet almost every day, but so did the adults. On rare occasions, adults and children played the game together. The region's many farmers frequently congregated across the road from the Taylor home, at the Glassburner farm, because old Mr. Glassburner was a blacksmith. While horses were shod, the farmers played croquet, and the

competition was fierce. Old Mr. Glassburner also hosted cock-fights, which drew large crowds of men. The bloody fights and steep wagering meant occasionally some farms were lost in the process. We kids loved to watch all this activity, even if the men tried to keep us out.

The enterprise later passed into the hands of Bob Glassburner, a son. Bob converted the blacksmith shop into a modern gas station for cars, whose numbers increased during those years. Bob was always friendly, and I liked to hang out at his place. He introduced me to a soft drink unavailable in Michigan, birch beer, which I loved.

The Hempstead's dairy farm was just north of Grandma's. The Hempstead sons, young adults during my childhood, taught me to milk the cows by hand, which I thought was a big deal. When they converted to milking machines, I lost the bragging rights to my milking prowess.

A rail line bordered the backside of Grandma Taylor's property as it ran along the west bank of the Thames. A cove of the Thames formed in that area and required a trestle to carry the rail line across the neck of the cove. The trestle spanned a length of only about twenty feet, but it provided us some hair-raising experiences. My playmates and I would sometimes stand in the middle of the trestle, listening for an oncoming train. We challenged each other to stay on the trestle as long as anyone dared, before dashing off to safety on the side opposite the train's approach. This was great fun, but we all made sure not to tell our parents about this little game. I sometimes went to the trestle to practice by myself.

The water under the trestle was never deep, even at high tide. One day I learned that a boy about my age dived off the trestle at high tide and struck his head on a passing log. He died instantly. I went to a funeral for the first time, and also made my first appearance at a Catholic church.

As a child, another death difficult for me to comprehend was that of Joan Grubar's father. Joan was my age. One summer when I returned to Quaker Hill, my friends eagerly shared some big news. On the previous Christmas Day, Joan came downstairs into her living room, anticipating the joy of opening presents. She found her father hanging from a rope in front of the Christmas tree.

This image dominated my mind for a long time. I still wonder if Joan was ever able to emotionally recover from the shock.

During several summers, I enthusiastically participated in a camp sponsored by the Junior Midshipmen of America. The camp was located at the back of the Hempstead farm property and faced the Thames River. My cousins Bobby and Jimmy Brown and I learned to tie knots and to understand many naval terms and duties. We dressed in full naval attire to parade with pride in the New London July 4th celebrations.

Captain Cabral, the camp director, tried to turn the camp into serious naval training for us. Each night some boys were assigned to guard duty posts, which required us to be alone and in full uniform, to protect the campsite and to deter any would-be intruders. One night, when Jimmy served guard duty at one of the entrances to the camp, he heard some rustling in the under-growth nearby. In a trembling voice, he commanded as he had been taught, "Advance and be recognized!" After he uttered the command several times, out from the brush came a mother skunk trailed by three baby skunks.

As I look back on the Junior Midshipmen organization, I guess our elders thought they should prepare us to become the sailors in the war that felt imminent in the 1930s. Captain Cabral devised an activity meant to simulate the real Navy experience. To any of us who wanted to go home or elsewhere for part of a weekend, he granted "liberty." Before leaving the camp and also upon return, we needed to undergo a "short-arm inspection." This meant we, who probably ranged in age from ten to thirteen years old, stood in a line and dropped our trousers and undershorts to allow the Captain to look at our privates, supposedly to ascertain our cleanliness and health. I think now this was unnecessary, but not perverted or abusive; I believe that the Captain truly wanted to teach us all aspects of naval life. But I recall intensely disliking the experience.

My favorite summer activity was to fish for crabs off an old stone dock on a cove of the Thames. My father bought me a row-boat and he arranged with Louie Ginsberg, the local grocer on the same cove, for it to be tied behind Mr. Ginsberg's store. I bought all my twine and fish heads for bait from Mr. Ginsberg. I rowed out there alone. Through the inner portion of the cove, I used the

net handle to pole my boat forward through the shallow water while I looked for crabs. When I spotted one, I quickly reversed the handle so I could net it. My family was very appreciative as I contributed the essential ingredient for the crab feasts we all loved in Grandma's back yard. Side dishes, like corn, potatoes and clams, roasted in the nearby pit dug by the adults.

My family heavily patronized Louie Ginsberg's store, as did most of our neighbors. Times were financially tough for many Quaker Hill residents as the Depression wore on in the 1930s, though the Taylors survived with their finances unscathed. The Ginsbergs were friendly people, and apparently too kindhearted; their store closed soon after the Depression because Mr. Ginsberg extended too much credit that remained unpaid in time to save his business.

Once each summer, people from New York and other areas in the East gathered at various spots along the Thames to watch the annual Yale-Harvard boat race. Our family had only to go to the back of Grandma's property to join the visiting spectators for this event.

The 4th of July celebration highlighted our family's wonderful summer vacations. My father always purchased an immense quantity of fireworks and set them off in the evening with all family members present, along with other adults and children from the surrounding area. He loved being the center of attention and admiration. I loved the fireworks.

As I got older, my parents allowed me to explore beyond our family enclave. Compared to Quaker Hill, New London was a prosperous and sophisticated city. My Aunt Fanny, my father's youngest sister, had married a successful businessman, Louis Markow, and they lived in New London with their only child, Lois, two years older than me. The marriage of Fanny and Louie caused tension for their families and also for their daughter since the Taylors were New England Baptists and Louie came from a Jewish family in New York City. The Markows came frequently to the gatherings at Grandma Taylor's home, but I detected an undercurrent of non-acceptance and mistrust, especially on the part of the Taylors.

Aunt Fanny and Uncle Louie frequently invited me to visit at their new, luxurious home in New London. It overlooked the Pequot Beach Club and the Long Island Sound. Nearby was the

famous Lighthouse Inn, a hotel that attracted wealthy movie stars and successful New York businessmen of the time. Also close to the Markow home was Admiral Bullard's Naval Academy, a private, expensive boarding school devoted to preparing high school students for the U.S. Naval Academy at Annapolis.

From Fanny and Louie's home, I often went to the Pequot Beach Club, explored the shore and swam in the Sound. Because of Louie's religious heritage, the Markows were not allowed membership in the Beach Club, but the Taylors were long-standing members. So we could swim there and include the Markows as our guests. Louie never came to the beach with us, and Fanny and Lois only came along three or four times in all the summers I was there, and then they did not swim, but merely sat under the beach umbrellas. The prejudice at the Beach Club extended beyond the Jewish faith to the working class. I felt I could not invite my Quaker Hill buddies there because I knew that Beach Club members would make my friends from the country feel uncomfortable.

At the Beach Club I met a boy my age, Jimmy Wagner. He was from a well-to-do family who owned a lovely home on a hill overlooking the beaches. Just as I felt unable to include my Quaker Hill friends in the Beach Club activities, I also felt the same reticence to invite Jimmy into the Markow home and to Quaker Hill, as I presumed this would make everyone involved uncomfortable. Maybe I was wrong in my assessment at that time; maybe Jimmy would have been as comfortable as I was in bridging three worlds. My early experiences of ethnic, religious, and class discrimination were duplicated later in prison. It made me as sad then as it does now. Human beings make way too much of their differences; I have little faith that this will ever change.

Both Aunt Fanny and Uncle Louie doted on me. When I was quite young, Fanny liked to get me all dressed up to go to Peterson's Tea Room on the main street of New London, where she showed me off to the other ladies. She was a regular customer at Peterson's, and was accorded many extra courtesies. Because she was married to a Jewish man, some places did not accept her, but she adopted a supercilious manner at Peterson's. She bought me expensive gifts there, and once she really splurged and presented me with a beautiful model yacht, about thirty inches long. I took

that motorized toy out into the water at the Beach Club more than once, each time attracting much attention from both children and adults.

Louis Markow owned and operated The Sport Shoppe in downtown New London. The shop catered to well-to-do women with time and money to spend. Louie did his own buying, traveling each year to Europe to select the latest fashions. The matronly saleswomen wore black dresses with white collars and cuffs and gave the women customers extravagant service. When Louie was in the store, the customers received his individual attention and he treated each one like a queen.

Louie himself dressed conservatively, but he always had the biggest and best Cadillac on the market. Later Cadillac models became so long that they did not fully fit within his garage. Louie also owned a forty-eight-foot motor yacht and kept on twenty-four-hour call an experienced man who captained the yacht and managed any needed repairs.

On those summer days when Louie was at Grandma Taylor's and felt the tension in the atmosphere there, perhaps the stress of social discrimination, he often turned to me and said, "Let's go for a ride, Jimmy Pete." And because I felt the family tensions, too, and wanted to get away from them, and because I loved Louie so much, I always agreed to go.

Uncle Louie and I grew very close. He often took me out on his yacht, and we, along with "the Captain," motored out via the Thames into the Long Island Sound. We fished. Louie and the Captain drank beer while I gulped down soda pop. Before we boarded the yacht we usually bought a bucket of clams to use as bait for our bottom fishing in the Sound. When a quarter of the bucket remained we then had ourselves a picnic on the boat. Louie and the Captain ate raw clams on the half-shell; I waited until they cooked up the remainder into chowder, which I devoured.

Uncle Louie owned many rental properties in the Ocean Beach area of New London, populated predominantly by Jewish people. Ocean Beach attracted numerous visitors with its large boardwalk along the ocean and an amusement park. When Louie took me in his car, sometimes we went to Ocean Beach, where Louie was well-known and respected. He collected rent from some business and residential tenants, and these people always wanted to please

me. I received hot dogs, soda pop and ice cream, along with fawning attention. I loved being with Louie, and I could not help but love the food. However, so much attention embarrassed me.

One summer I owned a new baseball glove and I proudly showed it off to all my buddies. I carried the new glove with me wherever I went, including one day on a ride with Uncle Louie. As we drove, I pounded a baseball into the glove, over and over, in my efforts to break it in. Louie watched out of the corner of his eye as he drove along toward Ocean Beach. Just before we got there, Louie offered me a deal: "Say, Jimmy Pete, tell you what I'm going to do. I'll get you one of Izzy's hot dogs, a big mug of root beer and some ice cream, if you'll let me hold your ball glove until you can pay me back."

I did not think about the part of paying him back, because in my mind I only saw, smelled and tasted the hot dogs and other foods in the area. I said, "Sure."

I consumed all the goodies that Uncle Louie bought me at Izzy's. I had a very full stomach as we got back into the Cadillac and I expected Louie to hand the glove back to me. But he did not. He did not even give it back to me when he dropped me off at Grandma's house. I hardly slept that night and I could not play ball without my glove the next day. My dad asked me where my ball glove was and I told him I left it in Uncle Louis's car. Louie stopped by the house a few times in the next days, never mentioning the glove. I looked at him with questions in my eyes and finally I asked, "Uncle Louis, can I have my glove back?"

Louie said, "Well, Jimmy, what were you thinking when you gave it to me? I thought a deal was a deal. Now that you've eaten all those goodies I paid for, you want your glove back. Free, for nothing?"

I could not believe it. Had I really lost my glove for those few treats so long ago I could not even remember them? He let me stew for a few more days and then he gave back my glove, with a big grin. "Don't give up something of real value and lasting pleasure, for the sweet of the moment. Remember this."

Uncle Louie gave me many invaluable lessons in my youth. But they did not stick with me into my young adult years. If Louie had only lived long enough, I could have gone to him when I started having real problems in my twenties. Perhaps with his wisdom I

might have never gotten involved in criminal activity. But Uncle Louis died suddenly from a cerebral hemorrhage at age forty-five, when I was about ten. He was like a real father to me, and likely, he felt I was the son he never had. In my late teens and early twenties, the voice in my head was always my father's voice, not Louie's, and that produced only negative results. My father gave advice when I asked for none, and anything he advised I only considered a roadmap for doing the opposite.

After Louis Markow's death, it soon became apparent that Aunt Fanny could not manage The Sport Shoppe. Another aunt, Edith, had long ago established herself as a professional in the women's clothing business. Edith gave up her job as a buyer for Lord and Taylor in New York City, and she, along with her husband, Harry Sloan, moved into Grandma Taylor's home and took over management of The Sport Shoppe.

Shortly after Uncle Louis' death, I experienced another great loss. Grandma Taylor died when I was eleven, in 1936. This did not occur in the summer, so I was not with Grandma Taylor in her final days. She spent the last months of her life in the Markow home, where her youngest child and namesake, Fanny, took care of her. She too, I think, might have reached out to provide effective guidance to me in my early adult years had she been alive. I know that she loved me dearly, and would have been greatly disturbed to watch me choose the wrong roads. Losing Uncle Louie and Grandma Taylor before I became a teenager left me feeling abandoned and vulnerable in the summers, not just at home in Michigan. These guiding lights were snuffed out and not replaced.

During the summer I was fifteen, a major disruption came to the Taylor family of Quaker Hill. The State of Connecticut decided to build a highway, and by eminent domain, took some of the land through the eastern third of the Taylor property. The road was constructed through the old apple orchard, leaving the family distraught over the loss of the property, as well as the resulting traffic and noise. My father and I felt the same outrage about this travesty and we agreed on a response. We planted a row of pine trees on the west side of the creek in order to provide a shield from the intrusion. This is the only time I can recall my father and me in agreement on a project.

seeking sanity in hell

ALTHOUGH I WAS never a good student in grade school, high school, and college, I had an independent interest in history. I read extensively during my formative years, including stories about India and Mahatma Gandhi. Being a natural rebel, the stories about this old man of slight stature who led his countrymen to a standoff with the British Empire, and won, impressed me. I remembered this and the fact that Gandhi used passive resistance as a weapon.

Within a year of my beginning to serve my life-plus sentence in the federal prison system, I decided I would try the Gandhian approach. It was my way to make a statement that I did not agree with the Government's belief that I was a cold-blooded murderer. Active rebellion would not have furthered my cause. In fact, the superior forces of the Government would crush me easily if I acted out my frustration violently. It would also play into the Government's hands by giving them evidence that their impression of me as dangerous was correct.

My first act of passive resistance was silence. I decided to speak to no one, neither staff nor inmates. None of the inmates became angry when I did not respond to them. Some of them concluded I was crazy, and avoided me. Others, probably the smarter ones, soon realized my plan, and they appeared highly interested in how

the authorities would respond. Immediately the staff, angered by my silence, took action. Within a day of the beginning of my silence, the staff demanded that I speak. The next day, staff members threatened me with dire punishment if I did not. By the third day, they put me in "the hole" for refusing to obey a direct order. In the hole, one would have a hard bed, maybe some bed linens, and a toilet. Over the next years, I found myself in the hole many times. As I recall, this punishment was generally meted out with a specified time, such as three days or three weeks. I remained even more stubborn when handled this way.

When I was deemed sufficiently uncooperative in the hole, they confined me to a strip cell in Unit 2-1-EAST, the place where the psychiatric treatments in vogue at the time were available in ample supply to those diagnosed as very mentally disturbed or behaviorally unmanageable. It would not be long before sores from lying naked on the grooved concrete floor covered my body. I learned never to ask for treatment for my sores because the one time I did so via a note, the staff said, "Okay, we'll bring you some treatment." The "treatment" was also called "a baseball game." Nine guards charged into the strip cell, slamming the door behind them. They tightly encircled and pummeled me with their fists until I fell to the floor, and then, with their boots, they kicked me into oblivion.

While in the strip cells in 2-1-EAST, the staff sometimes took me to a separate area to receive hot tub baths and ice packs as legitimate forms of treatment. I was lucky, I guess, to escape the electroshock and the lobotomies, reserved for those inmates who violently resisted the hot tubs and ice packs. I did receive, in great abundance, the psychotropic medications of the time: Thorazine, Stelazine, and Prolixin. Staff had a creative technique for administering unwanted medications to an uncooperative inmate. They used it on me a few times while I was in a strip cell, perhaps for fighting an order to take some oral tranquilizers. Resisting the medication was foolish because staff would have their way. A group of guards entered my cell pushing into the room ahead of them a framed screen, which expanded to the full size of the cell wall as soon as it cleared the doorframe. Then the guards pushed the screen across the room, forcing me, naked, up against the opposite wall. A physician or physician-assistant entered the

room with a large syringe and administered a massive dose of the tranquilizer. As a hardhead, I suffered this indignity a number of times.

I warranted the above punishments and treatments not only for choosing silence but also for other behaviors deemed bothersome. Sometimes as part of my silence, I wrote answers to the guards' questions in a small notepad I carried in my pocket. Then I would show the pad to the guards, which was never satisfactory from their point of view. I didn't care; in fact, my purpose was to frustrate them. But when Larry Nelson addressed me as a man and recognized positive values in me, I wanted to cooperate and converse. For the most part, that ended my silence and reliance on a notepad.

I felt particularly irritated by the uniformity imposed on inmates at the time, and wearing military-style attire was one of the requirements. I decided to employ the passive resistance strategy to this issue. One day I took off my cotton-web belt, cut it up and flushed it down the toilet. I left my cell and walked down the hall toward the mess hall, not because I had any particular business in the mess hall, but just because I wanted to walk past the guard whose job it was to check for dress-code compliance.

My silent challenge drew the expected response, "Hey, you, come over here." I looked around to ascertain if he was talking to me (like a dog, not a human). I walked toward the guard with a sullen look on my face and stood before him. He said, "Where's your belt?"

I mumbled and acted as if I was trying to feel for the belt somewhere in the vicinity of my waist. Then I put on a real stupid look and replied, "I don't know where my belt is. These guys around here steal everything. They must have stolen my belt."

The guard sort of grunted his disapproval and said, "Well, go ahead now, but you'd better find a belt because I don't want to see you without it again."

The next morning, I walked down the hall, hoping to encounter the same guard. He stood at his post and again hailed me down, "Where's your belt? I told you yesterday to get one for yourself."

I replied, in the aw-shucks manner I had used with him the day before, "I did get a new belt yesterday from my unit officer, but it was gone this morning. Those guys must have stolen it again. Why

would guys steal my belts? Do you think someone is planning to make a long enough rope with them and then escape?"

The guard did not want to engage in a conversation about why my belts were stolen, but this problem I presented frustrated him. He may not have believed that I had obtained a second belt from the unit officer, and he wanted to be sure that I had a belt now. He said, "Come here, I'm going to be sure you have a belt because I don't want to see you again without one." And he took me to the clothing room where I was issued a new belt.

Back in my cell, I cut up the belt and flushed it down the toilet. The next time I walked toward the guard, he did a double take when he saw my belt-less waist. Then he pretended he did not see me. I continued on my way that day, and for years after that, without a belt, gaining some satisfaction from not doing things their way. They have a place for guys who say, "I refuse to wear a belt." But they had little idea what to do with a guy who acts too stupid or too sick to know how to keep possession of his own belt. Other inmates observed this and some of them copied my methods. There may have been other factors that led the authorities to gradually relax the rules about clothing, but I tend to think that my little acts of non-cooperation played a part. With actions such as these, I earned a reputation as an "inmates' man," gaining respect and sympathy from them. At the same time, to the custodial personnel I was a troublesome inmate, and often punished beyond the reasonable.

I cannot recall exactly what behaviors sent me into segregation and strip cells so many times, but it was never for any acts of violence toward guards or inmates. In the strip cell I experienced what I believe most inmates experience from the darkness and solitude there. Besides the physical discomforts and pain, my thought processes became unclear and even somewhat paranoid. A group of guards could come into the cell and I would not know if they were coming to release me or to inflict some further physical punishment. So to hear the sound of the key in the lock of the door was frightening. (The key for those cells measured about a foot long.) Guards knew that this sound produced fear in the inmates and some guards played "rattling the cage." This meant that they would stroll down the cellblock, make a lot of noise with their keys, and then insert the key in a lock, jiggling and manipu-

lating it as if the turning process were difficult. The inmate inside the cell would shake in fear, and then the guards would not open the door, but rather go on to the next cell and do the same thing. Eventually they might open someone's door for some purpose, but before doing so they had jangled the nerves of many more inmates, just for the perverse pleasure of doing so.

Guards never entered a strip cell alone, but only in the company of five or more others. There may have been some kindly guards among those who worked in the strip cell area, but to me it seemed they were picked based on their proclivity for sadism. More than once while I was in strip cell confinement, I received the fingernail treatment. Guards entered my cell and demanded I stretch out my hands for inspection. "Oh, those fingernails are much too long. Here, use this clipper to take care of those nails. We'll be back in about five minutes." Sure enough, in five minutes they returned and, no matter how short I clipped them, my nails needed to be shorter. Soon there was almost nothing left but the quick. Apparently the guards played this little game to provoke some defiance that they could use to justify further punishment. In this situation I felt that defiance could never be productive, and so I did as they said. But you can bet that this kind of treatment only fueled the fire in my belly.

Another time I was in a strip cell under the influence of a huge dosage of a major tranquilizer. I felt so heavy and groggy that I could not lift a finger. All I could do was lie on the floor and let my mind wander. I became aware of guards outside my cell in an argument about whether I was conscious or unconscious. The debate raged and finally, one of the guards who thought me unconscious said, "Come on, let's go in and I'll show you." I recognized the guard's voice as that of Officer Lou Carpenter. With that, the cell door opened and in came the squad. Carpenter led the charge, bent down over me, and said, "Look, I'll put my lit cigarette on him and he won't even know." All of a sudden I felt an intense burning pain on my upper left arm, but I could not raise even a murmur of objection.

After I came out of that period of segregation, I never directly confronted Officer Carpenter about how he had violated me. But I instilled fear in him, because whenever I was near him, I maneuvered myself into a position behind his back. I never performed

any act of overt aggression toward him, but he exuded fear in my presence and even seemed to curry my favor. Obviously, he never figured out if I knew who put the burning cigarette on my arm, and he never brought up the subject to me. I still bear the scar of that burn.

Passive resistance requires mental strength. I acquired a certain amount of toughness from dealing with my father in my youth, from the development of my athletic abilities, and from my earlier experiences in penal confinement. But I needed far more strength than what I had already gained if I intended to survive the many years ahead of me in federal prisons. I thought a lot about my situation and concluded that I had to develop every possible mental tool.

Sharpening my intuition in the prison environment was one of my first goals. I had always operated intuitively on the football field and the basketball court relative to other players around me. Now the players were often dangerous or insane. My intuition for perceiving these threats needed further development. I taught myself the art of reading the body language of people around me. I watched their behaviors and checked these against my intuitions, adjusting and refining my assessments as I noted what actually happened in various situations. I became proficient in quickly determining friends and foes, although I never became infallible in this. I also learned to listen closely, not only to the voices of people near me, but also for the general sounds emanating from a cell or the larger area of a cell house. A low buzz of sound was normal. If a place was too quiet or too loud, I looked around for trouble and usually found it.

Another self-protective behavior I decided would be part of my routine was to always sit near the door in places where many inmates gathered, such as the mess hall, with my back as close to a wall as possible. This position afforded me the greatest possibility of seeing all that was happening in my environment and of exiting from a dangerous situation quickly. I also chose not to attend movies, since they occurred in a darkened room where inmates could, and often did, engage in violence toward one another. In all ways, I tried to maintain a heightened awareness of my back, and what went on behind it.

To act in these self-protective ways, yet not convey to others fear or even apprehension, was my goal. To show fear is to be vulnerable to predators looking for their next victim. One way to cover up my apprehension was never to tell anyone why I acted in certain self-protective ways. I also tried to portray myself as a relaxed, self-confident person who knew he could handle any threatening situation.

Another mental tool I developed was not to allow the stresses of my situation to interfere with my needed sleep. If I knew I was in a fairly secure place, such as a single cell or room, or even in a strip cell on cold concrete, I learned how to put all mental distractions aside and clear my mind so that sleep could come over me. In a cell with one, two, five or nine others, it was more of a challenge to relax and sleep. In those situations, I made the acquaintance of all my cellmates and showed each how I could be useful to him so that he would not turn on me while I slept. If I found a cellmate I could not trust this much, I finagled a way to move to another cell. No matter what occurred on any day, or what might occur the next day, I knew that mental and physical rest were my allies, and that only I could ensure these for myself.

In order to survive a horrible present, a person needs to have a dream for the future. I did not start my long federal sentence with any hope regarding my future. But when I decided I would not kill myself and I would live as meaningful a life as I could, I knew I needed to formulate a plan for a reality which would be bigger than the limited world I inhabited in prison. I knew release from prison was only a remote possibility, but I decided I wanted to fight for it. A release to a better future became my all-consuming goal, and everything I did related to that hope.

I could not construct any specifics for a future that remained still so distant. To keep hope alive, I nurtured my memories. In a secure room or cell, I let my mind wander, almost always to the happy times in my childhood. I thought about Christmases at my childhood home on Berwyn Road in Birmingham, Michigan, and about all the summers filled with fun at Grandma Taylor's home in Connecticut. I also thought about the many loving relatives, and about my sister, my cousins, and friends whom I enjoyed so much as I grew up. I mentally replayed the games of my earlier childhood, as well as the athletic contests I participated in as a teen and

young adult. These indulgences provided a balance to all the pain and negativity that was so much a part of my life. The fact that I had known happiness, and could tap back into my past to remember this feeling, was enormously helpful to me; sadly, a memory bank from better times was not available to so many of my fellow inmates who came from backgrounds of complete neglect and deprivation. Perhaps those inmates enjoyed the Christmas festivities in prison more than me. The feelings I enjoyed from reliving the past formed the basis of the dream I worked to develop for the future. I knew that I wanted somehow to recreate these feelings in whatever future I might have outside the prison.

As a result of my first job in Larry Nelson's office, I moved on to other office jobs for Unicor. I developed my skills, becoming fully capable as an industrial cost accountant, and later adding computer expertise to my repertoire. Working for wages boosted my self-esteem and mental attitude immensely, just as it would for any man regardless of whether he lived in an institution or in free society.

Working for Unicor often resulted in the additional privilege of placement in a unit occupied only by other Unicor inmate-employees, generally the more stable inmates. We often had single rooms in these units, the ideal living condition to have in the prisons. An office setting was also the calmest and safest environment for employment, due to the nature of the work and the fact that there were generally more civilian employees than inmates who held those desk jobs. We even had air conditioning, and in some offices, piped-in background music. I enjoyed working around the civilians because they were often intelligent, educated people. Some seemed to respect me for my hard work, intelligence, athletic knowledge and concern for them as individuals. Some of my fellow civilian employees enlisted their wives to do a little extra baking so that they could bring in goodies to me. To supplement the prison diet with anything homemade was a greatly appreciated treat. One civilian sought my advice and assistance in finding the right college and an athletic scholarship for his son. All this helped me to live a life outside a cell house.

From the beginning of my federal incarceration, I worked for legal relief of my situation. I needed to start from scratch in my knowledge of the law and the courts. I made virtually no progress

during the first few years because punishment and "treatment" for my mental problems interrupted me. But after I left the strip cells behind and went to work for Larry Nelson, I never turned back. I continued to avoid direct personal confrontation with the custodial staff, thus almost always enjoying as much freedom as possible permitted within the walls of a federal prison. I had time now to spend many, many evenings and weekends in the law library. I started my legal education by working on my own case, seeking relief from the long sentence based on arguments that the sentencing court had not adequately considered my mental condition.

In the 1960s, the progressive movements that surged through civilian society found their way into the federal prisons. Rehabilitation of prisoners came into vogue and we saw an increase in educational opportunities for ourselves. I did my best to take advantage of these opportunities, completing many college-level accounting and business administration classes, along with liberal arts courses.

Besides finding ways to feel good about myself and avoid depression through working, legal efforts, and education, I decided that becoming a valuable asset to my fellow inmates increased the likelihood of my own survival. I thought about what might bring me the true appreciation of these men. I offered my own expanding knowledge of the law to others. I worked on the legal cases of many inmates over the years, and realized that I was often more successful with others' cases than with my own. I also helped and encouraged others in their education, over the years tutoring a good thirty to forty inmates as they prepared for their high school equivalency tests. Occasionally, I lent other inmates money for some of their worthwhile pursuits, but lending is risky business in this setting, so I did it judiciously. I even ran a "store" for a while. I had money from my earnings, which allowed me to buy many items in the commissary as well as some used property from inmates who wanted to unload it. This provided me with merchandise to resell, at a little profit to myself, to inmates who wanted to buy things when the commissary was closed or to purchase something at a second-hand price. I did a lot of business on weekends and holidays and I gained the appreciation of my fellows, although I will say a few inmates resented my success.

As my skills expanded in bringing legal issues to the attention

of federal courts on behalf of individuals, I realized that I could also help groups of inmates through legal actions. One of the first times I took leadership in bringing an inmates' issue to the courts regarded the matter of hair length and style. A very short haircut was the requirement for everyone when I entered the system in the 1950s. At that time, short haircuts were the style in outside society. Prisoners are not immune from the desire to keep up with the changing times, and as the 1960s rolled on, we wanted to let our hair grow. I was one of the inmates who rankled at the requirement for short hair, so I decided to use my legal skills to take the matter to the nearest federal district court.

We filed a class action suit, seeking the right to wear our hair at any length and style. The matter lingered in the court for many months, probably longer than a year, during which time I decided not to cut my hair. The rules had already relaxed a little so that inmates could wear hats indoors. Wearing a hat allowed me to cover my fast-growing hair. I used baseball caps on the yard and stocking caps indoors, and very few people knew just how long my hair was.

I kept track of our action with the court and finally received word that we had won our suit. I spread the news to just a few people and waited for the notice of the rule change to be posted on the appropriate bulletin board. The wait was difficult because we had worked so hard on an issue we really cared about, plus I wanted to pull my surprise on the staff. Eventually, probably weeks after I first knew we had won, I found the rule-change notice posted on the bulletin board, indicating that as of the next day, we could wear our hair any length and style provided it was neat and clean. I washed my hair that evening. The next morning I brushed my shoulder-length hair out to its fullest, and walked casually out into the rotunda, the center of the U.S. Penitentiary at Leavenworth. Staff gawked. I smiled. Staff advanced. More than one pulled on my hair, suspecting a wig. When they found real hair, they immediately realized that I had been putting one over on them for quite some time. While they could have punished me for this, they apparently decided to overlook it since, at this point, I was in compliance with the rules. Most inmates took great delight in both the new rule and in my defiance. But just as some inmates at times resented my successes, so, too, did some

guards resent my victories in the courts, especially when the legal process drew attention to their repressive policies and actions.

Another class action suit I led was one that did not turn out so successfully. After I had worked for Unicor for some time, albeit at low prison wages, it occurred to me that we inmate-employees were not contributing to Social Security. Many inmates with lesser and determinate sentences definitely expected to be back in free society and working. Although the likelihood of my parole was less than theirs, I felt that all of us, by not contributing to Social Security, missed out on the work credit that would likely benefit us greatly in our older years. I checked with the institution's officials regarding whether we could sign up for Social Security deductions from our wages. The staff said the law did not permit us to be part of the Social Security program. Now, how wise is this, especially considering that sentences have increased over the years and men serve much longer sentences, sometimes only gaining release at retirement age? Felons have enough going against them when they are released, and losing out on credits with Social Security while working full-time hours in prison hardly needs to be added to their deficits.

I talked with my fellow inmates and many agreed that we needed to fight for the right to participate in Social Security. We filed a suit, but lost. We took the matter further on appeal, but never won. Involving myself in this, and other such actions over the many years of my incarceration, helped to maintain my morale, but this particular loss was a bitter disappointment.

Another serious injustice that came to the attention of the federal courts was the use of federal prisoners as involuntary subjects for pharmaceutical experimentation. I contributed knowledge from my own experiences and worked with others to bring this to a successful conclusion. The federal courts stopped the practice as I had experienced it, allowing experimentation only with knowledgeable and willing inmates.

A choice I made which suited my personality, and which I felt would work toward my greater safety, was to avoid membership in any group. Most inmates choose to affiliate with a group, usually based on race, geographic origin, and sometimes philosophy or religion, believing there is safety in numbers. But I am by nature

not a joiner, and I made the decision to be friendly to everyone, or at least, not to be an enemy of anyone based on his affiliations. For my efforts, the NAACP (National Association for the Advancement of Colored People) awarded me a Certificate of Appreciation for my assistance in convincing the authorities at the Lewisburg penitentiary to allow a chapter for the inmates. Likewise, I assisted an American Indian inmate when we were both at the Federal Correctional Institution at Phoenix in his fight with the U.S. Government about housing promised to the Indians in exchange for some land. In gratitude, this man presented me with a chalk drawing of myself, which he drew without my posing or giving him a photo from which to work. The drawing is very well done, and I feel honored that he somehow made this blue-eyed, blond-haired Anglo-Saxon look like an American Indian.

warning signs

WHEN I WAS TWELVE, my eight-year-old sister Sally dropped a bombshell: "Mom told me we're adopted." I was stunned. This possibility had never crossed my mind. Incredulous that my pesky little sister knew vital information about us and that our mother told her before telling me, I ran directly to my mother and confronted her. "Is it true? Am I really adopted?" Rather matter-of-factly, my mother verified that she and my father, the only parents I knew, had adopted me when I was about three. I was furious, but said nothing.

I wanted to know about my beginnings. I waited for a chance to be alone in our house so I might rummage through my father's big desk. When the opportunity came, I discovered legal papers documenting my adoption by Esther and James Taylor through the Children's Aid Society of Detroit. There was no information about why my birth parents had given me away. Though still angry about my parents' choice not to initiate any discussion of this with me, I kept it to myself.

I did not learn any more facts about my birth or my birth parents until many years later. Sometime after the Freedom of Information Act became law in 1966, I requested documents kept by the federal government relative to my case and my sentencing. I gasped when I came upon one of the documents: a copy of an

FBI report labeled *James Peter Taylor's Real Mother*. I immediately and eagerly read the report, probably prepared as part of the pre-sentence investigation. It indicated that during her teenage years, my birth mother (no name provided) was a resident of the State Industrial Home for Girls, in Michigan. When she was seventeen, the officials of the Home arranged for her transfer to the University of Michigan Hospital, Psychopathic Ward, for observation and treatment. The University Hospital declared that she suffered from "psychopathic personality, unstable type." The FBI report then mentions "a male child was born to her on June 13, 1925." It says that in 1926, my mother's husband (no indication of whether this man was my birth father or my stepfather) resided in a sanatorium and that they had marital trouble. She apparently told someone, because it was quoted in this report, that "she couldn't live with him, that her husband did not like her boy, even though he was good to him, or tried to be good to him at times." I was placed in the Taylor home in January 1928, at age two and a half, and formal adoption occurred later. The report also says that my birth mother had a nervous breakdown in November 1930. Two years later, on Christmas Day, 1932, she died of lobar pneumonia, at age twenty-seven.

James Walter Taylor left his family home in Connecticut be-cause he saw no future for himself in the fishing community of New London. He came to Michigan as a young man to seek his fortune in the early stages of the automobile industry. James se-cured a job with a road construction company in the Saginaw area where he met Esther Norton, a telephone operator. James mar-ried Esther. Her parents believed enough in their new son-in-law's abilities that they mortgaged their home in order to lend James money so he could establish his own road construction business. My future adoptive father enjoyed quick success and soon sent for his younger brother, Jack, to come to Michigan to be his part-ner in the business. The Taylor Brothers Construction Company, located in Birmingham, a suburb of Detroit, eventually became one of the three largest road construction companies in the state of Michigan.

James and Esther had no children until I joined their family. My father was then forty years old and my mother thirty. Two years after I arrived in the household, Sally was adopted as an

infant. I remember being all decked-out in a navy blue sailor suit and told we were going to pick up my little sister. Isn't it odd, that even though there is in my brain this memory of driving somewhere to get Sally, I never thought about her being adopted until she revealed this to me years later?

I remember the first house I lived in with my new parents. It stood on Madison Avenue, in a pleasant, well-established neighborhood east of Woodward Avenue, the main north-south artery through Detroit, Birmingham and other suburbs. Our home felt comfortable. I remember enjoying a sandbox in the adjoining vacant lot. Uncle Jack and his wife, "Jose" (short for Josephine) lived right across the street. They had two daughters: Mary, who was about my age, and Joanne, a few years older. My mother's brother, George, known always as "Curly," and his wife, Dorothy, lived without children just around the corner from our home. Curly was an osteopathic physician in the area, as was his older brother, Joseph. Uncle Joe, his wife, "Ted" (Theodora), and their sons, Bud and Jim, lived about ten miles away, in the suburb of Farmington. This family joined us for Sunday dinner almost every week for years. Bud and Jim were about four and six years older than me.

Sally and I grew up during the Depression years without ever wanting for anything. Looking back, I recall a lot of movement of families in and out of their homes in Birmingham. I think now that the movement was due to the declining fortunes of many families during the 1930s. But the Taylor family thrived. Before I began first grade, my father had a home built for us, west of Woodward Avenue, in an area with only a few new homes at that time. Our new five-bedroom brick house, at 497 Berwyn Road, is the focus of almost all of my childhood memories, many of which are very happy. We had a live-in maid, and dined out at the Fox and Hounds and other nice restaurants on Thursdays, the maid's day off, and Sundays. We vacationed in Connecticut almost every summer and in Florida many winters. We occasionally spent time at a Michigan resort. I was sent to summer camp for a few weeks, probably during three different summers. We always had two cars, purchased new and traded in every two years. My mother drove the Buick sedan and my father the Ford Coupe. My parents bought a grand piano to adorn our living room and then arranged

lessons for Sally and me. Neither of us responded with any enthu-
siasm or talent so my mother took lessons herself.

I loved our home on Berwyn Road. There were other families
living near enough so I always found playmates. But there were
also wide-open spaces. Looking west from the second-floor win-
dows, I could see the Oakland Hills Country Club a mile away.
Just south were open fields and woods where I roamed, look-

ing for pheasants in season, hunting snakes, and harvesting wild strawberries from the patches in the fields.

Whenever I announced I was "running away," usually because my mother had denied me something, I headed for the strawberry patches. My mother, on these occasions, usually said, "Okay, you go, and have a good time. Here's a snack for you to eat while you travel. Oh, and by the way, we'll be having hamburgers and sweet potatoes for supper, but I guess you won't be here." In the strawberry patches, I ate the berries, pouted and considered a return home. Staying away never seemed an option by the time I heard my mother ringing the dinner bell for me.

Our home was built on a large, deep lot with plenty of space for my dad to plant flowers and vegetables. He favored roses and planted them so they climbed the many trellises around the garden. My father also placed benches around the garden's perimeter, where we could sit and admire his work. In the side yard, we had a wooden glider-swing, where my parents, and sometimes Sally and I, sat and swung on late spring and early fall evenings.

I loved dogs as a kid. My first was Tommy, an overprotective Heinz 57 mutt; he bit anyone he thought threatened my toys. Even my parents feared him, but they put up with his aggressiveness for a few years before they got rid of him. I do not recall a specific incident that triggered his sudden disappearance. I missed Tommy, but my parents found a quick substitute. My next dog was a gentle little collie whom I named Cliquot, after Cliquot Club ginger ale, my favorite soft drink. Everyone loved Cliquot (pronounced "*Clee*-ko"), my mother so much so that she willingly took on the daily responsibility of brushing his long hair. Cliquot, however, had a flaw, one that was especially unsuited to a suburban dog: he loved to chase cars. Seemingly, he could not help himself, and no amount of instruction or discipline was effective. After a car hit Cliquot once too often, I came home from school one day to find that he was gone. My parents told me they gave Cliquot to a family in the country where he would be safe from moving cars. I cried at the loss of my Cliquot, even though I understood my parents' reasoning in finding another home for him. But I was not present for any of the transactions regarding Cliquot's new home, so there remains in me some doubt that they truly did move him to a safer place.

Sally always had a cat, and we usually had a canary, too. I remember the time one of our maids found a wounded baby squirrel in the nearby woods and brought it home. My mother agreed that the squirrel could stay in one of our extra birdcages while she and the maid nursed it back to health. At times, Mother was kind enough to let the canary and the squirrel out of their cages. On one memorable occasion, Sally and I came into the house to find quite a scene: the canary perched on top of the living room drapes, the chattering squirrel running up the drapes, closing in on the canary, the cat halfway up the drapes, and Cliquot below, yelping excitedly. Not surprisingly, the freaked-out canary discharged white excrement down the dark red velvety drapes. My mother and the maid tried to catch the animals, while my father barked orders. Sally and I laughed ourselves sick.

Sometimes I bought goldfish and kept them in a big glass bowl. I also found snails and frogs in the ponds and swamps at the edges of the field south of our house. I brought some of these critters home, and was usually met by my mother, who set some limits on what kinds of animals could come in the house. On an occasion my mother did not stand guard, I brought in fifteen or twenty turtles that I carried home in a bushel-basket from nearby Quarton Lake. I brought them to the basement, filled a laundry tub with water, and set the turtles in the tub. I played with them for a while and then went upstairs to find something else to do. Alerted to trouble by the sound of my mother shrieking, I knew she had found my turtles. I came down the stairs and saw Mother standing with her arms crossed and a stern look on her face. "Get these out of here fast, Jimmy, or I'll tell your father." I gathered up those turtles into the bushel-basket as fast as I could and took them back to their home in the lake.

When I was seven or eight, my mother took me along on one of her shopping expeditions to an open-air market in Royal Oak, a suburb next to Birmingham. As we browsed through the aisles of stalls, we came upon a farmer selling live chickens. I announced that I wanted a chicken, and Mother humored me by buying one. I carried the chicken home in the car and set about building a coop for my new pet. A few days later, I went out early in the morning to check on my chicken, and by gum, in the nest lay an egg! I ran into the house, carefully carrying the egg, and showed

it to my parents with excitement. "Look at my chicken's egg!" We put the egg in the refrigerator. Next morning, I went outside to see if my chicken had repeated her feat. To my amazement, she had doubled her production, for there lay two eggs! Over the next four days, I found first three, then four, then five, and finally, six eggs. I decided to go into the egg business, so I started going door to door in the neighborhood.

Though we were not poor, I guess my parents decided that the joke had become too expensive. One day when I came home from school, I found no chicken in the coop. Instead, a trail of blood led from the coop down our cement driveway and across the street. My father had apparently slaughtered the chicken and given the dead bird to our neighbors, the Moses, who probably asked their maid to prepare it for dinner. But my father never acknowledged the truth about what happened to the chicken, and I was angry with him for weeks.

I have no recollection of my mother's father, but I do remember Grandma Norton well. She came to visit our family about twice a year, each time staying for several weeks. My mother clearly resembled her own mother; both were sweet, loving and peaceable. Grandma Norton was a great hugger--she hugged everyone she could, and I felt great warmth toward her. She became the family baker while she visited. I could not wait to get home from school when she stayed with us, so that I could stuff myself with doughnuts and other luscious goodies, fresh from the oven. She had a little mischief in her, too. One time my mother told me to go upstairs and retrieve something she wanted from the closet in the guest room. I did as I was told that day, and when I opened the closet door, out jumped Grandma Norton, arms outstretched to hug me, shouting, "Boo!" I nearly had a heart attack at that young age, while Grandma and my mother chuckled. I did not find it funny.

When I was nine or ten, my parents told me that Grandma Norton had cancer, and that she would die soon. Grandma came to our house to live out her last days in my mother's care. My mother nursed Grandma Norton in our guest bedroom. Uncle Curly came by every day, and Uncle Joe came about three times each week, but they had no cures for the cancer. I watched my

mother's hair turn gray that year. Finally Grandma died, which saddened the whole family for a long period. For some reason, a few years later the guest bedroom became my bedroom. Even as a teenager, I retained fears of the closet, imagining that Grandma might jump out at me.

Uncle Curly and Aunt Dorothy had no children of their own. Much later, after I was all but grown, they adopted two children. But in my early childhood, Uncle Curly doted on me. He played Santa Claus for me while we still lived on Madison Avenue, so close to him and Dorothy. Often they were visiting at our house when it was my bedtime. I would be sent to bed, and Curly would come into my bedroom to tell me a scary bedtime story, which I enjoyed. After that, he would bid me good night and act as if he was leaving the room, turning off the light and closing the door. Within about a minute, a low, scary voice would then intone, "This is Doctor Fu Man Chu, and I'm here to get you." He would carry on some more, scaring the daylights out of me until I would damn near wet the bed. And then Curly would turn on the light to show himself, bid me a real good night, and leave me alone with my fears.

My Uncle Curly was also our family doctor. Whenever any of us developed an ailment, he appeared in a flash. As I got a little older, he liked to show me wrestling moves. Curly stood about five feet, ten inches, and probably weighed two hundred pounds, a big man. I learned the moves and one day, when I thought I perhaps had surpassed him in strength and agility, I decided to try to pin him in one of our matches. It happened in our kitchen on Berwyn Road and I was sixteen or so. Curly and I started to wrestle and just as I had him pinned to the floor, Aunt Dorothy came through the swinging doors into the kitchen. I detected in an instant that Curly became incredibly embarrassed for his wife to see him as weaker than his nephew. I had not intended to hurt him, and immediately regretted putting him in this position. Something vitally important changed between us that day and never again did we roughhouse.

My first friend in my neighborhood on Berwyn Road was Skippy Fader. Skippy and I made excellent partners in mischief. We were about six when construction of a new house took place on our

block. One day, after all the windows of the new house had just been installed, we played in the surrounding piles of dirt and rocks. I picked up a stone, and not thinking much, threw it at a window. My aim was good, the window shattered, and a shower of glass fell to the ground. The noise and destruction that followed so simply from a thrown stone exhilarated us both. Skippy wanted his own experience, so he threw the next rock, with the same dramatic result. We laughed and threw stones until there was not a single window left unbroken on the entire first floor. Skippy and I shattered some very large windows, along with many small ones, in a short period of time, leaving us exhausted but satisfied. We walked away, talking with excitement about our fine aim. I had not really considered the wrongfulness of my actions while I threw those stones, but as we walked home, I decided not to inform my parents about what had happened.

Later that day a policeman came to our door, inquiring whether I might have been the window-breaker. My father asked me if it was true, and I immediately confessed, deciding not to implicate Skippy because he had only followed my lead. My dad told the officer that he would take care of both payment for the windows and my punishment. As the officer walked toward the door, he gave me a little wink and said, "Now, Sonny, don't break any more windows." I was relieved because I thought the worst was over. But my dad was irate. He swore and yelled at me. When he slapped me, I fell to the floor, and he gave me a few kicks. This was not the first time my dad physically punished me, but it is the first incident that I remember clearly.

My father's unpredictable, violent personality hung over my youth like a thundercloud. I have almost no recollection of my father as a warm, loving person, not just in relation to me, but also in relation to my mother and sister. I cannot count how many times I heard, "If I've told you once, I've told you a thousand times, don't ..." He jabbed his strong, straight index finger into my chest, over and over, in rhythm to his tirade. "Do you understand me? Do I have to tell you again?" His approach created fear in me, at first, and then later, a need to stand in opposition. I vowed to deny him many pleasures that my abilities might otherwise have provided. Because I loved athletics so much, I could not give that up,

even to hurt him. In athletics, I was determined to be the best, to surpass whatever my father's accomplishments were in that arena, so as to gain some gratification. Paradoxically, I strove to be an excellent athlete, in part, because I desired to gain his approval.

But in many other ways, I refused to fulfill his wishes for my success. I was perfectly capable, for example, of doing well academically, and he wanted me to be a good mathematics student. So I deliberately failed math. He wanted me to be interested in his road construction business, and he expected me to accompany him and learn by watching his employees build roads and do various kinds of office work. I went along grudgingly and learned little. He used a completely ineffectual approach, authoritarian and demanding, and he finally gave up. Had he engaged me in a loving and positive way, I think I would have shared many of his interests.

In my early grade school years, I sometimes lost a mitten or one of my galoshes. Then, realizing I needed to return home without a lost item, I would become paralyzed by fear. I knew I would have to answer to an angry father and no answer would be good enough. My report cards became another occasion for me to dread his reaction, although I acknowledge that I quite consciously produced bad report cards for the express purpose of thwarting any pride he might have in my academic career.

His responses to my intentional and unintentional provocations were not only verbal outbursts, but also physical assaults. As a young child, I often received blows to the head from my father's open hand. Whenever my mother observed these actions, she pleaded with him to stop, but with little effect. When she objected too much, he invariably turned on her, thrusting his fingers into her chest and shoving her, all the while screaming orders and obscenities.

The man never once voiced an apology. Rather, if he was particularly abusive to me one day, I might find a new baseball glove or some other new plaything on my bed the next day. I did not decline these gifts. In his own way, my father was good about providing me with extra opportunities to learn. He and my mother bought many books, including all the children's classics, which I devoured eagerly. Many times, on our trips as a family, my father stopped the car so that Sally and I could visit historical sites or

other tourist attractions along the highway. I loved learning in these ways, much more so than in the confines of a 1930s class-room.

The community elected my father a Justice of the Peace, with part-time responsibilities that he could perform while still running his business. He constantly harped on me to be honest and trustworthy, so as not to sully the dignity of his position or his reputation in the community. However, my father was not entirely an honest man. We crossed the Canada-U.S. border numerous times in our summer travels to and from Connecticut. At these times, he expected the complicity of Sally and me as he hid bottles of whiskey under the front seat and told the border guard that he had nothing to declare. He also hung Hudson Bay blankets, newly purchased in Canada but undeclared at the border, on the cord stretched across the rear of the front seat. Besides the fear I felt, I also became intensely angry at his hypocrisy.

I dared not reveal my father's deceptions to the border patrols nor even privately question him. But I would have enjoyed it if he had been discovered and punished. Occasionally he met his comeuppance. The time I remember best happened in Grandma Taylor's house in Connecticut. My father had a distasteful habit of opening the icebox, pulling out a large container of soda pop, taking a big swig, and then returning the bottle to the shelf. One day, my mother prepared a large volume of potassium permanganate, deep purple in color, for the purpose of treating the poison ivy to which Sally and I were susceptible in the summer. Mother put the solution into a large, dark green ginger ale bottle, and placed it in the icebox. My father walked into the kitchen from the hot outdoors, reached into the icebox by the door, and quickly took a big gulp of what he thought was ginger ale. My mother, an aunt, and I all sat around the table, none of us aware of his actions. All of a sudden, my father spewed purple liquid from his mouth, all over himself and the kitchen, screaming at my mother, "Esther, what is this? Have you done something stupid again?"

My mother became extremely solicitous and tearful. "Oh, Jim, I'm so sorry, it's the stuff for the kids' poison ivy. Here, quick, wash your mouth out with water." She guided him to the sink. My father pushed her away, and my mother cried, "Don't you remember? I always put the potassium permanganate in a dark bottle."

He screamed that was no excuse. Feverish activity ensued, as my mother, aunts and grandmother scrubbed the purple off the cupboards, appliances and floor. My father continued his rage for some time thereafter. I took great delight in watching my father suffer, although as usual, my concern for what my mother had to endure tempered my pleasure.

My father seemed to enjoy seeing me suffer, too. I had no interest in boxing, for example, but he bought me a punching bag, erected it in the basement, and encouraged me to practice. I was then eight or nine. I developed no interest in the sport and never practiced. He then bought me two pairs of boxing gloves and suggested that I box with my friends Tommy, Jack or Bruce. The gloves remained little used until my father had a new idea. One Sunday when Uncle Joe, Aunt Ted, and their two sons, Bud and Jim, were at our house for dinner, my father suggested that Bud and Jim take turns boxing with me. These cousins were several years older. I recall that Uncle Joe and his sons expressed their reluctance, but my father insisted. From that point on, every time the Norton family came to dinner, boxing stayed on my dad's agenda and only occasionally could I extricate myself. I felt powerless to refuse outright my father's command that I put on the gloves, and Bud and Jim, though initially reluctant, became willing to routinely give me a sound thumping.

I enjoyed exploring the woods, marsh and open field to the south of our house. If I wandered all the way to the southwest corner of the open area, I could inspect the city dump. As many kids would, I invariably found fascinating objects in the dump, so I disregarded my parents' wishes that I stay away from that area. I found old military medals, rusted car frames, worn household items and much more. One day, I found some old, greasy rolls of film, and decided to bring them home for further inspection. I took the film to our basement and set the rolls in my tool chest, which sat on my workbench. The chest of tools had been a gift from my father, and he had the workbench built especially for me to spur my interest in handicraft. As with so many other activities to which he introduced me, I demonstrated very little interest in using the tools. Now there was so much film that the lid of the chest could not close, so I rested it back against the wall.

Several days later, I remembered my stash of film and decided to look at it more carefully. Since the basement was quite dark,

I thought I would try to illuminate the film with some kitchen matches I had stored on a ledge close to the ceiling just above my workbench. I had to climb up on a nearby storage cabinet to reach the matches. When I stretched to grab a few of the matches, I brought my hand down, and one of the matches scraped against the rough concrete wall, burst into flame and dropped into the tool chest. Instantly, the greasy film caught fire and exploded into a fiery mass. I jumped to the floor and tried to put out the fire, but quickly realized it was beyond my capacity to extinguish. I ran to the foot of the basement stairs and hollered, "Dad!"

My father came charging down the steps, grabbed a fire extinguisher, and quickly brought the blaze under control. "What did you do?" he screamed at me. I tried to explain as well as an eight-year-old could, but he neither believed nor cared that it was an accident. He started to wallop me, but I got away. I ran up the basement steps and then to my bedroom on the second floor, where I stayed for the rest of the day. I guess my mother interceded, since my father did not follow me. When I came down the stairs the next day for breakfast, facing my father filled me with apprehension. But the matter did not come up, and I breathed a sigh of relief.

Another incident which remains vivid in my mind occurred a year or two later. I was in the kitchen when I heard my father call to me, "Jim, come here." I located his voice as coming from the garage, and so I went there and saw him down on his haunches, deeply involved in tinkering with something. He turned his head toward me and said, "Go down in the basement and get me my pipe wrench." He said it with such firmness in his voice that I knew he felt he needed that particular tool right away. However, I did not know a pipe wrench from any other kind of wrench, and I dared not ask him for clarification. I panicked, but went down the steps to the basement, to the area where my father kept his tools neatly arranged in rows on the wall. I looked at those tools, desperate to know which was the pipe wrench, but had no idea how to make the right selection. Seconds went by. My fear intensified as I heard him yell, "Get up here with that wrench." I shook with fear. I grabbed several wrenches, all that I could carry in my two hands, and ascended the steps slowly, hoping as hard as I could that one of these tools was the one he wanted. He kept yelling and I slowly approached him with my offering. As I entered the

garage, he turned around from his crouched position and saw my presentation. He bellowed, "What the hell is the matter with you? Those aren't what I want." He came up out of his crouch and smacked me so hard that I lost my balance, my feet left the floor and I tumbled into a nearby radiator, opening a large gash in my head.

My mother came flying out of the kitchen, across the back entry, and down the three steps into the garage where she saw my bloody head. She went wild. "You stop that!" she screamed at my father, and she put herself between him and me. I used the opportunity to scramble to my feet and run up to my bedroom. As I ran, I heard my father hitting my mother, and I heard her crying. When I got to my room, I went into the adjoining bathroom and locked the two doors into it. Again, I stayed upstairs for as long as I could—many hours.

Due to repeated incidents like these, my fear and my anger grew. I thought that I knew exactly when I was in trouble and likely to be walloped. But occasionally my father surprised me. One summer I decided to plant cantaloupes in one of our gardens. My dad approved of this, perhaps because I showed interest in one of his hobbies, gardening. The cantaloupes made good progress under my care and were almost fully-grown, when one day, Tommy Rupp, a neighborhood bully about six years older, came through our back yard into my garden. Tommy started to taunt me about being a gardener. I wanted to chase him out of the yard but he was too big for me to take on directly. He escalated the encounter by picking up one of the cantaloupes and smashing it to the ground. Before I could figure out how to effectively respond to his attack on my cantaloupe, he picked up another and hurled it to the ground. He then proceeded to smash every one of the cantaloupes by stomping them, or crushing them with a fallen tree branch, all the while jeering at me, "What are you going to do about it, you little squirt?" I frantically tried to deal with the situation by talking back; I could not attack him physically. Then I spotted one of Cliquot's half-eaten bones. I grabbed that big old bone off the grass, ran up to Tommy as close as I dared, and flung the bone as hard as I could right at his head. My weapon landed in his face with a sickening crunch, and he ran off, howling. Our maid, hearing some of the racket from the kitchen, came out of the house and witnessed most of the encounter. She comforted

me, and because my mother was not at home, she telephoned my dad at his business and informed him of what happened. She may have given him her opinion of the justification for my action, but when she got off the phone, she told me that my father ordered me to my room. I knew that my father would deal with the matter when he came home.

I waited in trepidation. Finally, during the evening, the maid came to my bedroom and said that my father wanted to see me in the screened-in back porch, where he often sat in the evenings reading his newspaper. I came down the stairs and slowly approached the back porch. My father took off his glasses and looked at me intently. He told me that Tommy needed medical treatment, including many stitches across his cheek. Tommy's face would likely be scarred for life, and he, my dad, would be paying the medical bills. All this information heightened my anxiety considerably. My dad let the silence mount before he finally said, "Jim, if you hadn't thrown that bone at Tommy, I would have punished you. You did the right thing." He patted me on the shoulder while he said, "Good work, son." So very rarely did my dad side with me, or understand my point of view, that this incident also remains vivid in my memory. I think that my father wanted to teach me that defending one's property with some violence is justifiable.

At home, my father's tyrannical outbursts occurred frequently, while in the community he maintained an aura of respectability. One of my father's best friends was Ralph Mouthrupp, who owned the only lumberyard in Birmingham. Ralph and his wife, Bernice, became frequent visitors in our home. My mother enjoyed the friendship of the Mouthrupps as much as my father did. The Mouthrupps had no children and they became "Uncle Ralph" and "Aunt Bernice" to Sally and me.

When I was about nine, I woke up one night with a start, having a sensation that something was wrong. I got out of bed and headed for my parents' bedroom. I was surprised to run into my father also heading into the hallway. He asked me what was wrong. I told him I had awakened suddenly because something felt strange. This was about the only time I can recall that my father reached out to me in a kindly, familial way. He put his arm around my shoulder and suggested that we go down to the kitchen and get ourselves a hot drink. He had a cup of coffee and made me a cup of Postum. We sat at the kitchen table and wondered out

loud why we both awakened at the same time, with similar feelings of unease. We drank our beverages and then went back to our respective bedrooms. The next morning we learned that Aunt Bernice died during the night, at the very hour my father and I had awakened. This is the first time in my life that I remember having a clear and correct intuition something was amiss without any tangible evidence. Over time this happened more and more.

The community appreciated my father because he made a practice of patronizing the many small businesses in town. Once he bought me a bike from the man who owned the Firestone store, not because it was a particularly good bike, but because he liked the store's owner. While others in the community discriminated against Jews or Italians who may have owned businesses, my father did not show this prejudice. He patronized Sam Bruni's Italian grocery store. One day he came home from Dave Levenson's clothing store with a pair of purple corduroy pants for me, perhaps because Dave, a Jewish businessman, was unable to sell those pants to anyone else. I protested, but he insisted that I wear the pants. I knew if I appeared at Quarton School in purple trousers, I would be ridiculed and possibly forced to fight. Determined that I would not wear those pants in the company of my peers, I promptly went outside in them, and when I could not see home, I rubbed my knees hard across the grass and the rough sidewalk. This created stains and tears to the point when no parent would allow a child of theirs to be seen in such disreputable attire. I returned home telling a tale about the strenuous game of touch football in which I had just played.

One of the more unusual of my father's friends was Ken Bingham, an unmarried man somewhat younger than my father. I detected something different about Ken, which at the time I could not put into words. I enjoyed his visits because he had an engaging personality, plus he usually brought me extremely generous gifts of some of my favorite things, including a carton of Dentyne chewing gum. He often brought bananas, and once actually brought me a huge stalk of about fifty bananas. As time went on, I realized that Ken was quite effeminate. I never really understood the nature of the relationship between my father and Ken.

By the time I was thirteen, my father stopped hitting me, but he continued to stab his long bony finger into my chest to make

his various points. We were miles apart emotionally, and he virtually never seemed to act in a truly paternal way. A couple of times when I was involved in accidents while driving a family car, my father inquired about the condition of the car before my health. The priority of his concerns saddened me. On another occasion, I came home late one evening from a date with a girl. I entered the kitchen and heard my dad call to me from the screened-in back porch. I went out to the porch, expecting him to show disapproval of my late arrival, and found him in his usual position, sitting on the swing along the north wall. I greeted him, hoping that all he wanted was to see that I was home. Instead, he quipped, "I know what you've been doing. I used to put my hands into the girls' panties, too, when I was your age." His comment disgusted me. I could not imagine the fathers of my friends Bruce, Jack, or Tommy ever talking this crudely to their sons.

My sister Sally watched the interaction between Dad and me and then played her cards differently. She worked to please him, and showed great interest in learning from and helping him. For her efforts, she had room to verbally challenge him on occasion. He never hit her, even when she was mouthy. I was always a terrible tease with her, typical of a brother with a younger sister. My teasing probably became more intense as I became jealous of her success in establishing a workable relationship with our father. In addition, our mother irritated me whenever she told me to take Sally along when I went out to play. I think I took my frustration at this parental command out on Sally. She whined and complained to Mother about my teasing, but Mother did not respond with any strong admonitions to me.

One year our parents hired an older couple, the Saunders, to live in our home and take care of Sally and me while they wintered in Florida. One evening we all sat at the dining room table eating dinner. From across the table, I made some smart remark directed at Sally. So quickly and so uncharacteristically did she react that I was totally unprepared. She flung her fork at me with such force that its four tines embedded themselves in my forehead. The Saunders' jaws dropped and they remained silent as I pulled the fork from my skull.

a loose cannon

THE BEST ALL-AROUND ATHLETE
NEW LONDON, CT
James Walter Taylor
1904

ROM THE TIME of my earliest memory, when I was six or seven, a small silver cup with handles on both sides, engraved as above, stood on the middle shelf of a bookcase in our home library at 497 Berwyn Road, Birmingham, Michigan. The words on that cup might as well have been engraved on my mind, as my father continually brought them to my attention from my early boyhood onward. Even after our family moved to Fort Lauderdale, Florida, in 1943, this small silver cup, attesting to my father's athletic prowess as a youth, earned a prominent place in our new home. My father repeatedly let me know that nothing I did in the realm of athletics could ever equal, much less surpass, his own athletic accomplishments. To the best of my knowledge, my father never competed in high school football, much less in any college or professional sports as I eventually did, albeit briefly. He was strictly a high school basketball player and track star. Yet, his assertions of superiority rang in my ears long after I left home.

In 1943, I played football on the Fort Lauderdale High School team, and we had a particularly memorable game with Belle Glade High School. In the first half of that game I scored five touchdowns, each a result of an exceptionally long run. At the halftime intermission in the locker room, Coach Clois Caldwell turned to me and said, "Great job, Jim. Relax now, take a shower, change your clothes, and join your family in the bleachers for the second half."

I accepted the coach's unusual suggestion, showered, dressed, and went to the section of bleachers where my parents sat. The minute my father saw me, he sprang to his feet and shouted, "Well, Stupid, if you had just faked running to the outside, and then cut back to the inside on that one run early in the first quarter, you could have scored six touchdowns, not just five. Next time, open your eyes and use your head for something besides a hat rack." All the spectators within hearing distance appeared stunned when they heard him berate me. I was irate, but I sat down with my parents. Not then, nor ever, did he give one word of praise for the five touchdowns I scored in the first half of that game, which we won 75–0. For what it is worth, Belle Glade delivered a decisive beating to Fort Lauderdale the following season when I was no longer on the team.

Even today, I can still hear my father's caustic remarks from that night and feel the sting of his criticism. And while the memory is painful to revisit, it points clearly to the reason why I spent the best part of my boyhood and young adult years doing my utmost to surpass the athletic exploits of my father. Long after any outsider would have thought I achieved this goal, I felt compelled to press on, as I continued to replay my father's belittling commentaries. I seriously wonder how much time and effort I would have devoted to athletics had it not been for my obsession to surpass my father's inflated perception of his boyhood athletic feats.

My dad did encourage me in his own way, though. When I became interested in basketball at about age 12, he installed a backboard and basket over the garage, in front of which the driveway provided space equal to about a basketball half court. He also mounted a floodlight so I could use the court after sundown. For the next several years, I spent endless hours, daytime and eve-

nings, summer and winter, shooting baskets from all distances and angles, perfecting my shooting ability.

Some adults in Birmingham recognized my football and basketball potential and wanted to direct me toward the University of Michigan. However, my classroom record indicated that I would not be prepared for college-level work when the time came. These local people arranged a partial scholarship for me to attend Cranbrook Preparatory School, located in nearby Bloom-

field Hills, hoping that I might respond positively to the greater academic challenge there. Cranbrook, and its sister school, Kingswood, were high schools which, along with an elementary school, an Academy of Art, and an Institute of Science, occupy three hundred rolling acres of campus donated in the 1920s by the newspaper publishing family, George and Ellen Scripps Booth. This entire private educational community is well-known far beyond Detroit, primarily for its emphasis on sculpture and ceramic arts.

I entered Cranbrook Preparatory School in the 1941–42 school year as a tenth-grader, at age sixteen. During favorable weather, I commuted by bicycle. Responding to the challenge and the opportunity, I started the school year determined to get good grades. From the first, Coach Elmer Raymond treated me like a son. He noted my self-discipline in athletics and he praised me. Soon I confided in him about the problems I had with my dad, and thereafter it seemed as if he went out of his way to give me special attention. Coach Raymond was the only adult I ever told about the verbal and physical abuse.

One day Coach Raymond called me to a practice field. He set out a straight line of about fifteen metal folding chairs spaced five yards apart. The coach handed me a football and instructed me that each chair represented a defensive player. He told me to run at high speed, weaving to the outside of each chair, shifting the football to my outside hand and arm. This drill developed an ability to always hold the football on the side away from a defensive player and to make the inside arm available as a straight-arm to fend off any tackler. As I had previously spent endless hours on the basketball half-court at my home, now I spent many more hours mastering this new football skill. I was a starter on the varsity football and basketball teams that year. We achieved only a mediocre record as a football team, but our basketball team became the champions of the District Tournament. Coach Raymond expressed his belief to my parents that I had an exceptionally bright future in both football and basketball.

When spring came, I made the varsity baseball team. In one of the early games that baseball season, Cranbrook hosted a Canadian high school team. In the game, I hit a double and stole third. With two men out in the inning, I stole home and scored. However, in performing this act, I incurred my first serious athletic

injuries. Sliding into home plate, the third baseman's frantic throw to the catcher hit me on the back of the head. I was knocked unconscious and suffered a concussion. I believe I was already unconscious when the spikes on my right shoe caught and stuck in the hard rubber of home plate. My body swung to the left, and as it did so, people later told me, it sounded like a tree limb breaking. When I came to, I found myself in the school infirmary where a broken ankle was diagnosed and treated. That ended my participation in baseball at Cranbrook.

After starting off that school year at Cranbrook determined to pull myself up academically, I lost my motivation mid-year when my parents told me that I would have to board at the school for the winter semester because they were headed to Florida. After attending many local high school basketball games with my parents when I was younger, I was angry and sad that my parents did not have much interest in watching me as a high school basketball player. They watched other kids in earlier years, but they did not even come back from Florida when our Cranbrook team made it into the District Tournament. I took my resentment out on them by slacking off in the classroom. After becoming disabled with the broken ankle in the early spring, I gave up altogether.

Another Birmingham native son was Hugh Mack, a lad a couple years older than me, an excellent football player. He later played the blocking back position at the University of Michigan, replacing Forrest Evashevski. The year I attended Cranbrook, Hugh prepared for playing on the collegiate level by attending Kiskimenitas Springs Preparatory School in Pennsylvania as a high school post-graduate student. Kiski had become, under Coach Jimmy Marks, something of a training ground for future University of Michigan football players, and it offered an academic year beyond the twelfth grade to potential collegiate football players who wanted to mature physically and athletically before entering college. The Kiski-Michigan connection had been established because the Michigan coach, Fritz Cristler, previously coached Jimmy Marks at Princeton. About the time Cristler moved from Princeton to Michigan, Marks took on the job from which his father, Jimmy Marks, Sr., was retiring at Kiski. The senior Marks had prepared Kiski boys for Princeton. Now, the junior Marks prepared boys for Michigan and the "Cristler System," which

he had learned at Princeton. Hugh Mack told Jimmy Marks, Jr., about my football and basketball promise, and so the Kiski athletic program courted me that summer. My poor grades at Cranbrook posed no obstacle.

Kiski Preparatory School, in Saltsburg, Pennsylvania, awarded me a scholarship for the 1942–43 school year. I was pleased to leave my parents' home and live in a new environment. But when I arrived at the Kiski campus, I was shocked and disappointed at its physical appearance. The classrooms and dormitories were housed in three or four old, shabby buildings. I played varsity football during the fall of 1942 with teammates recruited from across the country. For the first time I played running back, rather than as an end and pass receiver. As a result of playing the running back position at Kiski and on all other teams thereafter, I developed the practice of using my head as a weapon to deter tacklers. Since the helmets of that day offered virtually no protection, I incurred many head injuries.

Kiski's archrival in football was Mercersburg Academy, another prep school, located in Mercersburg, Pennsylvania. Our team traveled to Mercersburg for the last game of the season, a distance of about one hundred miles, over narrow winding roads through the Allegheny and Appalachian mountain ranges. I rode in a car with Coach Marks and a couple of the other players. At one point, our car slid off the road and into an icy ditch. The coach stayed at the steering wheel while we younger folks pushed the car out of the ditch. In the process, another guy and I at the rear of the car broke through the ice and found ourselves immersed in frigid water to our waists. We finally made it to Mercersburg. I played despite an obvious onset of illness. Whenever we huddled, I shivered so badly I could not control my limbs. During the game I received a violent blow to my head, leaving me dazed and giddy for the rest of the contest, which we won. I missed a week or more of school after that because I was hospitalized in Pittsburgh for pneumonia.

Very shortly after my return to school, my parents informed me that my dad had sold his half of the Taylor Brothers Construction Company to my Uncle Jack. They also had sold the family home in Birmingham to retire in Florida. I deflated like a punctured balloon. The only home I knew, fraught with good memo-

ries and bad, would be gone. I felt rootless. I also felt betrayed, because my parents had made the decision without warning, or any discussion with me.

I never played basketball for Kiski. Instead, I quit school in early December. When I informed my parents of this decision, they saw it as abandoning my education, which displeased them. But mostly I recall my father was angry that I left behind an upholstered chair he had purchased for me to use in my dorm room.

First I went to Connecticut to spend the winter of 1943 with my relatives there. One fine day in March I joined in a pick-up baseball game with my friends. During the game I was hit in the head with the baseball, fell unconscious, and, when my buddies realized I would not come to quickly, they called an ambulance. In fact, I remained in a coma for eight days before regaining consciousness. When the doctors discharged me, I traveled to Florida. I wanted to check out my parents' new house, located, as I discovered, on a small peninsula of land jutting into the Tarpon Bend area of the New River in the heart of Fort Lauderdale. I did not know if I could consider it my home. It was so different from the home I knew on Berwyn Road in Birmingham. So, not immune to the patriotic fervor of the times, I decided to join the Navy. My parents did not object. My father probably thought it was a great stroke of luck for the military to be taking me off his hands.

Before enlisting, I made some acquaintances by hanging around the local youth center. It so happened that the son of the center's director, a young man about my age, had attended Mercersburg Preparatory School in Pennsylvania. He had been a student there the previous fall when my Kiski team had whipped Mercersburg. This young man did not play football but was an experienced boxer. He and his Fort Lauderdale buddies thought the new Yankee in town should get his just desserts and so they challenged me to a boxing match. I felt a need to prove myself, and although I was no fighter, I accepted. I figured that if I allowed the guy to box, he would knock me out cold. So I did not let him box—I fought like a street fighter, throwing punches as fast as I could so that all he could do was defend himself. The center director, Mr. Kidder, refereed the match and I won the decision, but not before I took some heavy blows to the head. I felt satisfaction

with myself, and the Florida guys accepted me as one of them. Soon thereafter, in early May 1943, I went to Miami to enlist in the U.S. Naval Air Branch, but never mentioned to the enlisting officers my history of head injuries. They sent me to boot camp at the Jacksonville Naval Air Station.

One day at boot camp, I was part of a group ordered to report to an outdoor athletic area that included a boxing ring. Our Physical Training Instructor, Dwight Moseley, a former All-American football player (from the University of Alabama, I believe), had a plan for toughening us up. Moseley placed a former professional boxer in the ring and called for volunteers to fight this man. We were to fight three two-minute rounds, with the winner to stay on in the ring to fight the next challenger. The pro disposed of the first few "volunteers" quickly and they were carried out of the ring. They called for more volunteers and no one came forward, attesting to the good sense of the majority of the recruits. I moved in behind a very large fellow standing near me. Moseley saw my attempt to evade and immediately chose me to be the next "volunteer." I thought quickly about my predicament. It was just like the one I faced in Mr. Kidder's youth center in Fort Lauderdale. I decided to employ the same fighting strategy. My plan was successful, too successful in fact. As a result of my efforts, I won the decision in that fight and thus I had to remain in the boxing ring and accept all challengers. I took care of a few before another recruit, in a wild exchange of punches, landed a solid blow to my head that knocked me unconscious. When I came to, my head felt like a vice gripped it. Not long after that incident, the Naval Shore Patrol picked me up wandering the streets of Jacksonville in a daze. I landed in the base hospital. After numerous neurological examinations, doctors determined that I had sustained serious brain damage. I was subsequently given a Medical Discharge, under Good Conditions, on August 12, 1943, after serving only ninety-eight days.

During my three-month period of military service, my parents purchased a different home—more modern, larger, but with one less bedroom. I got the message; they had not planned on my return. But there I was at age eighteen, with some mental problems related to head injuries, without a high school education and no job. I needed their care for a while. I felt my parents' reluc-

tance to take me in. They converted the screened-in porch into a bedroom for me by installing blinds inside the screens. This insured some privacy but not much weatherproofing.

In September I entered Fort Lauderdale High School to resume progress toward a high school diploma. I intended to continue playing football, so my dad had a special helmet made in the hopes that it would protect me from further head injuries. I had no problem making the varsity football and basketball teams that year.

The 1943–44 Fort Lauderdale High School basketball season was not particularly eventful. I maintained fair grades and made many friends, starting with the group of guys I had impressed with my fight at the youth center the previous spring. I dated a couple of girls before I settled on my favorite, Mary Bea, a petite, dark-haired beauty. In April we discovered that Mary Bea was pregnant. At first this dismayed me because this would disrupt my life, which had temporarily stabilized. But soon my concern changed only for Mary Bea, whom I truly loved. She dropped out of school that spring, since she knew her pregnancy violated policy. We told our parents, and my father immediately called for an abortion. My parents bitterly opposed any idea of marriage for us because they did not perceive Mary Bea's family as good enough for our family. Mary Bea and I totally rejected the abortion option on moral grounds.

I was torn up emotionally during all the ensuing communications and decisions, but Mary Bea's family supported us throughout. Her parents were the classy people during these events, in contrast to my father, who seemed ruled by what I perceived as false pride. I dropped out of the high school that spring, angry with my parents, and with the system that discriminated against pregnant young women. That spring, while I argued with my father, my mother made some comments that my dad interpreted as supportive of me. He switched his wrath to my mother, yelling at her to stay out of the conflict, while jamming his bony fingers into her chest. My indignation hit its limit. I screamed at my father, "I'm leaving. I'm getting out of this house. If I ever hear that you have touched Mom again, I'll come back and I'll beat the living hell out of you." I turned and left, never to live with my parents again.

I did not take any belongings. I wound up that day playing pick-up basketball somewhere in town, perhaps on the court by the beach. Lots of teenage guys hung out there, as did a kid named C.M. Newton, who was about four years younger. C.M. often tagged along behind me, as he aspired to be a good basketball and football player. I usually obliged him when he asked to shoot some baskets or throw a football with me. That day, C.M. was at the court and heard me tell the older guys that I had just walked out of the family home. Eager little guy that he was, C.M. promptly suggested a solution: "Come on over to my house. We rent rooms and I'll ask my mom if you can stay with us for a while." That was the best prospect I had at the time, so I accepted. I stayed at the Newton home for a few weeks, before moving in with Mary Bea's family. My mom brought me some clothes and other necessities in a couple of days, and she told me that after I threatened my dad so convincingly, he went to their bedroom and did not come out for three days.

After I gained a little physical and mental space from the influence of my parents, I asked Mary Bea to be my wife, and she accepted. We married, and our daughter Jackie was born in December 1944. After failing to provide well for my young family with a series of low-paying jobs, I decided that I needed more education so that I could attain better employment. In order to get into college, I first went to night school to attain my high school diploma. I figured that with a diploma, my athletic skills would provide the financial assistance to enable me to attend college. I was right. The University of Miami in Coral Gables, a Miami suburb, awarded me a football scholarship and wanted me to participate in their spring practice in 1945. The University at that time consisted of only three or four old buildings, one of which previously had been a hotel. I went to spring practice in Coral Gables, but after seeing the sad shape of the campus, I decided not to attend or play football there. While growing up I saw several colleges and universities in New England and in Michigan, and the University of Miami did not measure up to my idea of a university. I went next to the University of Florida in Gainesville to demonstrate my skills to the coaching staff, which resulted in another offer of a football scholarship. However I did not accept, because by then I had received what I considered to be a more attractive offer.

I had contacted my old coach at Cranbrook, Elmer Raymond, to seek his help in attaining an athletic scholarship at some established college or university. He agreed to make some contacts on my behalf, and soon the University of Southern California offered me an athletic scholarship for the 1945–46 academic year. Coach Jeff Cravath authorized additional money for my transportation costs to the West Coast. Several of my former teammates from Fort Lauderdale High School previously had traveled west to play college football and study at the University of Nevada in Reno. Apparently they told Coach Jim Aiken about me. They filled Aiken's mind with glowing tales of both my basketball and football abilities and achievements. So when the bus stopped in Reno on my way to USC in Los Angeles, there at the bus station congregated a group of University students, including the one former high school teammate still attending Nevada, and University band members with their instruments. Also on the platform were coaches, as well as, unbelievably, the president of the University. Everyone greeting me suggested that I interrupt my travel and visit their campus. Overwhelmed, I accepted the offer. I visited the pretty little lake-dotted campus with my old friend and new acquaintances, and the school asked if I would consider a scholarship. I decided to stay in Nevada and forget USC.

Coach Jim Aiken had a volatile temper and little self-control. When I met him at the bus station and in my subsequent first days on the campus, Aiken seemed to be an affable fellow. I soon saw another side of the man. In the locker room at halftimes, particularly if our team was not way out ahead in the score, he ranted and raged, singling out individuals for his wrath. One halftime I remember clearly, Aiken told us to stand, shoulder to shoulder, and he worked his way down the line, berating and occasionally slapping players across the face. As he approached, I felt myself becoming enraged. While I had never responded well to criticism, this guy's abusiveness triggered extreme anger. I made up my mind that if Aiken touched me, God help him, I would let him have it. My resolve to fight back probably showed in my face, because after smacking the player before me, he stepped in front of me, glared, and went on to the next player.

During the football season, I suffered more serious injuries, but like others in my day, I played through the pain. I remember sustaining another concussion, but I cannot recall the details.

Perhaps more serious were the broken ribs, which caused constant pain. I played the balance of the schedule, and then blood started showing up in my urine. I was sent to a hospital in Reno and learned that a broken rib had nicked my kidney. This began a very long course of illness and treatment as infection set into my urinary tract. When the football season ended, I knew I could not go on into a basketball regimen, feeling as weak as I did. I am not certain if funds were still available for me to continue my education at Nevada, but I lost any motivation I had for scholastics, and so I left Reno and headed back to Fort Lauderdale.

It felt good to be with Mary Bea and little Jackie again, but my kidney and bladder illness soon required hospitalization. The infection waxed and waned for several months before my physicians decided I should take advantage of my status as a veteran. They referred me to the Veterans Administration Hospital in Miami Beach, because the antibiotic that would most likely be effective, streptomycin, was only available at VA hospitals. I stayed in the Nautilus VA Hospital for the better parts of May, June and July 1946, and the streptomycin treatment was successful. I cannot recall specifically, but Mary Bea's parents must have been providing for her and our child during my time in Nevada and then again as I battled the infections.

About this time, my family celebrated my mother's birthday at a Fort Lauderdale supper club. During our meal, we became aware of much commotion around the bar. My Uncle Curly got up from our table to check out the cause of the disturbance. He returned to our family group to announce that at the bar sat Jim Thorpe, the famous American Indian athlete. Thorpe had distinguished himself in college, Olympic, and professional sports, and he was my boyhood idol. I went to the bar where Thorpe sat drinking soda, introduced myself, and told him he was my hero. He shook my hand, gave me his autograph, and engaged in some short conversation. I noted that Thorpe looked older than the newspaper photos I had seen. I learned he was in the midst of touring the country, making appearances on behalf of the Ford Motor Company. Ford had learned that Thorpe was in the pits of his alcoholism and wanted to help him gain some self-esteem. At the same time Ford wanted to give the American public the opportunity to meet perhaps the best all-around athlete in this country's history.

In the late summer of 1946 I headed out of Fort Lauderdale on a bus bound for Birmingham, Alabama, discouraged with my failures as a family man and an athlete. I job-hunted in Birmingham and soon gained a position with Southern Ribbon and Carbon Company as a traveling salesman for a five-state area. I lived out of suitcases, staying at one hotel after another. The owner and top salesman for the Southern Ribbon and Carbon Company had just died, and I inherited his territory. I do not remember his real name, but he was known throughout the area as "The Dutchman." He had emigrated from the Netherlands and he continued to dress in very conservative, European-style suits. On his right hand he wore a huge ring, which he claimed was a family heirloom from the old country. He never lost his Dutch accent or his marvelous personality. In both appearance and manner, The Dutchman stood out and everyone remembered him.

It might appear that my job, following in The Dutchman's footsteps, would have been easy. But this was not the case. The Dutchman, knowing he was a dying man, had not disclosed his serious illness to any of his accounts, but had sold them enough office supplies to last for several years. I soon discovered that Southern Ribbon saw me merely as a "good-will ambassador" to the company's clients and I would be unable to sell any appreciable amount of office supplies for some time to come. Since my compensation was heavily commission-based, with only a mediocre salary, I was discouraged to realize that I could not make any good money for at least another year or two.

I was still on the job in Greenville, North Carolina when I heard one day about a local college, East Carolina Teachers College. I went to the campus to check out athletic scholarship possibilities. The basketball coach had me shoot a few baskets and he offered me a scholarship on the spot. I gave Southern Ribbon a call to inform them of my decision to quit their position effective immediately. I played that basketball season, 1946–47, and our team was successful, with a fourteen-game winning streak.

One of my ECTC basketball teammates, Charlie Bill Moye, asked me one day to accompany him to the local airport to meet his high school sweetheart who had returned to the area. We traveled out to the airport in his car and met this young lady as she got off the small plane. She was a glamorous beauty named Ava

Gardner. Charlie Bill and Ava met and dated at Farmville High School, near Greenville, and Ava went off to Hollywood and became a movie starlet. She was already twice divorced from her husbands, which included Mickey Rooney, when she returned to her hometown that evening. We sat in the Airport Inn to have some refreshments. Then we got into Charlie Bill's car, with me in the back seat. Charlie Bill told Ava that he knew she had been sleeping with various industry moguls to further her movie career. She did not deny his allegations and Charlie Bill told her he was finished with her. About that time, Charlie Bill dropped me off at the campus and they drove off. Charlie Bill and I never discussed this later, but I believe that was the end of his hopes for a life with Ava Gardner.

The following summer, 1947, I worked as a Recreation Counselor at the Charlotte News and Observer Fresh Air Camp for underprivileged boys. The YMCA of Charlotte ran the camp and its director, Mr. Robert Coons, hired me. The camp itself was located in South Carolina, just across the James River from North Carolina. I kept in excellent physical condition that summer, while assisting many young boys develop their own athletic and social skills.

The camp proved to be an opportunity for learning about the real world. Those little campers were happy to get out of their poor home environments and the facilities left them overjoyed. But during a softball game one day, a little guy, Danny, was sitting on the sidelines, head on his knees, weeping. I walked over to him and asked him what was wrong. He told me that his Daddy was at home, dying. I told him that on my next day off, I would take him into Charlotte to visit his dad. That day in the city I encountered the most abject poverty I have ever seen. Danny's large family lived in a very dilapidated dwelling. My foot went through a porch plank as we approached the front door. The odors of decay and feces and the sweltering heat permeated the tiny house. I gagged and gasped for air. Danny's father lay in bed with a soiled sheet covering him. He hugged Danny while his wife hovered nearby. He was obviously very ill, yet he expressed his great appreciation for the opportunity that the camp gave his son. He cried as he said how happy it made him that Danny had milk to drink while at camp, because milk was an unaffordable luxury for his family.

This saddened me immensely as I thought how poor some people could be within a rich country like ours. I promised the dying man that I would contact the Sunshine Ladies of Charlotte and see to it that the family be supplied with milk in the future.

On the other end of the spectrum was a wealthy Jewish boy whose father sent him to this camp for the experience of knowing some less-fortunate children. Allen was initially very inept at all camp activities, especially sports. I gave him some personal attention, hoping that he could acquire more coordination. Allen's father attended the camp on one of the final days when the boys showed off the skills they had attained during the summer. For this special occasion, Allen entered a rowing competition, but he had never mastered the use of both oars together, and so he could only row in a circle. The father watched and shouted his approval, "That's my boy!" as Allen tried his best. I was struck with the pride and encouragement Allen's father demonstrated toward his uncoordinated son, and the open affection Danny's father had bestowed on his son.

When the summer ended, I went to Charlotte and secured a job as a salesman for Lincoln National Life Insurance Company. My boss advised me on the importance of community notoriety if one was to succeed in selling insurance. He knew about my athletic skills and so he suggested that I contact the Charlotte Clippers, a professional football team. I played for the Clippers during the 1947 season, earning a pittance by today's standards. To supplement my income, I coached the backfield for Charlotte Central High School and was hired to be the assistant head coach of the first football team of the University of North Carolina–Charlotte. This University was in its infancy and virtually without facilities. The football team used the Central High School practice field, and the small student body used the high school classrooms in the late afternoons and evenings. I re-broke an ankle and some ribs playing with the Clippers and needed to quit the team, but I carried on with my two coaching jobs and the insurance business through that fall. My former campers followed me like the Pied Piper, from high school to college to pro games. I facilitated their free entrance into most of the games after the paying customers were seated.

When I was away from Fort Lauderdale, my thoughts, memories and feelings centered on those I had left behind, Mary Bea and our baby. I would remember the tender moments caring for Jackie, and I recalled the feel of her little hand grasping my fingers and the fragrance of the baby oil we used. My heart tugged me in their direction, and I longed for reunion with those I loved. I think I returned to Fort Lauderdale, to Mary Bea and Jackie, about three or four different times over a two-year period. For some reason, my parents finally seemed to want Mary Bea, our child and me together. They gave some emotional support for this, but never offered to provide monetary assistance or help for me to find employment.

Mary Bea wanted to resume our life together. I knew I wanted to be with her, but yet I also felt I could not provide a good future for us—that she and Jackie would have a better chance without me. On each of my return trips to Fort Lauderdale, I would spend time with Mary Bea and we often made love at night, usually on the front porch swing at her parents' home, after the other family members had gone to bed. The porch seemed best for a few reasons. Mary Bea and Jackie's shared bedroom was separated from her parents' bedroom by only a flimsy door. Also, the balmy Florida nights could be especially beautiful with the pervasive odor of night-blooming jasmine. After making love, I would say good night to her. But I did not feel comfortable staying with my wife in her parents' home, as I felt unable to make a commitment. I always told Mary Bea that I would see her the next day, but often before dawn I would slip out of our bed and leave Fort Lauderdale. I would give no sign of my intentions to anyone, but just disappear. Then I would return many months later, with no warning, and repeat the cycle with my long-suffering wife, who always took me back. Each time I held out the promise of togetherness, and each time I broke the promise, leaving behind all that I loved. I cannot even begin to think of the shame, the embarrassment and the hurt I caused Mary Bea and her family. There must have been many questions impossible for Mary Bea to answer. "Why did Jim leave?" "What did I do wrong?"

I could not have answered these or other such questions myself. But I think now, that I left so many times, and ultimately for good, out of a growing sense that Mary Bea and Jackie would

be much better off without me. I found plenty of proof that I was not capable of being a good provider. I absolutely did not leave due to any lack of love for them, for I did love them both dearly. To contemplate these past events even today causes me indescribable pain, because all the old feelings of loss and inadequacy return and overwhelm me.

On my last return visit to Fort Lauderdale, I had no intention of seeing Mary Bea or Jackie. I decided that it would be truly the best for them that I leave their lives. With Mary Bea's attractive appearance and her outgoing personality, I felt sure she would find another man who would be better able to provide. On this visit, I went into a drug store in the southwest section of the city to use their phone. I called my parents to let them know I wanted to pick up some of my clothes. In the middle of the conversation, I happened to look up and see my wife. She sat at a table facing me with her long dark hair and wistful smile. She saw me, too. Our eyes met and spoke volumes for us both. These were positive, beautiful things. If I had approached her at that time, I would have abandoned my resolve and certainly we would have repeated the cycle again. Much of me really wanted to go to her. And yet I got up, took another route to the door, and walked away, never to see her again.

I still had a yen for playing college athletics, and I was not ready to settle down into the insurance business. I decided to return to East Carolina Teachers College in Greenville, remembering what a good basketball season we had achieved the previous year. However, this time a new coach had been hired for the basketball team and he insisted on my shooting all shots with two hands. He even wanted free throws to be shot underhanded with two hands. I had developed a very successful one-handed shot for all my shooting, and used this skill to lead the team in both scoring and shooting percentage the previous season. I objected to the coach's instructions for the two-handed shot and he let me know that it was his way, or none. I chose to leave before the regular schedule of games began.

My ECTC roommate, Tom Flythe, invited me to accompany him to his family's farm home in Conway, North Carolina, for a holiday. I accepted the invitation, and went home with Tom. His

parents were exceptionally cordial people and after meals we sat and talked for hours. While I visited the Flythe's, I learned that the high school basketball coach had either died or otherwise left the community, and though I had not graduated from college, I applied for the job of coaching basketball and baseball at Conway High School. I had no real desire to return to ECTC and was hired. I might not have accepted had I known that my job also included coaching the girls' basketball team and teaching academic subjects.

I heard from friends that the new basketball coach at ECTC sought practice games. I immediately wanted to get a team together to accommodate him so that I might show off my one-handed shooting. We put together a team composed of some other young coaches and ex-college basketball players in the area, and I arranged the use of the Conway High School gym for the event. The competition drew a large, loud crowd, as tiny Conway rarely hosted any public events. Our local team beat the college team decisively, in good measure because I was hot that night and scored forty-eight points. My former teammates and friends at ECTC seemed quite happy at their new coach's visible embarrassment. They had badly wanted me on their team that year and were angry that he had alienated me with his insistence on an outmoded shooting style.

Though not a college graduate or much of a student in the classroom, I had done a lot of reading about government and history. These were the subjects I was expected to teach at Conway High School. I devoted considerable time and effort to my teaching duties, and my principal and students considered me a good teacher. However, I did not feel that teaching was my forte. I did not have a great deal of patience either for the academic preparation required or for the student behavior problems. I lacked patience in every respect at this stage of my life.

Murfreesboro, a small town a short distance from Conway, offered me a position as strictly a coach at Murfreesboro High School, and not a teacher of academic subjects. I accepted. I moved into Murfreesboro early in the summer of 1948 and rented a room in a private home. To supplement my coaching income, I took a job at a local hardware store.

Before the school year began, I picked up a newspaper one day and saw an article about the street-cleaners of New York City,

with an accompanying photo of these men, dressed in white, carrying brooms and pushing little carts. I read that these workers earned higher wages than schoolteachers in North Carolina at that time. I was indignant and decided not to work for such substandard wages any longer. I handed in my resignation letter before ever teaching a day at Murfreesboro High School.

Before I could fully consider my next move, I met a young man traveling through the various small communities of several southern states, trying to put together a team to compete in the National Fast-Pitch Softball Tournament, in which he would pitch. The district tournament was scheduled to play in Virginia Beach, Virginia, later that summer. He told me that a Richmond doctor sponsored the team. This was as good a prospect as anything I had at the time, so I quit my hardware store job, moved out of the rented room and traveled to Virginia Beach. I arrived in Virginia Beach about sixty days in advance of the softball tournament. I had no idea where I would stay or how to support myself, as I had not saved any money.

On one of my first days in Virginia Beach, I went into a restaurant to have a bite to eat. I had only enough money to pay for one good meal. I ordered and waited for my dinner. When the food came and I started to eat, a man came to my table and asked if he might sit down and talk with me for a moment. I invited him to have a seat and soon he told me that he owned the restaurant and also a small hotel on the nearby beachfront. I was surprised when he confided in me that he felt he could not manage both operations effectively, then shocked when he asked me if I would consider managing one of his two businesses. He knew virtually nothing about me and did not ask for any work references. I told him that his offer certainly piqued my interest, but needed to explain that I was in Virginia Beach for only a few months, primarily so that I could play in the National District Fast-Pitch Softball Tournament. If my team won, I would move on to Richmond to play in the National Regional Softball Tournament. I also told him that if my team lost in the District Tournament, I would probably remain in Virginia Beach and continue working for him. Despite all these possibilities, he wanted to hire me. He even asked me to choose which business I wanted to manage, the restaurant or the hotel. I chose the hotel. He instructed me not to permit prostitutes to work in his hotel under any circumstances.

My new boss sweetened our deal by advising me that I could earn more than the base salary he planned to pay me. He said that there were a number of military installations in the area. If I wanted, I could purchase some army cots, put them on the screened-in verandas at night, and rent these temporary overnight places to servicemen who might appreciate inexpensive sleeping quarters on the beachfront. He added that I was welcome to use the hotel's sheets, blankets and pillows. As long as I admitted the servicemen not earlier than midnight and had them out by 7:30 A.M., I could pocket the profits. I got a good business going there with the military men; I did not need the prostitutes.

Barbara, an attractive young woman, stayed at my hotel on vacation. I took her out a few times and soon she told me she was pregnant with my child. She did not put any outright pressure on me, but I certainly sensed she wanted our relationship to progress to marriage, and soon. She returned to her job and home in Richmond, while I made no promises.

I enjoyed my job and playing softball that summer and early fall. Then came the tournament. When our team won, I said good-bye to my employer with ambivalent feelings and went with my teammates to Richmond to play in the Regional Tournament.

In our first game of the tournament, my team went into the bottom of the final inning leading 3–0. The opposing team was batting and our pitcher struck out the first two men. The next two batters walked. The next player hit an easy ground ball toward our shortstop, who unfortunately bobbled the ball and the bases were loaded. The next batter hit a home run. I played left field that night and that homer continued heading upwards when it went over my head and out of the ballpark. My heart sank to my shoe tops as I realized there was nothing I could do. We lost 4–3. Fifty-something years have passed and in my nightmares that ball is still soaring up and away.

So there I was in Richmond, without a job, with no money in my pocket and no family or friends nearby. Once again I turned to sports as the solution to my dilemmas. I contacted the Richmond Rebels and they invited me to work out with them. I played several exhibition games with this professional football team. Again a head coach decided to use me as a running back. Again I was injured seriously; I fractured my left collarbone, which rendered

me unable to play any further. I stayed in Richmond for many months, got a sales job at Morton's Jewelry Store, and obtained less-than-adequate medical care for my injuries.

The woman I apparently impregnated in Virginia Beach, Barbara, found me in Richmond and she invited me to dinner at her home. She lived with a married couple, friends of hers, and she told me she had the house to herself that evening. I accepted the invitation but got cold feet when I arrived at the front door of the house. I peered in the front window and saw a dining room table prepared for an elegant dinner. I could not ring the bell. I knew that if I walked back into her life, and especially if I shared her hospitality, I would need to stay. So I walked away, and never saw Barbara again. I heard from someone later that she was devastated when I did not appear that night. I also heard that Barbara returned to her family home in North Carolina, to receive the support of her family as she prepared for the birth of the child I never saw. I pray that Barbara and her child have had a good life. At the time, I did not let myself think of my impact on her or anyone.

As I now look back on those earlier years of my life playing football, I think I had extremely "soft hands," that is to say, I could catch anything I could touch, in any weather—cold or hot, rain or snow. That, combined with decent speed, meant I evaded most opponents and put points on the scoreboard. If I had been utilized strictly as a pass receiver and not as a running back, I might have gone on to become a household name in football, since there would have been less chance of my incurring serious injuries. I was just not physically sturdy enough to withstand the rigors of a running back in those days of the single-wing and short-punt formations. Only in later years did the T-formation and passing game, with its trickery and finesse, become more prevalent. This style would have suited my physique and my skills much better than the older power-style football. There has also been tremendous improvement in protective equipment for football players, which certainly could have benefited me in my playing days. I might also have protected myself by choosing to focus my efforts on basketball, where I had equally well-developed skills, but even these were diminished by my football injuries.

The break in my collarbone did not heal properly and the Rebels organization refused to pay for additional surgery. I decided to return to Florida, to a Veterans Administration Hospital, which I hoped could provide me the care I needed. I checked into the VA Hospital in Bay Pines, near St. Petersburg, on June 6, 1949. I remained there for most of the next ten months, until March 26, 1950. While in that hospital, I underwent major surgery, with bone removed from my left hip and grafted into the area where only a shattered collarbone existed. A Kirschner pin was inserted into my left shoulder to secure the graft. While in a complete body cast for over six months, two wretched catheters were stuck in my penis, resulting in a series of urinary tract infections and the charming experience of undergoing nineteen cystoscopies.

In the body cast, which extended from my ankles to my throat, I could not move since movement might disturb the graft. A steel bar built into the cast kept my legs spread apart. Upon removal of the cast I was weak all over and unable to move my left arm away from my body. My left hand was positioned on my right shoulder. All types of physical therapy were employed to help me regain the use of my left arm and shoulder, but to no avail. I weighed about 130 pounds, fifty pounds less than normal. I felt embarrassed by my shriveled shoulder and arm and my overall emaciated appearance.

One day my surgeon asked me to come with him to a window overlooking the staff parking lot. The doctor, pointing to his car in its space, informed me that this was where he parked his car each day when he came to work. He said that he always left the car door unlocked and the keys under the front seat on the driver's side. He further said that as long as his car was back in its assigned parking space at 4 P.M., he would be fine with me using it. He told me that my medical record indicated I had been an excellent swimmer at one time, and he believed that swimming might have a positive effect on my left arm and shoulder. He finally suggested that I ought to attempt to swim again, and though the hospital had no pools, there were many beaches along the Gulf coast within driving distance.

Several days later, I acted upon the doctor's not-so-subtle hints, borrowed his car and went looking for a swimming beach. I initially drove to St. Petersburg, but the crowded beaches made me sensitive about my starved appearance. I kept driving. I arrived

within the hour at Clearwater Beach, where only a few people swam and sunned. I parked the doctor's car, made my way to the shoreline, waded out and let myself down into the water. I settled into a sort-of sidestroke using my right arm predominantly and my crippled left arm very gingerly, since I could barely move it away from my right shoulder. After a bit of paddling about, I suddenly realized that I was out in the water much further than I intended and the tidal current was sweeping me out into the Gulf. I looked to the nearest shore and saw no one. I began to feel real fear, but when I looked out toward the Gulf again, I felt the greatest fear I have ever known before or since. Not more than fifty yards away, and coming toward me fast, was a large shark fin. At that moment, all thoughts of my crippled limb evaporated, as I raced toward shore, using the Australian crawl and approximately eight strokes to a breath. I do not know what the world record is for the distance between that beach and where I started but I am sure that I equaled or surpassed the record that day. Finally my hand struck a sandy bottom. I attempted to stand up and walk to the beach, but my adrenaline had depleted. I crawled to shore, where I lost consciousness.

When I awoke a short time later, a small group of people surrounded me, inquiring how they could help. I assured them I was okay and thanked them for their concern. I actually needed their help as I rose and staggered to the doctor's car. I drove back to the hospital, where I immediately found the doctor and related the story of my narrow escape. He laughed and told me that if it had not been for the shark, in all probability I might never have recovered the use of my left arm and shoulder. I would not be surprised if the doctor continued to relate my "shark therapy" story to his patients, but would hope that none of them ever had to practice it.

Many nurses at the VA Hospital in Bay Pines treated me exceptionally well. They saw to it that I had enough pain medication. I was given morphine, but later switched to Demerol, a drug thought of as less addictive. Nevertheless, I became addicted to both these drugs as I used them regularly and heavily for months, under doctors' orders.

One of the nurses, Anna, invited me to live in her apartment upon my release. I accepted her invitation, figuring she would supply me with morphine and Demerol, even though the doctors

by this time had ordered me off the drugs. I was not disappointed. One day I ran out of Demerol and Anna was late with another supply. I started sweating, then shaking, and then wildly hallucinating. In a rage, I cut up all her clothing, smashed her glassware and china, and destroyed her furniture. Had she come in the door during that time, I am sure I would have killed her with a knife I had laid aside for just that purpose. Fortunately, she did not come home then. Eventually I calmed down and saw what I was, a fool and a monster. I felt immense shame and sorrow. I left money to cover all the damage I had done and threw in some extra cash. Then I left her apartment and never saw nor heard from Anna again.

Immediately after leaving the apartment, I rented a room in a private home. I locked myself in that room with the full intention of kicking my drug habit. I sat in a chair, lay in a bed, and paced the floor for a week or ten days, sweating, craving, hallucinating and rarely eating or sleeping. I was successful. I have never used another narcotic or controlled substance since then, unless prescribed by a doctor. In fact, I hesitate to take even prescription drugs to this day because of my intense hatred for what addictive substances can do to a person.

Another nurse on my hospital ward at Bay Pines, Helen, indicated a personal interest in me. Helen invited me to go with her on vacation to her family home in Phillipsburg, New Jersey. Since I had nowhere else to be, I accepted her invitation. One day while visiting Helen's family, I was tossing a football around the yard with a young neighbor and accidentally ran into a heavy steel fence while looking back over my shoulder. This unique mishap caused the Kirschner pin holding my clavicle in place to break. X-rays showed that a jagged part of that sharp pin was extremely close to an artery in the area. I needed to undergo emergency surgery, this time to remove the broken Kirschner pin.

Helen and I stayed longer than originally planned and while we were there, she and her parents began to believe that we should get married. She notified the VA that she did not intend to return to her employment. Helen secured another nursing position in the Phillipsburg area. I used Helen. I liked her as a person but felt no love for her. After I became aware that Helen and her family anticipated an early marriage, I left their home and hospitality,

without proper farewells, in the new car that Helen had bought me as a gift.

When I left Helen and her family, I headed for Pennsylvania and settled briefly in Abington, a suburb of Philadelphia. I believe I stayed in Abington only about a month or two. While working out in local gyms, I met some young basketball players and coaches in the area. They asked me to join their team for a game scheduled against the Harlem Globetrotters. I played in that game, which we won. I attribute our success to our decision not to allow ourselves to be drawn into the clowning, showmanship tactics of the Globetrotters, for this would only play to our opponents' strengths.

I became a true vagabond, and increasingly, a loose cannon. I left Abington and next settled at Campbell Junior College in Buies Creek, North Carolina, with plans to play basketball at the college. However, very soon after arriving there, I met an attractive young lady, Mary Lou. She soon invited me to visit her family's home in coastal North Carolina. I never even started classes or basketball since not long afterwards Mary Lou became pregnant and we got married. We lived in her parents' home briefly and I secured a job selling insurance, which required travel. We lived in a number of small cities including Elizabeth City, North Carolina, and Lynchburg, Virginia. I suffered serious kidney infections during this time, which required hospitalization several times at different hospitals in Virginia and North Carolina. I cheated on Mary Lou even after the wedding. My bizarre thinking and decision-making processes at that time included a plan that if Mary Lou gave birth to a male, I would stick around; if the baby was a girl, I would leave. A female child was born in February 1951, and true to my plan, I deserted. I am still ashamed of this. (Like Mary Bea, Mary Lou eventually initiated all divorce proceedings when it became obvious I wasn't going to return to her.)

At this juncture of my life, I made more and more poor decisions. Law enforcement authorities became a part of my life, and in June 1951 I entered prison for the first time. From that point on, until I committed major offenses in November 1955, I was in and out of three different penal facilities, becoming angrier, more desperate and more defiant. After my arrest in December 1955, and after receiving a lengthy sentence in July 1956, I began a penal

odyssey that lasted forty years. I do not understand all the reasons I fell so far off course, but I believe that the impairment of my athletic abilities resulting from my many injuries was part of the problem. Athletics had consumed me from boyhood through early adulthood, and I believe sports best channeled my intelligence and creativity. Participation in sports provided an outlet for my intense feelings of confusion, anger and depression. Without athletics as a career possibility and without any particular educational accomplishments, yet still with a burning desire for financial success and positive recognition from my father, I floundered. It took me many, many years to recover and gain a philosophy of life that would save me from the bleakness and depths of my despair.

I left a trail of tears and anger during those years, about which I continue to feel great sadness. In every town and city where I lived, I found young women to use for my own sexual and emotional gratification. I courted women, persuaded many to give up their virginity, took some right up to the altar—and deserted them all. I impressed the women and their parents with my look of respectability, and invariably I betrayed their confidence. I find it no wonder that by the time the Law had a reason to hold me accountable for something, community pressure was there to see to it that I received severe punishment.

an unusual journey to manhood

BEFORE I WAS THREE, my parents were not particularly concerned that I develop my masculinity. They let my blond hair grow very long before they brought me to the barber for my first haircut. I recall being distraught at losing my long, curly locks, and I cried and struggled with the barber. I do not know why this disturbed me so. As a preschooler, I played mostly with my female cousins. In Birmingham, my cousin Mary Taylor was almost exactly my age, and we spent most of our time together. When we went to Connecticut each summer, my cousins Mary, Joanne, Jane and Lois, along with their girlfriends and my sister Sally, were my constant companions until I grew old enough to explore beyond the family property. Trips to the bathroom and getting dressed happened with all of us together. Young children do not feel the need for modesty.

My parents first took things somewhat outside the mainstream one summer day when I was about seven, on a vacation with Uncle Joe and Aunt Ted at a Michigan lakeside cabin. One hot day my parents suggested that we all go swimming nude in the lake. The adults seemed comfortable with this plan. Sally, who was only three, offered no opinion, but I lagged behind. Soon everyone else splashed happily in the shallows, while I remained in the cabin in a mental struggle to take off my underwear. I could hear

the adults calling to me from the water, "Come on, Jimmy Pete, take your clothes off and come on in." Finally I did so, but I tried to cover myself with my hands as I sidled into the water. It felt wrong. I think that my parents perhaps had read somewhere that this type of exposure was a good way to eliminate kids' future curiosity about the male and female bodies. But they never suggested another nude activity.

Not long after this swimming incident, my father called me into my parents' bedroom early one weekend morning. I was still in my pajamas, and my parents were in bed. My father motioned for me to come around to his side of the bed, further from the door, and then he told me to get in beside him. I did as he said and he put his arm around me. It felt odd, especially when he pulled me up against his body. I think I went to sleep. On a few future Saturdays, my father repeated this activity and I became increasingly comfortable with my part in it. Then one morning in their bed, with my father in the middle between my mother and me, he reached over my back and started to fondle my genitals. A whole rush of feelings—shock, embarrassment, fear—flooded my body. I had some sense that this was wrong, but I did not really know for sure. I let him do what he wanted, then when his arm relaxed, I squirmed out of the bed and went back to my room.

This scene repeated itself weekly for a year or more. I don't know if my mother was aware of what my father was doing to me, but I feel at some level she must have known. I do not remember why this sexual behavior by my father stopped, but it may have been that I finally resisted his call to participate, even though at that time I did not understand it as abuse. Or perhaps my mother finally became aware and effectively called it to a halt.

My parents hired a teenager named Elaine to baby-sit Sally and me several times. After she put Sally to bed, Elaine invited me to sit next to her on the living room davenport where she touched my genitals. She repeated this action each time she babysat. I had a similar experience with a girl named Judy, who lived down the block on Berwyn Road. Judy was a few years older than me and apparently she wanted to explore her sexuality. She invited me to the recreation room in the basement of her home and there she fondled me. I did not tell my parents about either of these older girls' activities with me since I rather enjoyed the experiences.

I did refuse to participate the day a male stranger approached Sally and me, along with our playmate Jack and Barbara Hamel, in a desolate area about a mile from our homes. We had gone on our bikes to where the River Rouge runs through the Birmingham Golf Course to catch crawfish in the river. The stranger offered candy to any of us who would pull down his or her pants and show him our privates. Barbara alone did as the stranger suggested. Later that day, as Sally and I ate dinner with our parents, I mentioned the incident. My parents, particularly my father, asked several questions and seemed very concerned. After dinner, he made telephone calls to the Hamels and to the police. Soon I was at the Birmingham police station with my father, explaining what happened to an officer. Apparently the police had already picked up a suspect based on my father's telephone complaint, as immediately after the conversation, an officer took me to a room where I could see a man through a glass window. Told that the man could not see me, I verified that this was, in fact, the pervert.

Sometime after the sexual activity with my dad (and with the older girls), I started to recognize within myself a dislike for the clothing that boys and men were expected to wear. I did not care for the dark colors and coarse fabrics of the male wardrobe. To my envious eyes, girls and women enjoyed considerable freedom in choosing their attire from a range of colors, fabrics and styles. My fascination with this difference led me to explore some of the clothing in the closets and dresser drawers of my cousins, Joanne and Mary. My parents often took me along when they visited Joanne and Mary's parents, and I found many occasions to spend a few moments alone in the girls' bedrooms examining their clothing.

One day when I knew the Jack Taylor family was away from their home for an extended period, I figured I could ride over there and explore some more in private. Biking along, I thought about the time I would have there alone, and how exciting it would be to try on some of my cousins' clothing. That day, at age ten, I experimented with dressing in female clothing and jewelry for the first time, and tried to imagine what my life might be like had I been born a girl. After this day, I found further occasions in the next year or two to get back into that house and dress in the girls' clothing. I always stayed within the house however, keep-

ing this strictly a private pleasure. While this did not strike me as morally wrong, I had some recognition that my behavior was not typical, so I never told others about it.

When I was twelve and just into seventh grade, Tommy Spiegel and I liked to sneak into the senior high school early on Saturday mornings to shoot baskets in the big gymnasium. After checking various entrances, we could usually find an unlocked door. The janitor discovered us in the gym on several occasions and chased us away. One day when he found us, he told us we were free to stay and shoot baskets as long as he worked. We thanked him for this privilege.

After a few such practice sessions, the janitor approached us one Saturday and invited us to the basement furnace room where he kept most of his equipment. He offered us seats and started telling us stories about his life, especially tales of his sexual escapades in Pontiac, a city about ten miles from Birmingham. Our ears perked up as he regaled us with graphic descriptions of the Pontiac prostitutes. After we both became quite excited, he suddenly reached over and put his hand on Tommy's crotch. The janitor then said that when we returned to shoot hoops the next Saturday, he would have the door open for us, we could have some fun together, and he would someday take us to Pontiac with him. When Tommy and I left the school that day, we agreed we would no longer use that gymnasium for our basketball practice.

By this time in my early adolescence, I focused almost exclusively on developing my athletic abilities. Basketball and football were my first loves. My father seemed to believe I paid too much attention to athletics, to the exclusion of other normal social pursuits. Unlike the sons of my father's friends, who noticed girls and wanted to drive a car, I had no interest in these things.

One evening at the dinner table, my father announced that he had spoken with an older teenager, Bob, who lived several blocks from our house. He had made an arrangement that he would pay Bob to teach me to drive. He had already given Bob a set of keys to one of our cars and a key to our house. I had no idea why Bob might have needed our house key. Why did he get one when I did not? Also, I did not appreciate that my dad made these arrangements without any discussion with me. But I did not actively resist my father's expectation that I learn to drive from Bob.

So my relationship with Bob began. I was thirteen at the time and Bob was probably seventeen. Though a strong young man, he had no interest in participating in athletics. Rather, he was a sportswriter. He wrote not only for the high school paper, but his articles also appeared in the local *Birmingham Eccentric*. Even the *Detroit Free Press* had printed a couple of Bob's pieces. We commenced the driving lessons, but I was a reluctant learner. I would have much preferred spending that time perfecting my basketball shots.

Very oddly, not only had my father given Bob the house key, he had told Bob that if our driving lessons lasted late into any evening and he did not want to walk home, he was welcome to stay overnight in the extra twin bed in my bedroom. Again, he had not asked how I felt about Bob staying in my room. Often my parents socialized in the evening and would return home quite late. One evening after the driving lesson, Bob said he would spend the night at our house, in my bedroom. What could I say? I prepared for bed and so did Bob. I got into my bed and he into the other twin bed. One of us turned off the light, and within minutes, Bob jumped in my bed. Not particularly sophisticated in his approach, he smothered me with touches and kisses. I resisted his advances, but I was hopelessly overpowered. He finished with me and returned to the other bed. I lay there, overwhelmed with feelings of disgust, anger, and confusion. I felt betrayed by my parents for setting up this situation and I felt I had no one to talk to about this.

Bob came to our house regularly after this, giving me a driving lesson and then staying overnight. He became more aggressive with me, having a preference for oral sex, but occasionally engaging in penetration. All of this he accomplished first through brute force, but over time my resistance became quite weak as I learned the pointlessness of my own defense. After some months passed, I came to the startling realization that I found some pleasure in Bob's lovemaking. I began to look forward to Bob's overnight visits.

As time went on, the sex became more intense. One night, as we undressed and prepared to shower, Bob opened his overnight bag and took out a pair of ladies' white silk panties, a lacy nightgown, and some perfume. He wanted me to put on these things

after I showered. Though surprised by his desire, I remembered the pleasure I had enjoyed from my previous cross-dressing experiences. I wore the feminine attire that night, and thereafter Bob kept me supplied with women's lingerie and perfumes. Dressing in women's clothing as a prelude to our sexual activity was an unmistakable turn-on for both of us.

Bob definitely initiated our encounters, and always remained a step ahead of me. He next wanted to take my cross-dressing out into public. He brought over clothing then in style for young women, along with women's wigs, lingerie, breast-like padding, cosmetics and jewelry. He instructed me in how to dress in a pleasingly feminine way. I enjoyed the appearance I achieved under his tutelage and soon I was willing to go out in public with him, as his date. We never went to any places near Birmingham, but Bob drove us through Detroit to the Grosse Point area where he knew about various parties for teenagers. These parties took place in private homes, and in public places. Bob assured me how attractive I appeared to him and to others, and how no one questioned my true gender. Apparently he was correct, because I never detected any suspicion from others. I believe that all the other teenagers at these parties were perfectly straight so I felt a need to be on guard. But I did become more comfortable as Bob's "girl," even to the point that I danced with other boys and felt I "passed."

Soon I began to think that I wanted to be a female for real, and permanently. I had no thoughts of transsexual surgery because I had never heard of such a thing; in fact, I do not imagine such surgery existed in the late 1930s. I felt that my true self was female, and I began to resent the expectations placed on me as a male by my family and by the surrounding society. I did not discuss this with anyone, even with Bob; in fact, our conversations were all quite superficial, so I have no idea what this period of our sexual involvement meant to him. He may have been just using me to explore his own sexual fantasies.

All this time, I ardently pursued my athletic interests. Bob told me that he enjoyed seeing me succeed athletically, and he urged me to develop my talents. But he also expressed some concern that the masculinity I developed through sports worked against the femininity he encouraged through our relationship. Once, after I played particularly well in a junior high school foot-

ball game, Bob rewarded me with some female clothing and cosmetics and enclosed a note, which read, "From the person who writes the headlines, to the person who makes the headlines."

The summer after all of these events occurred, I went with my family to Connecticut, as usual. My cross-dressing with Bob had become a regular practice and I started to reminisce about it. One day at my Grandma Taylor's home, I found myself alone for a few hours. I thought I would enjoy putting on some of my female cousins' clothing, so I went to the second-floor bedrooms. I donned some underwear, a blouse and skirt, and went to a mirror on the first floor to admire myself. All of a sudden, I heard the crunching noise of car tires on Grandma's gravel driveway. I rushed to the window to see who it was. Getting out of the car were Aunt Fanny, Cousin Lois, and a girl of my age whom I fancied, Jane. Panicked, I dashed into a first-floor bedroom and dived under my Aunt Elizabeth and Uncle Ernest's bed, which had a dust ruffle around the bottom to shield me. Aunt Fanny and the two girls came into the house calling my name. They entered the bedroom where I lay holding my breath under the bed. I was scared to death one of them might lift the ruffle and find me, but no one did, and finally they left the house, commenting that I must have gone out with some friends from the area. Although they had gone, I could not resume my previous activity. I took off those clothes as fast as I could and never tried that again at Quaker Hill.

At the end of the summer, we returned to Birmingham. I looked forward to resuming my relationship with Bob, but he and his family were gone. They no longer lived in their home near us, and no one I talked to could tell me anything about where they were or why they had left. Feeling lonely and confused, I tried to make sense out of my involvement with Bob. These experiences made me believe I had nothing in common with my peers. I fit in nowhere, and I had some feelings of wanting to die. While I did not make any suicidal gestures, nor did I ever develop a specific plan to kill myself, I felt miserable, and ultimately plunged back into my athletics. I never saw or heard from Bob again.

I threw myself into heterosexual activity with girls of my age group. I neither had nor showed any regard for their feelings, but wanted only to meet my own heightened sexual desires. I became very promiscuous, seeking any girl who would allow my advances.

Because I wanted to be liked and respected in my own locale, I did not choose girls from Birmingham or nearby Franklin Village, but I found girls in Pontiac, Detroit, and other places where my local friends were unlikely to hear about my pursuits. I think now that my hypersexual behavior served as an attempt to prove my masculinity to myself and others, and also to punish females, probably because I was jealous of their gender. But I am really not certain why I did some of these things.

After I attended Baldwin High School the next school year, I transferred to Cranbrook Preparatory School, located in Bloomfield Hills, the suburb next to Birmingham. During the winter term, because my parents and Sally went to Florida, I boarded at the school. The boarders were quite well supervised, which restricted my activities. The many road trips our football, basketball, and baseball teams made in the interstate prep school league kept me very busy.

I did not have much opportunity to pursue young ladies during this time, but I did become quite well acquainted with my schoolmates. One of these was Al Schwartz, whose family home was in Detroit. Many of the Cranbrook guys knew the reputation of Pontiac as a city with numerous houses of prostitution. Al and I decided to go to Pontiac and patronize a "house of ill repute." This was to be an inaugural event for both of us. While my parents vacationed in Florida for the winter, I had access to one of their cars. So we headed for Pontiac. We feared that if the police raided the whorehouse while we were there, our car could be traced to my dad and we would be in serious trouble. So we parked the car in the city and hailed a cab, asking the driver to "take us to a whorehouse." The guy reacted angrily, "Get out of here," as he pulled the cab door shut in our faces. We stood there and wondered whether we should try again. We still had hot pants so we hailed another cab. This time, the driver was a greasy sort. He obligingly drove us several miles to the outskirts of the city. As he collected the fare, he advised us, "Now you boys just go up to the door, ring the bell, and a lady will come to the door. You tell her that you want a date with one of her girls, and she will invite you in and set you up. Here, take this number, and call me to pick you up when you're ready."

Al and I walked, knees a-knockin', to the door of the big frame house while the cab drove away. After we assured each other that

we were up for this, we rang the doorbell and waited. A middle-aged woman opened the door, squinted at us, then asked, "What do you boys want?" We said we wanted to have sex with her girls. She broke out laughing and slammed the door in our faces. We stood there and heard the laughter of young females inside the house. Apparently no one wanted to earn any income from minors. We suddenly realized we were far away from any public transportation and had no access to a telephone. We set out on foot for the center of Pontiac. When we got to our car a couple of hours later, we were exhausted and shivering. Mission unfulfilled, we drove back to Birmingham.

The next fall I spent at Kiski Preparatory School in rural Pennsylvania. As at Cranbrook, we teenage males spent lots of time talking about how we might actualize our sexual fantasies with the girls in the nearby town of Saltsburg. Trouble was, by the time we managed to sneak off campus after our dormitory lights were out, then maneuver our way down a steep slope to the bridge leading to town, we never found any likely female companions awake. So most of our fantasies went up in smoke. However, I did manage to meet one young lady from Saltsburg, and we agreed to rendezvous outside her house one cool fall night, about 1 A.M. Walking around in the dark, I kept looking for a suitable place to engage in what I had in mind. There seemed to be nowhere for us to go, but then I spotted a cemetery. I persuaded the young lady to enter the cemetery with me. We lay down on the cold ground in front of a large tombstone. When I took out my erect penis to perform the act, the cold night air quickly reduced me to a shadow of my former self. Alas, no scoring here either.

I did not stay at Kiski for the full year. News reports told of the U.S. Navy taking a beating in the South Pacific. I had a particular interest in that branch of the armed forced because I had spent much of my youth in the Navy-centered town of New London, Connecticut, so I enlisted. During boot camp, the non-commissioned officer in charge of our barracks summoned me one day to his private quarters. He was a middle-aged man who had been in the service many years. He said, "I've been watching you, Taylor. I've decided that I want you to bunk in my quarters with me." Before I could ask why, he put his arms around me and attempted to kiss and touch me. I was startled and pushed him away, but his advances grew more insistent. I thought I had not much option

but to concede because this guy had indisputable authority over me. I quickly considered the possible advantages of his offer. It would get me out of the huge dormitory where privacy did not exist, due to the nighttime activities of the other recruits. This petty officer might also help me obtain some privileges and rank that I might otherwise not be able to achieve for a long time. I remembered that the experiences of five years earlier with Bob as rather pleasant, so I knew I could please this man while gaining some pleasure myself.

I moved into the petty officer's quarters and for the next several weeks I was his sexual partner at night. He treated me well. I did not have to go to the mess hall to eat, since he brought food into his quarters for us, and sometimes he took me to restaurants on the base, which served excellent food. This arrangement lasted only about two months, because I suffered a head injury in a boxing incident on the base, which resulted in an honorable discharge only three months after enlistment.

I left the Navy in August 1943, and went to live with my parents in Fort Lauderdale. I did not engage in homosexual activity the following decade, nor did I return to cross-dressing. I felt no attraction to males and considered myself fully heterosexual. I did, however, take out much of my considerable accumulation of anger on females.

At age twenty in 1945, I attended the University of Nevada in Reno on a football scholarship. The football players traditionally staged a show at a local theater after the season ended. I participated in the show that fall, and our group decided to put on a skit in which we dressed up as females in a chorus line. A member of the Reno Police Department happened to be in the audience that night, and apparently was impressed with my female impersonation. He approached me a couple of days later and asked for my assistance in apprehending a rapist. I was to be a decoy by dressing and acting like a young female, sitting on a park bench in the area where several of the sexual assaults had occurred. I agreed after the police officers assured me they would be nearby and come forth to make the arrest as soon as the prospective rapist put a hand on me. On the first try, the trap worked, and the man was arrested. The police expressed much gratitude for my willingness to play the role.

In 2002, my wife Katherine and I toured Ireland in a group of about forty people. At the social hour the evening of our arrival, people introduced themselves and I noted that a few of them mentioned they were from Michigan.

We ate breakfast in Galway one morning with some Michiganers when they told me that the woman who sat across from me, though now a Californian, lived in Birmingham as a child. I turned with excitement to this woman to ask if she, in fact, grew up in my hometown. She verified this and I pursued the conversation: "Where did you live? On what street?"

She replied, "On Berwyn Road."

"Really? Where on Berwyn? That street is only a couple of blocks long."

She described the house, and it dawned on me: this was Judy, the teenage girl who took me at age eight into her home and fondled me. And she was across the table from me in Ireland, seventy years later, denying any recollection of the little boy whose family built a new home and moved in down the street in the early 1930s.

After breakfast I kept talking to Katherine about how amazing this was, that on a two week sojourn out of the country I would run into someone from my childhood. Katherine, also amazed, told me that I must not discuss with Judy my memories of our youthful sexual explorations; the old gal would probably expire from embarrassment. But I knew that this eighty-something-year-old woman from California was Judy-down-the-street, and she acknowledged it too when a few days later she and I shared a memory of her family's gardener, Glenn, who loved to talk with us kids and even took me fishing on occasion.

the 1980s

I GAINED BOTH release from the U.S. Penitentiary at Lewis-
burg and parole status in 1980 with great expectations that I
might finally return to living a normal life in relative freedom.
My release at age fifty-five, after twenty-five years of incarceration,
was long overdue, but I cannot say I was in terrific shape mentally.
Surviving in the so-called Big House enhanced my ambition and
self-developed integrity, but scrambled my already confused sexu-
ality. In a way, cross-dressing led to my return to jail. I violated no
laws, yet my intermittent feminine appearance—which was dis-
concerting to many people—made me appear strange and perhaps
mentally unbalanced. My memory for the complicated and per-
haps incredible account of my short-lived "freedom" and its after-
math is fading. In fact, I have lost my memory of many events and
only when I re-read my own accounts do I remember. What has
not faded, however, is the remembrance of the emotions I experi-
enced, beginning in 1981, as I suffered the greatest injustices of my
life with dwindling resources for counteracting these wrongs. To
now retrieve those events from my faded memory and from vari-
ous documents I preserved brings back intense feelings of anger,
frustration and disappointment. It is a place I do not want to be.

I began my parole in January 1980 living in a halfway house in
Anderson, Indiana, a location recommended by my friend, Jean.

She and her friends encouraged me to enroll in Anderson College to attain further education in the field of business. I followed this advice but, at the same time, I started to implement a career plan that I developed while still imprisoned.

In the few years prior to 1980, I took college-level courses offered within the Lewisburg penitentiary, mostly those in administration. I figured that if I gained parole, I would have a greater chance of success in society by being self-employed. I pondered how I might set up my own business without much capital. One day while reading a business magazine, I found an answer in an article that described a new business opportunity needing little investment. It required training in the use of the latest voice stress analysis equipment in order to achieve competence in lie detection. I sought further information from the article's author and persuaded myself that this could be the right option.

While at the halfway house, I obtained permission from my parole officer, Mr. John Baker, to attend a training conference on voice stress analysis at Rutgers University in New Jersey. As I recall, a Rutgers professor developed the voice stress analyzer I read about and he provided the training in its use. Ironically, my classmates, perhaps twenty people, were mostly law-enforcement professionals. We socialized together outside the classroom and soon I divulged to some of them my status as a federal parolee. I don't think any of them believed me, since they responded to my revelation as if I was joking. I became certified as a voice stress analysis expert and purchased the necessary equipment with funds saved from my prison earnings.

I returned to Anderson and began to market my services, initially earning enough money so that when my parole officer allowed me to move out of the halfway house in May 1980, I could afford to rent a unit in a luxury apartment complex. My new business took off, as lawyers, businessmen, spouses in conflict, and even some local law-enforcement officials found that my knowledge could be useful to them. I supplemented my income by expanding into security products, such as personal defense sprays (similar to mace), and then becoming a distributor for Amway. I was almost manic in my energy level, probably unconsciously trying, in my mid-fifties, to make up for all those lost years in prison. I had virtually no time to enjoy my home or any leisure activities and ignored my spiritual self. I pursued transgender sur-

gery and hastily married a woman named Patsy. Admittedly, and to say the least, my lifestyle lacked balance.

One day, John Baker came to my apartment for a supervisory visit. Perhaps it had been some time since his previous visit, because he displayed amazement at my accomplishments. As he discovered the amount of money I earned, and saw my property, including two cars, he first assumed that I was engaged in illegal activity. He expressed great concern that I had succumbed to the temptations of crime. I assured him that all my income was legitimate and, in fact, the result of hard work. I showed him a several-thousand-dollar check as an example of what clients paid for my services. At that point, John Baker almost wept as he blurted out, "You're earning more money in just a few months time than I am, after all my years as a parole officer. It's not fair."

I doubled my income with each passing month. I felt proud that I was finally succeeding and doing so legally. With my parole officer's permission, I hired another parolee to work for me, "Joe." He then passed the word to another unemployed man with a felony record, Wesley Robinson, that I might have work for him. When Robinson approached me for a job, I did not know he had a criminal record, nor did I ask. Though not impressed with Robinson's appearance (which eliminated him as a candidate for a sales position), I thought he might have the necessary hands-on skills to install and repair the security equipment I sold. So I encouraged his interest in my business, but I did not immediately hire him.

My association with Wesley Robinson proved disastrous. Not only did I unwittingly violate the conditions of parole by associating with a felon without the express permission of my parole officer, but also Robinson soon accused me of crimes I never committed. Things began to happen very fast at this point which is partially why my memory does not now hold all the details of the events I will describe. I am well aware that the public does not want to hear yet another convict proclaim his innocence, since we all know that the penal institutions are full of innocent men if we were to believe each of them. But it is true that there are a few people who are framed by the system and only recently has DNA evidence proved this happens more than the public suspects. When a person in power wants to find someone guilty (and there are many motivations for this), it can be done. It happened to

me. I have no reason to lie at this time since my penal servitude is behind me and my story is interesting enough without exaggeration.

At first I assumed the truth of my innocence would be quickly discerned by the authorities but then I realized they were taking the false accusations seriously. I heeded the advice of a friend at the time: keep records. I started saving everything that might be useful to me. Although these records were disregarded within the system and thus not helpful in extricating me from it, they are available to me now as I try to reconstruct the sequence of events for this chapter of my memoirs. The police reports indicate, and I do not deny, that I met with Wesley Robinson a few times on the 24th and 25th of April 1981, the last time attired in the female clothing I was counseled to wear in preparation for transgender surgery. I cannot recall why I did this or how Robinson knew about my dressing in female attire. I only know that within minutes of Robinson leaving me in my car on the evening of April 25, Anderson police officers surrounded the car, and demanded that I open the door and get out. They searched and arrested me. Later the police tore apart the car to look for weapons. There were none, but they charged me with armed robbery anyway, and then soon they changed the charge to conspiracy to commit armed robbery.

That moment began the most maddening period of my life, accused of a serious crime I did not commit. I was held in the Madison County Jail and not allowed to post bail. All my efforts to explain my actions, and to contradict what law enforcement seemed determined to believe, failed. Most of the friends I had made in Anderson, including my wife, walked away, only too willing to trust the police and newspaper reports of the ongoing criminal behavior of a parolee—one caught in women's clothing at that. I asserted my right to a speedy trial but languished in jail for almost two years without one. I caused some of that delay by my own requests for continuances (to obtain a new attorney, to be evaluated by a psychiatrist), but mostly the prosecutors were responsible for the long wait. I watched helplessly as my business evaporated and my property disappeared. While I impatiently waited, I suffered a heart attack and a resulting chronic atrial-fibrillation condition.

The Anderson Police reports, upon which the conspiracy charge was based, alleged that Wesley Robinson came into police headquarters on the morning of April 25, saying that I had tried to engage him in a plan to rob a local grocery store with a weapon. The reports stated that Robinson told police I wanted to pull off the crime that evening, and I threatened him into agreement. They said that Robinson agreed to go ahead and meet with me as planned and thereby to assist the police in my arrest. I do not know if Robinson initiated those contacts with the police. For all I know, the police may have solicited Robinson's cooperation in their efforts to see me back in prison.

Twenty-three months elapsed with no progress, with a trial finally set for March 14, 1983. Four days before the scheduled trial, the prosecutor presented audiotapes to my attorney and me. He claimed these were made from an electronic monitoring device that Robinson supposedly wore on the evening of my arrest. We immediately filed a motion to suppress all evidence emanating from any tape recording. The basis for this motion was: 1) I had not been aware of any recording involving myself; and 2), if a court had authorized interception of any communication between Robinson and myself, I had not received notice of such an order at least ten days before trial, as required by the law which allows interception and divulgence of oral communication under some circumstances. Several days prior to filing this motion, I had filed another motion with the court to dismiss the charges as the prosecutor had not brought me to trial within the time period prescribed by law, considering that I had formally requested a speedy trial back in 1981.

On March 14, 1983, I was brought into the courtroom. The county prosecutor first made a motion to continue the case again because he could not find his star witness, Wesley Robinson. Judge Harry Sauce denied this motion. At that point, the prosecutor said that since he could not go forward without his star witness, he requested a dismissal of the case, without prejudice — meaning that he could later file the same charge against me. The judge granted the dismissal, but advised the prosecutor that any further filing of charges would need to be done within the next twenty-four days.

I continued to object to any use of the supposed tape evi-

dence, adding to my argument the fact that the prosecutor had failed to comply with the judge's previous orders to allow my attorney and me to listen to the tapes prior to any trial proceeding. Judge Sauce then ruled favorably on my motion to suppress all evidence obtained from the tapes so that if I was brought to trial later, none of that supposed evidence could be used. At a later time, we heard the tapes. Then I objected to them for reasons other than legal technicalities. The quality of the recording was very poor throughout, lacking real audible conversation. We counted 120 gaps. The voice purported to be mine was not mine. I believe the Anderson Police Department manufactured the tapes and the prosecution's threatened use of them was probably a ruse to induce a confession from me.

With Judge Sauce's orders, including one for my release from jail, I thought my ordeal had ended. My mind leapt to strategizing how I could resume my life. But I was not released. Instead, the U.S. Parole Commission reactivated the warrant that had been issued two years earlier at the time of my arrest. I was turned over to the custody of the U.S. Marshals, who took me to the U.S. Penitentiary at Terre Haute, Indiana, to await a parole revocation hearing. I quickly dispensed with my anger, gathered my resolve and settled down to wait a little longer, figuring this revocation hearing was only a formality since the charges had been dismissed, the tape evidence suppressed, and I knew I had committed no crime.

My parole officer, John Baker, recommended to the Parole Commission that additional charges be added to the one already considered by the court, i.e., conspiracy to commit armed robbery. The Commission accepted Baker's recommendation and additionally charged me with possession of a weapon, and associating with two known felons, Wesley Robinson and Joe, the ex-con in my employ who had sent Robinson to me for a job. Baker told the Commission that authorities now knew the whereabouts of Robinson and that Robinson had agreed to return to Indiana so that the county prosecutor could again file charges against me within the specified time period.

A preliminary parole revocation hearing needed to occur first, whereby an investigating parole officer determined if there was probable cause to sustain the charges. If so, he needed to refer me on to a final parole revocation hearing. I prepared for the prelimi-

nary hearing by verifying that my public defender would represent me and by communicating that I wanted any witnesses intending to present evidence against me, including Wesley Robinson, to be present for our cross-examination. However, I was not given any timely notice of the actual hearing date so neither my attorney nor I was able to notify the witnesses I wanted to call on my own behalf.

The preliminary hearing occurred on April 4, 1983. Before it formally began, I presented the investigator, Thomas Gahl, with written and oral statements informing him that Madison County Judge Sauce had suppressed all evidence from the police audio tapes and reminded him that federal law and the Parole Commission's own manual of procedures precluded him from using this evidence in the hearing. Mr. Gahl acknowledged receiving this communication, but proceeded to review the police reports, which relied almost totally on the suppressed evidence. He allowed me to present the one favorable witness I had managed to secure for the hearing, Robert Graham, a retired Anderson Police Department inspector and Past-President of the Indiana Fraternal Order of Police. Mr. Graham testified that Wesley Robinson had a reputation in the general community and with the police as a pathological liar, and that Robinson previously worked as a police informant as a way to garner some favor relative to his own law violations. But because Wesley Robinson was not present to give his evidence personally and for us to cross-examine, only his written statement to the police was introduced.

Mr. Gahl decided there was probable cause that I had conspired to commit armed robbery, that I had a gun in my possession without a permit, and that I had associated with Wesley Robinson, a known felon, without the permission of my parole officer. He did not sustain the allegation about my association with Joe because John Baker admitted he gave me permission to do so. With Mr. Gahl's decision, I realized in an instant that I could return to federal prison as a parole violator. This was now very serious, no mere formality, and while my outrage returned, I needed to focus on legal arguments for regaining parole.

A new attorney was appointed to represent me at the final parole revocation hearing set for May 31, 1983. That date approached and the assigned attorney, Barbara Rennolet, did not find time to meet with me although I was confined in the same

city as her office, Terre Haute. A few days before May 31, Ms. Rennolet submitted a written request to the Parole Commission that sought a continuance due to lack of preparation. The request was granted and another date, July 1, 1983, set.

As the July 1 hearing commenced with Hearing Examiner Henry Grinner, I brought forth my objections to the validity of the April preliminary hearing, and I advised Mr. Grinner that this final hearing could not make use of evidence suppressed by the Indiana judge. I further informed Mr. Grinner that I had not received any written notice of this hearing, as required by the Parole Commission rules. Ms. Rennolet stated that she had received notice, but had not met with me because she had difficulty locating me. In fact, authorities moved me four times during the month of June and she testified that when she found me in the jail in Indianapolis about a week before July 1, she was in a lengthy trial over 150 miles away and could not get back to the city. She asked for another continuance, based not only on her inability to adequately prepare the defense, but also on Wesley Robinson's continued absence. She noted that the Parole Commission had denied my request for Robinson's presence, stated a belief in the error of that decision, and told Mr. Grinner that I had filed a Writ of Habeas Corpus with the court, to demand Robinson's presence at this hearing. She argued that this final parole revocation hearing should not occur until the court had acted on my writ.

Mr. Grinner replied, "Okay. Ms. Rennolet, that's a very fine presentation, but I'm sure you know, as well as I do, that the rules of evidence that you are referring to, at least in part, do not apply at this type of an administrative hearing. The only request that you have made that would have—that would merit any consideration on the part of the Parole Commission is that you have not had sufficient time to confer with your client. I am not here today to debate legal issues with you, nor with Mr. Taylor, as you well know. I'm here to, first of all, share with you all allegations that have been made against you, Mr. Taylor, and to give you a chance to refute those. The Parole Commission has already reviewed the request to have Mr. Robinson here and has denied that, which is the prerogative of the Parole Commissioner. And that has absolutely no bearing on what we do here today, regardless of the law that you refer to there."

Following further conversation about his frustrations with my attorney, and our frustrations with the system, Mr. Grinner said he did not have the authority to grant another continuance, but he would telephone his bosses at the Regional Office of the Parole Commission in Kansas City and ask whether another continuance could be granted. He made the call and got the approval. My attorney and I agreed to hold the hearing at the Terre Haute penitentiary and Mr. Grinner told my attorney that the hearing would likely be scheduled for the second week in August, asking her if she would then be fully prepared to defend me. She promised the hearing examiner that she would be ready.

I waited in the Marion County Jail in Indianapolis and wondered when I would be transferred back to the Terre Haute penitentiary. When Ms. Rennolet had not contacted me by mid-July, I contacted another attorney, Marsha Shein, who worked with the National Legal Services Organization in Atlanta, Georgia, and asked her to help me find good counsel for this very important upcoming final parole revocation hearing. Ms. Shein assisted in engaging James Voyles, an attorney in Indianapolis, who agreed to provide my defense pro bono.

I do not know exactly when I discovered that the hearing would not take place in August in Terre Haute; instead, the Parole Commission decided to send Henry Grinner out from Kansas City to Indianapolis to conduct the hearing three weeks earlier than planned, on July 21, 1983. On that date, Mr. Voyles told the hearing examiner that he had only known since the previous day about the date of this hearing. Ms. Rennolet appeared in the hearing room and told Mr. Grinner that she only received notice of the new date when she happened to go into her office on Sunday, July 17, and opened her mail. Although she had not contacted me until the hearing date, she stated her willingness to either represent me or to withdraw. I advised Mr. Grinner that I had engaged other counsel, due to the fact that I had no opportunity to meet with Ms. Rennolet since July 1 and I felt she could not adequately represent me. Mr. Grinner, obviously irritated with this situation, made it very clear that he would not grant another continuance if requested. Grinner asked me if I still wanted to release Ms. Rennolet. I affirmed that was my wish.

My new attorney, despite knowing that his request would be

denied, argued for more time, until the date previously suggested by Mr. Grinner, during the second week of August. Mr. Grinner replied that he had been advised "before I came down the hall today that Mr. Taylor would no doubt be releasing Ms. Rennolet and retaining you [Mr. Voyles] ... And, I then wanted to do things by the book, and I established telephonic contact with our regional office, so as to be prepared to entertain your request for a continuance or proceed with the hearing. And, I was directed by my supervisor that because of the two prior continuances that we would be required to proceed and that's what I have to do and in view of that, then I have no choice but to deny your request for a continuance, and as I said before, I have to proceed ... I understand that Mr. Taylor makes a valid point that there has not been contact between he and Ms. Rennolet ... through no fault of Mr. Taylor's."

I told Mr. Grinner that I understood and appreciated his explanation. Nonetheless, I said, "I protest. I do proclaim my innocence of all these charges. I enter into [this hearing] because I am forced to enter into it ... I'd like to ask you a question. Are the adverse witnesses present today?"

Mr. Grinner responded that two police officers were there to testify, but he said that the Parole Commission had denied Wesley Robinson's presence. "The commissioner, who is my boss, made the determination that he would not be here and that we would rely on documentary evidence ... And, the presence of Mr. Robinson was denied, as it happens in quite a few cases like this, but if you don't believe that that was a justifiable reason for the Commissioner to deny that, then of course that would be a matter that you could take up through another avenue; the court, the appeal process, or whatever. But, I don't make the rules, Mr. Taylor. I just try my best to carry them out as best I can."

Mr. Voyles and his associate, Mr. Jeff Paul, also present, again formally requested a continuance because they were not prepared to proceed. They also indicated that I had told them of my wish to present about twenty witnesses who could speak on my behalf, but who had not been interviewed by the previous attorney. Nor had they met them since they had been only so recently engaged in my defense.

Mr. Grinner proceeded to read the four allegations against me, including the one for which the investigator, Thomas Gahl,

at the preliminary hearing in April had found no probable cause. I denied all the allegations. I protested the absence of Wesley Robinson. Despite my informing Mr. Grinner that all evidence which emanated from the police audio tapes was suppressed, he read the long police reports replete with statements by Wesley Robinson and interpretations of what the police believed the audio tapes showed. The police reports implied that officers had themselves observed me, dressed in female attire, in my car with Robinson on the evening of April 25, 1981, where I handed Robinson a gun and waited for him to return following his supposed intent to rob the grocery store.

At one point in the hearing, Mr. Grinner snapped at Mr. Paul, who tried to prove that the police had not observed what they wrote in their report. Grinner said, "I'll point out to you, counselor, not to get involved in any philosophical discussions, but the police reports clearly state that the officers had taken up surveillance in a motel room overlooking the parking area where Mr. Taylor and Mr. Robinson were, and observed him leave the car with the weapon." Later, the two police officers were brought into the hearing where my attorneys cross-examined them. My attorneys used a hand-drawn map I provided them, proving the impossibility that any of the three police surveillance teams saw my car or me. The police officers admitted that they had not visually observed any behavior on my part that evening, except that they saw me pick up Wesley Robinson at his home.

Throughout the discussion of the allegations against me, my attorneys argued that all the evidence was merely hearsay, based on the representations of Wesley Robinson, who still had not been confronted and cross-examined. They also pointed out that I had languished for twenty-three months in the Anderson County Jail on those very charges, later dismissed partly because Robinson was not available for the scheduled trial.

Mr. Grinner excused himself from the room to deliberate. He returned with his decision. He said he believed that a preponderance of the evidence indicated I had conspired to commit an armed robbery, I possessed or had under my control a gun without a permit, and I had associated with a known felon without permission. He said that the guidelines for this behavior indicated a sentence of sixty to seventy-two months and his recommendation to the Parole Commission was for a sentence of seventy-two

months, with credit for the twenty-seven months I had been in custody since arrest. He clarified that my presumptive re-parole date would be April 25, 1987 if the National Commission affirmed his recommendation. My head spun, and with a lump the size of a baseball in my throat, I said, "Thank you," and the hearing ended.

I did not mean "Thank you." I cannot adequately relate what I meant. Within a week I returned, devastated, to the U.S. Penitentiary at Lewisburg, Pennsylvania, the institution from which three-and-a-half years earlier I emerged into free society after twenty-five years of continuous confinement. I did my best and committed no crime. Denied my constitutional rights to a speedy trial and a chance to cross-examine my main accuser, I found myself right back where I started, one of tens of thousands of federal prison inmates, looking at another four years imprisonment. When the National Commissioners reviewed the recommendation of Mr. Grinner from that Final Parole Revocation Hearing, they not only affirmed his findings, they more than doubled my sentence to 168 months, eight years longer, to April 1995. I reeled with a dizzying anger and frustration. The highest parole authorities in the country had themselves thwarted authentic justice, and I knew that my chances were minimal for rectifying this great wrong. In fact, nothing about this decision by the Parole Commission ever changed. But yet to come were many more calamities that required great faith.

On the same date I received the written notice of the action taken by the National Commissioners, August 18, 1983, I received notice that Indiana authorities had re-instated the charge of conspiracy to commit armed robbery. I fought the order for Indiana to take custody of me and lost, and then I filed a motion to dismiss the charge, with prejudice. A year and a half went by while these legal maneuverings dragged on, and then in March 1985, Indiana authorities appeared at the Lewisburg penitentiary to transport me back to Indiana. I sat in the same jail in Anderson where I previously spent two years waiting for my speedy trial, this time waiting over five months.

The same Judge Harry Sauce heard the case in Madison County on August 15, 1985, by which time there was a new prosecutor on the case who agreed with my motion to dismiss the

charges. Judge Sauce talked extensively about the injustice of this entire prosecution and how so many of my rights had been trampled. He reprimanded the State for its failure to adhere to the law in this case and he said that the State could not try me on the 1981 charges even if I wanted a trial, due to the huge time delays. He thanked me for the education I had provided the court. The new prosecutor, whom the judge did not hold responsible for the reprehensible behavior of his office, added his comments, "If Mr. Taylor had been accorded a timely, lawful trial by jury, he would have been acquitted. The Prosecutors' Office concurs with your Honor, in that we too have been educated by Mr. Taylor in these matters, and I also extend my thanks to Mr. Taylor."

It mattered not. The U.S. Parole Commission still maintained jurisdiction over me. Immediately after I heard all those affirmative words in Judge Sauce's courtroom, U.S. Marshals appeared with orders to transport me back to the U.S. Penitentiary at Lewisburg, Pennsylvania. Had the Judge not dismissed all the charges? Had the prosecutor not agreed I was innocent? I was caught in an absurd Kafkaesque web of intractability. The only hope I could cling to at that point was that I might possibly obtain some relief from an upcoming interim parole hearing, which ended up being held six months after it was due.

At that interim parole hearing on February 19, 1986, an attorney from the Lewisburg Prison Project, Robert Hauhart, represented me. When allowed to speak, I tried to explain how the revocation of my parole in 1983 occurred with the use of court-suppressed and faulty information. Hearing Examiner Newman asked me if I had appealed Mr. Grinner's 1983 decision to the National Commission. I said I had and that I never received a response. Mr. Newman then said that the National Commission must have decided that everything was proper. He grew impatient with my awkward attempts to summarize clearly all the injustices I felt had been done in my case. He did not address them, but just said he was in a hurry and needed to proceed.

Hearing Examiner Newman allowed Mr. Hauhart to speak on my behalf, but he quickly told my attorney that the time I had used would be subtracted from his. Robert Hauhart argued succinctly for a reopening of my 1983 parole revocation case and for the overturning of that revocation decision for "non-compliance

with the substantial preponderance of the evidence test. We do not think there was any evidence presented that the United States Parole Commission should have relied on, due to the suppression of the evidence by the Court in Indiana." Hauhart further argued that considering my superior program achievement, I should receive a presumptive release date as I had already served fifty-eight months where the minimum guidelines were sixty months. Mr. Newman took a brief recess, and upon his return told us that he had decided to recommend that no changes be made in my 168-month (fourteen-year) sentence. Two months later the National Commissioners affirmed this decision.

If it were not for Robert Hauhart and the Lewisburg Prison Project, I may have given up at this point. This organization worked on the legal issues of those imprisoned at Lewisburg unable to pay for their own legal counsel. The Project was a lifeline to many poor inmates, and Bob became almost a personal friend to me in those times when he saw how the system had so unjustly captured and suffocated me when it revoked my first parole. He encouraged me to file an appeal, requesting that the Commission re-open the 1983 parole revocation proceedings and reconsider its 1986 decision to continue my confinement for many more years. Bob submitted a brief in support of my appeal, outlining how the Commission had failed to ensure that I received the due process to which I was entitled under *Morrissey v. Brewer*, specifying that I was not allowed to confront and cross-examine an adverse witness, nor allowed a continuance so that an adequate defense could be prepared, and that the evidence produced at the 1983 hearing was insufficient to support a finding of fact. He further argued that the earlier 1986 decisions had not adequately considered my superior performance achievement during the previous years of confinement. On July 23, 1986, the National Commission responded to my appeal by affirming their own earlier decision, stating, "all relevant factors have been considered and no new or significant information is presented which would justify a more lenient decision."

The 1980s, which started out on such an upbeat note, had become a nightmare. I thought I had experienced every possible wrong, but I had not. When I returned to Lewisburg, about the only positive circumstance was that Unicor, Federal Prison Industries, rehired me. I acquired some computer skills by participating

in classes offered at the prison, and I applied some of this learning to my job. Specifically, I worked in the Unicor payroll office, where I was the primary person dealing with the payroll of about five hundred federal inmates. Two other men worked in that little office with me under the supervision of a civilian employee.

On March 2, 1987, I returned to my desk after eating lunch in the main mess hall. I became wholly engrossed in designing a computerized payroll program. An inmate, who did not work in the area, entered the office carrying a lead-filled pipe. He walked past me to the rear of the office and smashed the pipe into the head of the man who worked back there. Still I remained oblivious. I am told that the assailant then came up behind me where I was bent over my desk, concentrating on my calculations, and bashed the left rear portion of my head with the lead pipe. My skull opened up and the force of the blow drove my head forward onto the computer keyboard. My only awareness came days later when I awoke in a hospital bed. I was at Geisinger Medical Center in Danville, Pennsylvania, about twenty-five miles from Lewisburg, where authorities had taken me because neither the prison hospital nor the local hospital could deal with such severe injuries.

The first thing I recall when I woke was an awareness that a nurse stood by my bed. She placed a clipboard in front of me to sign a Consent for Treatment form. But I realized almost immediately that my left eye saw nothing and I had limited vision in my right. I then noted that the left side of my face felt very odd, mostly numb. I thought I should sign the form but I could not recall who I was. I asked the nurse, "What's my name?" I could barely form these words with my partially paralyzed mouth. The nurse kindly told me that I was James Peter Taylor. I had no idea how to start my signature, and I broke down and cried.

Then I noticed something slimy and liquid-like on the right side of my face that slithered down on the front of my chest. I grabbed it in my right hand and brought it up very close to my right eye. I saw a long, slippery blood clot that had come from my left ear. The nurse took my hand away from the blood clot and then, mercifully, I lost consciousness.

Whatever the medical staff at Geisinger did to put me back together succeeded in the short term. I learned that my left eye had been knocked out of its socket and that they had returned it.

The muscles around the eye were unable to hold the eye in place, so the doctors sewed my eyelid shut. In the year ahead, I worked hard to exercise those facial muscles to convince subsequent doctors to reopen the eyelid.

The blow on the back of my head caused immense damage to my nervous system. The left eye is blind not because there is anything wrong with the eye itself. Rather, what I have is considered "cortical blindness," meaning that the nerves from the eye to the brain are damaged. Likewise, I have balance and vertigo problems, and am deaf in my left ear, all due to the brain damage I suffered. Facial paralysis along the left side extends across half my mouth and lips so that chewing and eating remain difficult chores. I lost my senses of taste and smell, which further frustrates eating. My memory for spelling returned fairly quickly, but I never recovered my memory for recent events. My speech returned only after two years of therapy and hours of practice on my own. In my early days in prison I attained the highest score possible on the Beta IQ Test, putting me in the superior intelligence range. After my 1987 injury, the same test placed me in the low-average range of intelligence.

I moved back to the prison hospital at Lewisburg after only a few days of intensive care at Geisinger Medical Center, still in rough shape. Keeping a prisoner in a community hospital, with a guard employed to provide security, gets expensive. As my mind cleared, I began to ask questions about the circumstances surrounding the assault. Sympathetic authorities told me that the black man who wielded the lead-filled pipe on March 2, 1987, was angry with our office supervisor, a white civilian. A few days earlier, he alleged, the supervisor had cruelly denied him a job in our office, complete with a racial slur. When the outraged inmate came back to the office, our supervisor happened to be temporarily absent. This guy felt committed to venting his rage on "Whitey," and it did not matter at that point exactly who received the blows.

My long-time friend Jean came to visit me very soon after the assault. After expressing normal concerns for my health, Jean remarked, "This may be the best thing that ever happened to you, Jim. All your life you've relied on athletics. Now you'll have to use other aspects of yourself to survive and succeed." I would have

angrily rejected her suggestion had Jean not been such a close friend. I held my temper at the time and later thought about the meaning of Jean's words. Soon thereafter, a doctor suggested that I attempt to play tennis again. At first I was astounded at this challenge, because I could not even see a ball or racket, much less an opponent or the tennis court itself. But again, this remark got me thinking. Soon I decided I must make the best of the cards I was dealt and do my utmost to be as functional as possible. Though I made gains eventually, I was never able to work again as an accountant. The Unicor offices gave me a chance to continue doing this type of work, and I tried my best, but I could never add a column of figures correctly.

I spent the next two months at Lewisburg in recovery, with visits to various doctors in the community, whose assessments indicated permanent disability. Perhaps because the authorities did not want to consider what compensation might be due since I incurred these injuries while working on a Unicor site, they transferred me to the U.S. Penitentiary at Terre Haute. Evaluated again by the prison and community doctors, they verified the permanence of my disabilities. The officials at Terre Haute recommended that I go to the U.S. Medical Center at Springfield, Missouri, to participate in a long-term rehabilitative program there. And so I returned, in September 1987, to the Medical Center that I had left in 1968, some nineteen years earlier.

No longer did my peers seek me out for my athletic prowess. No one wanted or needed an inept person playing on his basketball, softball, baseball or football team, and of course I knew I could no longer compete effectively in those sports. My fellow inmates saw me as a "lame," useful to them only for sex.

But I could not reconcile myself to a mere existence of sexual usage by others. Remembering the doctor's challenge, I began by hitting tennis balls against a wall, hours each day, every day, rain or shine, hot or cold. The Medical Center had no tennis facilities, but I used an available outdoor handball court. At first I was extremely discouraged and frustrated. But gradually, after about two years of hitting balls against walls, I improved and could pretty well gauge the speed and direction of the oncoming ball by the sound and the way I had hit it. About that time, I was transferred again to a low-security facility, this time with tennis courts

available and the subsequent chance to compete against sighted players. When competing against either a right- or left-handed player, I consciously attempted to direct the majority of my shots, low and deep, to my opponent's backcourt. When I believed I had my opponent consistently going to, or leaning to his backhand side, I would do my utmost to hit a drop shot with considerable slice, just barely over the net on his forehand side. In time, I developed a number of cut and slice volley shots, along with a fairly hard serve. I started to beat most beginning tennis players, and even gave some mediocre players a good match, though not a defeat. But this took years of physical practice and mental planning.

By the time I was assigned to the Federal Correctional Institution at Fort Worth, Texas, in 1992, I wanted to have some fun. When I was quite new to the place, a tennis tournament for inmates was announced. I signed up, and enlisted a new friend to help me on a little joke. On the morning of the tournament, my friend pushed me out to the tennis court in a wheelchair we borrowed for the occasion. I carried not only my tennis gear but also a cane. My friend wheeled my chair up to the assigned court, and as my opponent for the match watched, I hesitantly lifted myself out of the wheelchair and hobbled onto the court with my racket and cane, calling out, "Let's get this match started." For the first few points, I played lame, letting the score reach 40-love. Then I threw my cane away, and started to play my best. It took my opponent a game or two before he got himself together from the psychological blow I had dealt him. I won the match.

There were many other disabled inmates since Fort Worth offered specialized medical services. I took up jogging upon the urging of a new friend. He tied a long cord around his waist and the other end of the cord around my waist for our jog. I always held the cord in my left hand as I jogged in synch with my partner's slow pace and direction. By this time my own rehabilitation had progressed to the point where I could assist others. I suggested to some of the men in wheelchairs that when any of us wanted to go somewhere, I could be the legs and could push anyone's chair, if he could see to direct our way.

For years, starting at Springfield, I went out in the early mornings and shot a basketball, often for hours. I listened to how my

shots hit the rim or the backboard. At first I spent more time retrieving the errant shots than shooting, especially if no sighted person was around to tell me where the ball went. I also listened for the sound of the bouncing ball in order to retrieve it before it stopped bouncing. Gradually I got better by using the knowledge I gleaned from one successful shot, feeling how I used my body to make the shot, and then trying, over and over, to replicate it. It was best if I avoided hitting the rim or the backboard altogether and instead softly arched the ball high so that it dropped through the basket with a swish—such a sweet sound, one I have always loved; the sound I would like to hear when I eventually take my last breath on this earth. Over time, I redeveloped my ability to make a high percentage of shots from the free throw line, then from the top of the free throw circle, and finally from the corners of the court.

On one occasion at Fort Worth, about six years after my blinding injury, I drew a considerable crowd of onlookers as I sank seventy-four consecutive free throws. Basketball is a game where touch is almost as important as sight. The moment I release a basketball from my fingertips, I have a good idea where the ball is going. This is particularly true when I have taken one or more shots from the same area. When a player dribbles a ball behind his back, he obviously does not see the ball, since he is too busy looking for a teammate or figuring where the opposing players are. I can still dribble behind my back because loss of sight is no obstacle.

Efforts to obtain my freedom had been put on hold on March 2, 1987 and I could only gradually resume the struggle. Because I was transferred out of the Lewisburg penitentiary, I did not have the assistance of the Lewisburg Prison Project lawyers. As I listen today to the audiotape of my interim parole hearing conducted on March 30, 1988, I can hear that my speech is labored and my thoughts are not well-expressed, obvious results of the assault of one year earlier. At the beginning of that hearing, which took place at the Medical Center, the examiner orally reviewed the history of my case. He said the earlier decision to increase my confinement above the guidelines was because the authorities deemed me a serious risk. I "repeatedly failed to adjust to

release in the community." Specifically, he said, back in 1955, upon release, I committed a murder. I attempted an armed robbery in 1981, just eleven months after my release in 1980. He went on: "And in 1985, you were released and within two weeks you committed a murder."

I queried, "1985?"

"Yeah," he said, "that doesn't look right ..."

We agreed that there was a mistake on the record, and that the 1985 behavior he read in my file actually occurred in 1955, over thirty years earlier.

The discussion then centered on my injuries and disabilities. I emphasized these as a possible reason that the Parole Commission might release me since none of the earlier arguments made on my behalf had ever been effective. I argued that I was no longer functional in the penitentiary in that I could not effectively defend myself in that setting, and there was no program within the federal prison system to properly care for someone in my medical condition. Dr. Kevin Puzio, the Chief Medical Officer of the Medical Center, appeared on my behalf to verify that I had neurological problems resulting from the assault and that I had worked diligently on my own rehabilitation. The examiner commended my efforts to rehabilitate myself, stepped out of the room to deliberate, returned and said, "Mr. Taylor, we are not going to do you any good today. The essential reason is that you have done substantial harm to the community in the past and we cannot lightly gloss over that ... I am recommending no change in your parole date of 1995."

I had learned to live with disappointment and frustration. Next I received the National Commission's Notice of Action relative to the parole hearing examiner's recommendation. It stated that they affirmed his recommendation that I remain in prison at least until 1995, because in 1985 I committed a murder two weeks after release. I would not have released me if that was true. But I had been in the custody of the federal government and the State of Indiana every day in 1985. Someone had either intentionally or accidentally changed the record to indicate that my 1955 crime occurred in 1985. While in the presence of the hearing examiner in 1988, I heard that assertion for the first time, but I never dreamed that anyone would regard it as accurate. The hearing

examiner obviously understood instantly as he read it that it was an error. But he also never corrected the records, so that when the National Commissioners reviewed them in preparation for acting on his recommendation, they took at face value the paperwork in the file that said I committed another murder in 1985. Rage and desperation enveloped my whole being. I had already suffered a life-threatening assault after my unjust return to prison five years earlier. Now the total incompetence of the system to keep accurate records kept me behind bars. Federal employees with exalted positions of trust (a bunch of imbeciles in my opinion) had just disregarded thirty years of my life.

I do not know how long it took me to gather up my strength for the ongoing battle. I still had issues with eating and speech alongside my vision problems and hearing and memory losses. And I needed someone to address the original problem of my parole being revoked unjustly in 1983. But I added an item to my to-do list—to bring the error regarding the mistaken records of a 1985 murder to the attention of the Parole Commission. I wrote to the Commission and asked them to check their own records of my whereabouts in 1985. Knowing that they would find that I was in custody, I asked them to please correct the records that said I had been released and committed murder in that year. It was so clear and convincing to me that the false record must be corrected, I assumed they went through with the change.

That is why, when my next Interim Parole Hearing took place four years later (yes, it was four years before I had another parole hearing) in 1992, I never verified that the false and inflammatory information had been removed from my file. Instead, I returned to my arguments about the injustice of my confinement, dating back to the 1983 Final Parole Revocation Hearing and the illegal use of court-ordered-suppressed information and how the Anderson police based all their reports on what Wesley Robinson, a witness I was never allowed to confront, apparently told them. The examiner indicated he only wanted to hear *new* information but that he would forward all my written documents to the Commission. In a routine I knew only too well by this time, the examiner stepped out of the room to think. When he returned, I heard those very familiar words: he would not recommend any changes, he would refer his recommendation to the National Parole Com-

mission, I would hear their final decision later, and I was entitled to appeal.

This 1992 hearing occurred in the Federal Correctional Institution in Ashland, Kentucky, but I did not get the written Notice of Action from the National Commissioners until I was in the FCI at Fort Worth. I could not believe what the Notice said: my confinement would continue because when I was released in 1985, within two weeks I committed a murder. The records had never been corrected despite my written notification to the proper authorities that their files contained wholly erroneous and inflammatory information on me.

It was only because I mailed a letter of outrage, with copies of the Notices of Action, along with Bureau of Prison documentation of my confinement during all of 1985, to each member of the U.S. Senate Judiciary Committee that I finally obtained some relief. Senator Edward Kennedy followed up with questions, the records were finally corrected in 1993, but I was not told of the correction for another twelve months, until 1994. Within a few months, the authorities informed me that I could plan on release from confinement in 1995.

I served the entire fourteen years, from 1981 until 1995, because I associated with Wesley Robinson on a few occasions. This violation of my parole should have cost me, at most, a twelve-month return to prison. To tell the events of these years and to thus relive my feelings is acutely painful and not good for my soul. Now that I have done so, I do not want to think about it again.

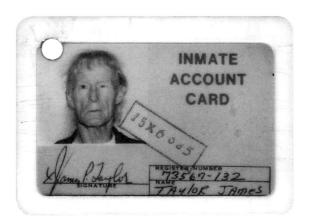

the last mile

A FTER MY SERIOUS INJURIES in 1987 in a maximum-security facility, the authorities moved me to a series of lesser-security institutions. I transferred in 1992 to the last of these, the FCI in Fort Worth, Texas, which was considered medium-security. However, the relatively relaxed atmosphere did not mean that my troubles ended.

I suspect I was targeted for personal harassment. When my twenty-seven boxes of legal papers, which had accumulated over the previous decades, finally arrived at Fort Worth from my previous placement at FCI Ashland, the staff told me that I could not keep this property in my room. The custodial staff said that all the boxes would be stored in a locked area within my unit manager's office, available only upon my written request. I wanted to work on my legal issues daily, primarily trying to gain parole, but I had to comply. What a continuous hassle—whenever I requested access to my boxes, I had to wait for a written response, and an "okay" meant that I next needed to make an appointment with the unit manager. My requests were handled on the unit manager's timetable, so I got access to my boxes only intermittently and even then for only fifteen minutes. I discovered that someone, certainly a staff member at Ashland or Fort Worth, had rummaged through the material I had kept quite well-organized. Given the great disarray of the files and the time limit, I needed assistance

from a sighted person. Sometimes I enlisted the unit manager's secretary and other times a fellow inmate to help me. Even with help I did not always find what I needed. I believe that these hassles were designed to frustrate my efforts to gain my freedom.

In 1993, I gained the attention of Senators Ted Kennedy and Carol Moseley-Braun, and they made inquiries on my behalf to the prison and parole authorities. I felt this was progress, yet remained irritated by what I viewed as harassment by some members of the FCI staff. I had the suspicion that some of the staff created a negative record on me to thwart my parole efforts. Also, during those three years at FCI-Fort Worth, I received an inordinate number of "shots,"—disciplinary reports—from custodial staff. All of these were bogus reports but required a ridiculous amount of my time and effort to appeal. Usually this meant I lost some privileges while I waited for the appeal to be considered. In one case, I earned a shot for "invading the privacy of a probation officer" because I placed some required paperwork into a designated in-box on her office desk while she was there. In another instance, an officer pounced on me for carrying a plastic bag of powdered Ensure, the nutritional supplement I took to help maintain my weight in view of my partially paralyzed mouth. I was accused of carrying cocaine, and the staff banished me to solitary. My release only occurred when an expert proved the powder harmless.

I have no direct evidence, but the similarities to the trail of false accusations and unjust imprisonment I endured beginning in 1981 seem undeniable. In these matters, I suspect George MacKinnon, the U.S. Prosecutor on my case in 1955–56, who in the 1980s and 1990s served on the U.S. Parole Commission and the First Circuit Federal Court of Appeals. During the proceedings in 1956, I ridiculed MacKinnon with the baboon picture. MacKinnon held his anger in check in the courtroom, but I believe he became personally vindictive toward me after this. During 1956, he exaggerated the severity of my crime in various reports he wrote and in what he told the media. Again, I must stress that I have no proof of my suspicions, but Mr. MacKinnon clearly had the means and may have had the motivation to manipulate the system to arrange my arrest in 1981 and to affect the outcome of subsequent parole considerations. He could still have been influencing my fate in the early 1990s.

George MacKinnon attended the University of Minnesota in the 1920s and then earned his law degree from the same institution. While in law school he became a close friend of two other law students, Warren Burger and Harry Blackman. Burger and Blackman had been friends since boyhood. When MacKinnon joined the friendship they became known as The Three Musketeers. After law school they each embarked on careers, but MacKinnon's was interrupted by his service in the U.S. Navy during World War II. While stationed in San Diego, he became friendly with another young lawyer from California, Richard Nixon. Sometime thereafter MacKinnon introduced Nixon to his two Minnesota buddies, Blackman and Burger.

In 1952 Nixon became Vice-President under Dwight Eisenhower, and soon his pals received plum appointments: Burger was appointed to the First Federal Circuit Court of Appeals in Washington, D.C., Blackman to the Eighth Federal Circuit Court in St. Louis, and MacKinnon to the office of the U.S. Attorney for the District of Minnesota. Nixon, as a "law and order" proponent, gave MacKinnon the task of bringing the death penalty back to Minnesota. MacKinnon saw my case as a means to do so, but he was not successful in convening a jury, and only a jury could impose death in the federal system.

Shortly after my conviction and sentencing in 1956, MacKinnon resigned as U.S. Attorney to run for Governor of the state of Minnesota in 1958. To the everlasting credit of the Minnesota voters, he was trounced at the polls.

The sixties began with Kennedy replacing Eisenhower. The Democrats held sway in Washington until Nixon won the presidency in 1968. Just like clockwork, Nixon's three friends quickly won appointments in higher positions: Burger and Blackman advanced to the Supreme Court, and MacKinnon replaced Burger on the First Circuit Court of Appeals. MacKinnon was later appointed to the U.S. Parole Board (known afterwards as the Parole Commission). So every time my case came up for parole consideration, my prosecutor sat in a position that allowed him to be sure I received unfavorable decisions. Further, with friends in high places MacKinnon could extend his influence throughout the law enforcement and Bureau of Prisons communities.

Several months before my March 1995 release, I was informed

that I would be freed. Of course this news pleased me, but also caused apprehension about what the future on the outside held for me. In those months before my release some of my inmate friends told me of the need to be very cautious with the medical staff. I heard from more than one source that other men scheduled for release had been called in by the medical staff and told about a medical decision to change their medication, usually a heart medication, to some "more-effective" drug. The men died of heart attacks, never to realize their freedom. One inmate in particular I heard about was a Puerto Rican who had served some forty years following conviction for the attempted assassination of President Truman. He died at Fort Worth following a change in medication just before his release date.

I took heed of the warning since, after my heart attack in 1981, I used the medication digoxin for my condition. The medication was obviously doing its job, as I had no further heart attacks. Just in case, I started a stockpile of digoxin. But before anything happened regarding my heart medication, I faced a different challenge. One day in January 1995, the medical clinic insisted I make an appearance in their office. A doctor said that I had a lesion on my lower back and I needed to have it surgically removed in the prison hospital. I totally and completely refused. I walked out of the clinic and onto the yard. The Chief Medical Officer of the institution happened to be out there and I approached him. I said loudly, "Doctor, please look at my back. What do you see there?" I turned around and pulled up my shirt.

The doctor rather reluctantly looked and then said he could see nothing.

I persisted, "Please, look again more carefully," and I slightly lowered my pants so more of my back was exposed. Several other inmates had by then gathered around, observing the conversation.

The doctor again said, "No, I don't believe there is any problem there."

Intending to draw an even larger crowd to witness this encounter, I shouted, "Doctor, I want you to look very carefully and be absolutely sure. Is there any lesion on my back?"

The doctor bent forward, visually scrutinizing and probing my back. Then he repeated, "No, there doesn't seem to be anything here of concern."

I said, "That's exactly right. There is nothing there. But your medical staff just told me there is a cancerous lesion on my back and they want to operate on me. I'm not going to let them touch me." I walked away, but later, when I obtained copies of my medical records, I found it noted in my chart that I had refused recommended surgical treatment. Had I required any medical attention while still at Fort Worth, I could easily have been refused as "medically non-compliant." Thankfully, no medical emergencies arose in those months. I have been thoroughly examined many times since by doctors in the Minneapolis community, and never has anyone seen a lesion or signs of cancer on my lower back.

Another curious incident occurred about a month before my March 29th release date, when the medical clinic changed my medication. The doctor said that I should stop the digoxin and begin taking a new medication for my heart. I smiled and said, "No, thanks, doctor, I have enough digoxin in my possession to carry me through March, and I intend to use it, not your new medicine."

One may question what I have just said. However, I submit that President Clinton's associate, James McDougal, a figure in the Whitewater case, died of a heart attack while in custody at the Federal Correctional Institution in Fort Worth. Newspapers later reported that a federal government report revealed that McDougal, the day before his death, was moved from his regular cell to solitary confinement as punishment for failing to provide a urine sample, though McDougal claimed he tried. Prohibited access to his nitroglycerin medication, he died of a heart attack in solitary confinement.

willow in a storm

I ENTERED A PENAL FACILITY for the first time in early 1951, when I was twenty-five years old. I had been sentenced to serve time at the State Farm of Virginia in Goochland, Virginia. This unexpected imprisonment left me in a daze; I could hardly believe that post-dating some checks had resulted in incarceration. The first day at the State Farm, I looked around me, talked to a few men, and realized this world greatly differed from anything I had ever experienced. There were many young first-time offenders, but also numerous older, career criminals serving the last years of lengthy sentences. I resolved to survive the ordeal, despite any difficulties.

Confidence in my ability was rudely shaken during the first night in my assigned dormitory. This place housed scores of inmates in bunk beds that filled a majority of the floor space. I saw images in dim light and heard quite clearly the sounds of young men preyed upon by older inmates, who prevailed through threats, knives and clubs. I heard the cries of these victims as they succumbed to the sexual abuse. How could I sleep? My mind raced and my apprehension grew as I thought about how to respond when my time came. I decided to fight off any rapist with all my strength.

Nothing happened at first. My first work assignment involved cutting down corn stalks with a machete to feed the institution's

cattle. But soon my job switched to the brickyard, which contained several large kilns. After a load of bricks finished baking, these extremely hot ovens cooled down for a day or so. The first day I worked in the brickyard, an older inmate told me to fetch a tool from Kiln #2. Not suspecting anything sinister about the request, I complied.

I walked into the kiln to look for the tool. It was very dark in there, and as I turned around to ascertain why daylight from the doorway had disappeared, I realized instantly that several men had followed me and now stood there, holding pipes and bricks. Further into the kiln a couple others snickered as they anticipated their prey. I stood frozen in the darkness, knowing that all my strength would never be enough to ward off the gang-bang about to happen. Before I could think much more, someone tackled me from behind. Several men took me down to the dirt floor, cut off my trousers, and raped me. Once alone, I picked myself up. I had no choice but to return to work before a guard would notice my absence. My cut-up trousers gave evidence to everyone in the work crew of what had taken place. I knew all the other sexual predators in this institution now considered me fair game.

However, before I knew about it, one of my abusers let it be known to the others that he planned to make me his "old lady." He let me know soon enough that if I refused the arrangement, I would continue to be the frequent victim of sexual assaults. I had seen what happened in the dormitory at night and this man offered protection from that. I quickly decided to be an old lady rather than community property. I never did get a good night's sleep in the dorm due to the vicious actions around me and my own apprehension that, despite the assurances of "my man," I might still be assaulted there. But I was not. Rather, for most of my one-year incarceration at the State Farm, one man regularly raped me in the brickyard kilns.

This experience rekindled the old ideas I had of feeling feminine and the enjoyment of the female role. I started to accentuate any feminine characteristics I had, since I believed this might offer me some protection in this crazy system. In fact, I was treated somewhat better than the men around me who fought the predators with all their masculine strength. Beatings, stabbings, and even murders occurred at Goochland, often due to jealousies and resistance to the established sexual practices there. I

look back on those times with great sorrow that I did not help any of my fellow young inmates with their dilemmas. Yet, I could not do so because I was so busy just trying to survive — to get through another day, another week, another month.

When I was released from the State Farm at Goochland, a federal court immediately sentenced me to a reformatory at Petersburg, Virginia. A few months after release from Petersburg, my short-lived freedom ended with the conviction for my involvement in the stolen car ring. This resulted in a sentence served at the U.S. Penitentiary at Terre Haute, Indiana. In neither Petersburg nor Terre Haute did any violent sexual activity occur in my presence. However, when I arrived at the U.S. Medical Center for Federal Prisoners in Springfield, Missouri, in 1956, I quickly learned to expect unusual and exploitative sexual behavior.

From my experiences at Goochland, I knew what lay ahead of me in the federal prison system with a longer-than-life sentence. For a year or more after my arrival at Springfield, I was very depressed and sometimes suicidal. But as I have explained, I finally made a decision that I wanted to live and work toward my eventual release. To attain release, I needed to survive. This meant, among other things, that I needed a strategy for dealing with my own sexuality and the sexuality and aggression of the other men around me.

I soon learned that, as at Goochland, to be weak was to be in danger. Other inmates considered a new or young inmate, unattached to anyone or to a group for protection, a prime candidate for sexual exploitation. The safest way to participate in inmate society, and thus to survive, was to be the feminine partner in a monogamous relationship with a strong masculine partner. The male in such a relationship had a difficult and dangerous role. He took charge, controlled his shemale, and allowed no other man to have any personal relationship with her. (I say "her" because the men playing the female role in these relationships adopt the feminine pronoun.) The male partner also secured a private place for the sexual liaisons. This often meant paying another inmate, or group of inmates, for access to a room or space which one of them claimed as his turf. Just like a man with a wife in traditional society, his responsibilities included providing for all the physical and emotional needs of his partner. He supplied her with clothing, jewelry and cosmetics — things she needed to wear and use in

order to play her feminine role satisfactorily. Also, just like in the outside community, many men viewed their women as property and were abusive to their partners, especially when angry with them about some perceived infidelity. This latter situation was about the only real hazard of the female role. I felt I could avoid this danger by being faithful in the relationship.

I decided to communicate to my fellows my interest in a monogamous relationship as a shemale. Due to my experiences at Goochland and with the older teenager, Bob, when I was thirteen years old, I easily adapted to such a role. I do not remember my first "running partner" at Springfield, but whoever it was, I set up a pattern with this person which worked for me, and which I lived for most of the next thirty years. I started my participation as a female in these relationships in order to survive. As time went on, I became more comfortable in the role. I attached myself to strong, reliable, respectful men who treated me well and who offered protection from many of the ordinary difficulties of being in the penal system, thus making my life simpler and easier than it would have been otherwise.

I was enormously grateful for this protection. I reciprocated by trying to be very physically attractive to my partners. I remained faithful, and so never put my "friend" in a position of having to defend his honor and reputation, which most of the other inmates respected. Because I have had no contact with my old partners upon release, I will refrain from identifying them here. Some may be dead, some may still be in prison, but others, old men like me, may be married with families. I don't want to cause them any embarrassment.

Relationships in a penal setting are always subject to end for reasons beyond the control of the participants. The federal penal system transfers inmates for its own reasons, and on a more positive note, inmates sometimes serve their time and are released. If my "friend" was up for transfer, or even release, negotiations had to occur relative to my next relationship. Even though my "friend" would be gone, he had an interest in seeing to it that I would be treated well in the future. When we knew in advance of such a change, I spent much time carefully assessing whom I might want to pair up with later. Luckily, my partners understood my wishes in this regard and then tried to arrange the relationship I wanted, with the proviso that if they came back to the institution where

I resided, they would have me again as their partner. Other she-males were not so fortunate. Some were treated more like slaves, and even sold to the highest bidder by their departing male.

Then there were occasions when I was transferred. Upon entering a different federal facility, I invariably recognized and knew other inmates from a common period of residency at another facility. As soon as I arrived, the pressure for me to enter into a relationship started. By this time, with my good reputation as currency, I had more autonomy in selecting a partner, provided I chose someone who was available and agreeable. At these times I felt like a rabbit pursued by greyhounds. I knew that I needed to make a decision promptly or my currency would be devalued, and I would become fair game for the predators. Usually I was plied with gifts and other inducements, which mostly I rejected until I decided with whom to partner. I always chose someone whom I felt would best assist my survival, rather than someone whose personality might be more pleasing. As I never contracted any sexually transmitted diseases, my choices were also lucky. The institutions notoriously allowed new inmates to mix in the general population without first ascertaining if they carried infectious diseases, such as H I V.

I do not know if more unfaithfulness and promiscuity existed in the prisons than in outside society, but I do know it resulted frequently in serious and violent consequences. Infidelity often resulted in death, and not only shemales were killed for such misbehavior; the shemales were capable of killing their mate, or seeing to it that the job was done.

The Goochland-style gang rape was an ever-present possibility too, not so much for me as an "attached" person, but more so for the unattached. Usually an inmate brandished a knife as the threatening weapon of choice, but alcohol and drugs could also render an unsuspecting subject incapacitated and vulnerable. Predatory behavior also occurred in the surgical recovery rooms, especially at the Medical Center in Springfield. Many homosexuals worked in this area, and after the civilian medical staff left a surgical patient in the care of inmate orderlies and nurses in the recovery rooms, group rapes of unconscious patients occurred. Inmates who knew this avoided even necessary surgery until finally the authorities took appropriate action by assigning the offending inmates to other jobs.

Occasionally guards became sexually involved with inmates. Any guard who succumbed to this temptation was a fool, for then he was vulnerable to a multitude of manipulations by inmates who knew. If an inmate could set up a credible situation that even remotely looked like an employee was sexually involved with an inmate, the first inmate had tremendous power over the employee, and thus, high recognition from his peers. Whenever an employee and inmate became sexually involved, or even were thought to be involved, the tension in the environment was palpable.

I never got caught in a sexual act by authorities. However, at the Medical Center at Springfield, while I worked in the institution's education department, staff discovered my large stash of female clothing and other accoutrements of my shemale role. I stored this collection in the empty space beneath file drawers in the office where I worked. Generally, I took many of these items out of their hiding place on Friday afternoons as I left my job, so they would be accessible for my use during weekends.

One Friday afternoon I walked back to my living unit carrying many items concealed in the several big pockets sewn into the lining of my coat. I stepped off an elevator into my living unit. Custodial officers waited to shake me down. There was no way to avoid the trap and so I said to the man in charge, "Lieutenant, just take me into that office over there and I will give you all I have." I did not want my fellow inmates to view the quantity of female clothing and jewelry I carried, because if they saw it all, the custodial staff would need to punish me for seriously violating rules against contraband. I had a better chance of securing lighter consequences if I could deal with the authorities out of the view of other inmates, so the officers would feel no need to make a lesson out of me.

Once in the office with the door closed and only the lieutenant present, I removed from the multiple coat pockets an array of women's clothing, jewelry and cosmetics. The lieutenant seemed astonished at the quantity, and said, "Taylor, you know what this means?"

I replied, "Yes, sir, I do." As it was all contraband, I could have been charged in federal court with a crime.

The lieutenant asked, "Well, do you have any more of this?"

"Yes."

"Where is it?"

I replied that there was quite a bit more in the filing cabinets at my workplace. The lieutenant dispatched a group of custodial personnel to confiscate all of it.

About two weeks later I stood before a disciplinary committee of the institution, and thankfully, not a federal judge. In the meantime, I regained most of the confiscated items through the voluntary help of an inmate who cleaned that office. So there was little evidence produced at the disciplinary committee, but still enough to proceed. The committee consisted of mostly higher-level authorities, not including the lieutenant, and only one or two of whom were original members of the confiscation team.

"Taylor, how did this material get in here?"

I said, "I can't tell you that."

My response noticeably disturbed them, and then someone asked, "Well, why do you have it?"

"Because it makes me feel good. It makes me feel more normal than wearing your prison attire."

Another one asked, "Why don't you have men's clothing?"

I replied, "I feel more comfortable in female clothing."

I left the room while they deliberated. I waited outside the committee room for a decision regarding my punishment. Soon a small red light flashed, signifying that I should come back. I did so and one of the committee members told me to sit down. As the first words were uttered, I knew I would not be severely punished. "You know, Taylor, we can't give this material back to you."

I smiled and said, "No, I realize you can't."

One of the associate wardens looked at me and said, "What are you going to do without this stuff?"

Very candidly, I replied, "I'll get some more." Surprisingly, they all laughed, and I received no real punishment. They sent me to Unit 10-East to live with the other labeled homosexuals of the feminine persuasion. I did not really fit in there because this population tended to be the promiscuous, flamboyant type. Within a few months, the authorities decided that I did not belong with this group, and I returned to my former living unit.

After twelve years at the Medical Center, the officials deemed me well enough to be transferred to a high-security prison. I was sent

to the U.S. Penitentiary at Leavenworth, Kansas, where I continued my lifestyle as a shemale partner in a monogamous relationship with a strong, responsible male. However, Leavenworth's inmates thrived on violence. When I had been there only a short time, on the flags (ground floor) one day, an inmate acquaintance called me aside and said, "Look up there." He pointed to an area of the surrounding cellblock about three stories up, where the men on holdover status were housed. At first I noticed a regular line of men on the walkway just outside their cells. I could see officers making a head count of the prisoners before they went to the mess hall. The long line started to move and my acquaintance laughingly asked me if I saw anything unusual. I looked as the line moved toward the stairwell, and all of a sudden, I noticed men disappearing out of the line. I realized that about one-third of the perhaps thirty men in the line got yanked back through the open cell doors as the line moved forward. My friend then told me that the more-permanent residents of that area, who went to meals at a different time than the men on hold-over status, snatched the hold-overs, who did not know their environment well, into the cells in order to use them sexually. Each victim was raped multiple times, and resisting resulted in a beating afterwards. The guards never realized what happened because the snatching took place after the before-dinner head count, and the holdovers were pushed back to the returning chow line before the after-dinner head count was made. If these had been cartoon characters, it might have been a funny sight, but not when real live human beings were involved. I realized that no matter how big, strong and resistant a man in this situation might be, he could not help but become a victim. And victims, all too often, decide to become victimizers.

Another fairly common scene I came across at Leavenworth, as well as at my next institution (Lewisburg), was a long line of inmates, waiting to rape some poor soul captured by a stronger thug. The would-be rapists could pay the thug for the victim with a pack or two of cigarettes. Whenever I saw this happen, I felt great sympathy for the victim and helplessness to do anything for him. One may wonder at this point how so much violence could occur within a prison—like, where were the guards? The reader knows by now that the number of guards is small relative to the

number of inmates; thus, inmates often rule within the cellblocks and guards frequently find it in their own interest not to see what is in front of them.

After being stabbed at Leavenworth in 1975, I was transferred to Lewisburg. Within a year or two of arriving there, I felt my chances of gaining parole had improved. I began to seriously plan for a life on the outside. I had become very accustomed to being the feminine partner in a sexual relationship and I decided I wanted to continue in a similar role in free society. In spite of all evidence to the contrary, I never considered myself a homosexual: I felt truly female. Years earlier I had learned about the experiments in transgender surgery at reputable medical clinics in the country and I wanted to explore the possibility of undergoing such surgery. Within the prison system, I knew a couple of men who so urgently wanted to become women that they took knives or razor blades to themselves. Horrible medical complications resulted. Though not that desperate, I thought I wanted to be transgendered into a woman when I got out on parole.

I was released in January 1980 to a halfway house in Anderson, Indiana. My good friend and faithful advocate, Jean, paved the way for me, including arranging my admission to Anderson College, a small school under the auspices of her church. Over the stated reservations of Jean and some other friends, I pursued my plan to undergo transsexual surgery. I enrolled in a sex-change program at Vanderbilt University in Nashville, Tennessee. Although I felt ready to have the surgery and could pay outright for it when I contacted Vanderbilt, the doctors wanted me to engage first in psychological counseling for about six months. By the spring of 1981, my counselors advised that I should wear women's clothing and apply cosmetics in a feminine fashion for certain periods of time, so as to become accustomed to what life might be like as a full-time woman. Due to my previous cross-dressing experience and the female persona I adopted in prison, I think I was more advanced in this process than other candidates for surgery.

During the summer of 1980, I met a woman, Patsy, in an Anderson College class. In talking with her day after day, I learned about the recent troubles in her life. She had divorced her alcoholic, abusive husband and was trying to support herself and her

four children. Their father offered little assistance. I felt sorry for Patsy, and I was lonely. I no longer lived in the halfway house, but had moved on to a rented apartment. Since developing my business and taking classes took up so much time, I rarely went home. I wanted to help Patsy, especially after the day I visited her house and witnessed first hand the family's desperate poverty. The house was in a housing project and the refrigerator contained virtually no food.

I offered to become very involved in Patsy's family. I suggested that we all move into a good-sized home I found available for rent in another little town a few miles from Anderson. I wanted to give the family physical, emotional and financial support. Patsy agreed, and soon after we moved in together we began a sexual relationship. I shared with Patsy my belief that I was emotionally and mentally more a female than a male, and I told her of my plans to undergo transsexual surgery. She accepted this, as she accepted my plans to cross-dress on occasion. I do not recall what went into our decision to marry each other. I was in no psychological condition to promise to be a husband to my wife. But we did marry in a small civil ceremony in December 1980.

I believe I treated Patsy with much concern and respect, and I took on the role of stepfather to her children in earnest. The older girl, a teenager, was more involved with her peers than with the family, but the twelve-year-old girl and the two younger boys soaked up the attention I gave them. My arrest in April 1981 for crimes I did not commit left me bitterly disappointed with Patsy, as she almost immediately ditched me. Perhaps the police authorities told her things she chose to believe. At any rate, she kept, sold or gave away all my possessions and only visited me once. On that occasion, she brought along her sister, and the sister blatantly wore some of my jewelry. I took legal action from the jail and divorced Patsy. Among my possessions were two articles very dear to me, an autographed copy of Karl Menninger's *The Crime of Punishment*; and an oil painting of the Franklin Village Cider Mill near my boyhood home, something I created from memory. I have received no response to my recent efforts to reclaim these cherished items from Patsy.

In 1983 I was returned to the U.S. Penitentiary at Lewisburg, Pennsylvania. With the exception of the other relatively short period in an Indiana jail awaiting disposition of the false charges against me, I remained at Lewisburg until the violent beating in 1987. During those years at Lewisburg, I resumed my role as a female sexual partner. After the assault and some recovery, I moved out of the high-security setting to the U.S. Medical Center at Springfield, Missouri, for a couple of years, and then was sent on to a series of FCIs, before my final release in 1995. After the injury, I never partnered with a protective male again. By this time I was sixty-two years old, disabled, facially disfigured, and therefore not so desirable. Also, a man could relax and make more of his own decisions in these lower-security settings. I had lost much of my desire for sex in any form as I was old and tired, and needed all my energy to rehabilitate from my injuries.

After recovering many of my functional abilities by 1990 or so, I devoted all my passion to gaining release from this unjust confinement that had begun in 1981. In 1994, I was informed that my efforts would result in a parole. I wanted to go to Texas where I knew people who promised to be supportive of me. However, the parole board decided to send me to Minnesota, the scene of the original crime, where I knew no one and feared living with my

disabilities in the severe winters. I protested, but the plan never changed. I began to work on that option in my mind. Again I needed to consider my sexuality and what I intended to do with it. Since I had become comfortable in the female role over so many years, it seemed to me that I should adopt this role again. I knew I was too old to be considered by medical experts as eligible for transgender surgery, and honestly, my desire for it had waned. Still, I had memories of feeling good wearing feminine attire, so I decided that when I was released on parole I would acquire a woman's wardrobe in order to cross-dress in private, and possibly in public.

While living in the halfway house in Minneapolis, I easily procured women's clothing, wigs and other accoutrements at a large used-clothing store nearby. It was during these first few months after my release that I met the woman I fell in love with and subsequently married. During our courtship, I told Katherine the basic information about my cross-dressing and transgender-planning history. Along with all the other parts of my history that I asked her to understand and accept, this was a huge additional chunk of information for her to digest. I assured Katherine that I no longer wanted to be a female and that I had no intention of cross-dressing if she would consider marrying me. She cried and said this required an enormous amount of faith from her. We continued to see each other, and she finally said yes to my marriage proposal.

I candidly admit that giving up cross-dressing and the feminine role was neither easy nor simple for me. I accomplished this radical change due only to my great love for Katherine and my desire to please her in every possible way. Katherine has provided me with purpose and reason to live as I was born, and she has been integral to the happiest period of my entire life to date.

Note: To corroborate my description of sexual violence in U.S. prisons, read *No Escape: Male Rape in U.S. Prisons*, written and published by Human Rights Watch in April 2001 (Library of Congress Catalog Number: 2001088989).

moving on

I N LEAVENWORTH in the early 1970s, I was first confined in Cell House A, in a ten-man cell, number 404. A cell house is a huge place, five tiers of mostly ten-man cells stretching about two hundred yards long. Among my first cellmates were Robert and Josephus. Robert's nickname was "Dodi Mite," which he adopted from some racy poem he loved to recite. "Josephus" had given himself that name; though unofficial, it was how the prison authorities listed him. Both these men were African-American. Josephus was a short and slight fellow with a great outgoing personality. He loved rock-and-roll music and fancied himself something of a musician with a horn. I referred Josephus to Chuck Berry, whom I met in Springfield. Chuck did not mind advising other inmates who wanted to break into the music business. When I told Josephus I could make this connection, he did a little dance in our cell. I know that contact occurred between the two men but I never learned the results of it.

Dodi Mite originated from the Washington, D.C., area and was a natural athlete, one of the first blacks offered an athletic scholarship at Texas Christian University. While in Texas he got involved with some young white men transporting a small amount of marijuana into this country from Mexico. The car they used was rented in Dodi Mite's name. Thus, when the car got stopped

and searched by authorities, Dodi Mite was the one charged, convicted and given a twenty-year sentence, while the others got off. I believed Dodi Mite's story and felt he had been treated unjustly. I offered to assist him in litigating his case, and we eventually gained him an early release.

As Dodi Mite and I lived, played, and worked on his case together, we became well acquainted. There were two aspects of our personalities that drew us together. One, we both loved all forms of athletics. Two, Dodi Mite and I both challenged authority figures when we believed they were wrong, no matter the cost. One day Dodi Mite told me he had written a letter to his mother and told her about a man in prison, me, who should not be there. Later, Dodi Mite came to me and said he received a letter from his mother and she included a picture of herself. He showed me the picture, and whatever images I already had in my mind of Dodi Mite's family were shattered, for while he had a dark complexion, he showed me a picture of a fair white woman. I said with a smile, "Well, Dodi Mite, there's a story here."

Dodi Mite told me more about his younger days. As a young teen he ended up in a reformatory, and while there, one of his teachers, Mrs. T., showed particular interest in him. Subsequently, while still a teen, he lived with Mrs. T., her husband and children as a foster child. From that point on, he regarded Mrs. T. as his mother, because she acted every bit the part of a mother to him. Although he later became involved in criminal activity, this woman, his mother figure, remained interested and supportive of him for years. Sometime after he related this story, Dodi Mite told me his mother asked him if she could write to me. I said, "Sure, if she wants to write to me, I'll write her back."

Mrs. T., whom I have already referred to as Jean, began a correspondence with me at that time (1972) which has lasted to this day, over thirty years. She is like a loving, trusted sister. Jean has done incredible things on my behalf, repeatedly going many extra miles, figuratively and literally. There is absolutely no way I can repay her for her continued love and support, because without her there is no way I would have survived or gained my freedom.

After corresponding with me for some time, Jean began to write to others in order to verify some of the things I told her. The prosecutor in my capital case had given grossly erroneous

accounts of my crime to the court and to the newspapers, most certainly in order to inflame the public and gain the death penalty for me. There existed accounts and records of my crime that stated I chopped up my victim into pieces with a hatchet. Jean placed a telephone call to the undertaker in Thief River Falls, asking him for a description of the state of Mr. Lindberg's body upon death. The undertaker said there was an open casket funeral with an intact body, showing no cuts or bruises on Mr. Lindberg's face or hands. I felt vindicated, and Jean began to trust me.

In our conversations I also told Jean that George MacKinnon advised the court and the press that I began my criminal career by committing some felony in North Carolina at the age of fifteen. This was another example of how he invented inflammatory information. Jean did her own research, this time contacting police and courts in North Carolina and learned that I never committed any crime in North Carolina in my teenage years.

After Jean apparently felt confident in my trustworthiness, she began to advocate for my parole to those who might have some influence in this regard. She wrote many people, including U.S. Senators, Bureau of Prison authorities, and members of the United States Parole Commission. Her efforts led to the positive involvement of Senator Charles Matthias of Maryland, and Senator Mark Hatfield of Oregon, among others.

In 1975, when the inmate at Leavenworth stabbed me, I could only breathe due to some piece of medical equipment. As described, after about six weeks, the prison doctors told me they needed to remove me from the pump because it would certainly lead to my death if continued. However, the complication of shutting off the pump was that I would probably die from drowning in my own fluids. A nurse brought me a phone to call Jean. I told her this might be our last conversation, I thanked her for all her support and then said good-bye. I learned later that she made emergency calls to her fellow church members and they gathered that evening for a special meeting to pray for my life. When the breathing machine was removed the next morning, I breathed without complication on my own. Jean thus taught me the power of prayer and the possibility of miracles.

After I recovered from the stabbing, the prison authorities decided to transfer me to the federal penitentiary at Lewisburg,

Pennsylvania. This transfer had a positive effect in that I met Jean, in person, for the first time. Lewisburg is about a four-hour drive from Jean's home in Maryland. I was profoundly humbled and grateful that Jean chose to visit me each month for the next several years. Jean's motivation to befriend me in such a meaningful way derives strictly from her Christian beliefs. I was one of the three or four fortunate people on whom she focused her dedication at that time. She works constantly, even now in her eighties, on behalf of a handful of needy people.

During those first few years of my stay at Lewisburg, I realized my unusual fortune. I looked around me one day, after being in federal confinement for about twenty years, and realized that none of the inmates who started their sentences at about the same time as me were alive. Those men had been given very long sentences, so I do not mean that my fellow inmates attained parole. I pondered what happened to them and concluded that they had died of illness, injury caused by others, or by suicide. Later I read some official report that only three percent of federal "lifers" are ever released. I credit Jean's constant interest and advocacy in my case over the years for my very survival. Not only did she bolster my spirits and efforts to win release, she also became known to many federal authorities as my advocate. If I ever met an untimely, suspicious demise, they knew Jean would lead a relentless investigation into the reasons for it. She was my shield in battle.

Only through her intense advocacy on my behalf did my efforts to gain parole finally lead to my release in January 1980. An example of this advocacy is her travel, at her own expense, to Atlanta, Georgia, in April 1978 and her presentation of her own twenty-page report in support of me before the U.S. Parole Commission.

Jean laid out "seven specific reasons why the decision of the National Commissioners to deny parole, which was made on January 23, 1978, should be reversed." First, she made an extended argument about the sources of information that the Parole Commission used in explaining their denial of parole, showing how they did not use "primary sources" but relied on "secondary sources."

Second, she asserted that I was unlikely to commit any more violent acts as I had committed one act of violence in my life and

even within the walls of prison I conducted myself in a nonviolent manner.

Third, she showed how the Commission used a report prepared by George MacKinnon, which contained errors leading to a false impression of me as a habitual criminal whose career began at age fifteen.

Fourth, Jean argued that accountability for my crime, as defined by Congress, was satisfied by the years already served.

Fifth, she gave a lengthy statement regarding the many professionals and politicians who advocated my release.

Sixth, she argued how I long ago assumed responsibility, guilt and remorse for my offense, and over the years made a conscious decision to reform myself with the help of God.

Her seventh, and last, argument was to describe to the Commission the man she had come to know "better than any living person today" through her own observations of records and documents but also her personal acquaintance with me over five years. She described me as "a practicing Christian," "a man of integrity," and "a man of talent and exceptional ability." She then quoted me, from a letter I had written her, in which I described myself. Forgive me if I double-quote here. It is not in the spirit of *The Magnificent Obsession*, but gives insights to my thoughts back then: "Jean, there are not many who could have successfully come through where I have been, and not been horribly scarred and twisted beyond recognition ... I have undergone, and come out, not a broken nor brutalized man, but as a very strong human being for such an experience ... The type of strength I refer to, can and will sustain me through matters beyond the imaginations of most of my fellow citizens out there ... God must have traveled by my side for all those many long years, for me to even be able to write about it now. I do not credit myself, Jean, I do not mean to blow my horn, or pat my own back, for I know full well where the real credit belongs ... God has sustained me, Jean. He will continue to sustain me, for what yet undisclosed purposes I do not know. All I am sure of is that I am fully prepared, I can handle it."

This personal and extremely thoughtful presentation by Jean in 1978 was significantly instrumental, I believe, in my release, albeit not until early 1980. I devised a parole plan, mostly utilizing Jean's church and college contacts in Anderson, Indiana, and

the Parole Commission finally accepted the plan. After twenty-five years of confinement in major federal prisons, I felt immense joy and great relief, knowing I survived one of life's most dangerous environments.

On the appointed release date, Jean, along with Dick and Liz Shelley from Wilkes-Barre, Pennsylvania, who became my friends through our common affiliation with Mensa, came to Lewisburg to transport me to Anderson, Indiana. We drove to Anderson, where I entered Re-Entry, Inc., the halfway house overseen by Dr. Val Clear, a professor at Anderson College. Through Jean's efforts, Dr. Clear became my sponsor in Anderson. Jean visited me a few months later when she came to town for her annual church meeting. By then, I had moved on from the halfway house into my own apartment and was self-employed, earning a decent income. With great pride I showed Jean my accomplishments,

A year later, in June 1981, Jean attended the church meeting in Anderson and again visited me. But this time, the circumstances had changed significantly. She had to visit me in the Madison County Jail as I was held for what would become a two-year period without a trial on a charge of conspiracy to commit armed robbery. This grave injustice put me in a constant foul mood. I had already spoken with Jean via a telephone call from the county jail during which I described what happened to me. Not long after the call, my jailers told me I had a visitor. I went to the visiting area and Jean appeared. I felt shame and embarrassment that we were to meet in a penal facility again. I expected recriminations or anger on her part. After all, she invested years of intense effort, and recruited scores of other people to demonstrate their belief in me in order to win my freedom in 1980. And now, she was confronted with this most questionable situation. I had told her in the phone call that it was all a mistake—that I had not committed any new offense. Yet, authorities and the media repeatedly proclaimed my guilt. All she had was my word against all of that. I am sure she was incredibly disappointed that all her efforts had come to this. But Jean did not shake her finger, much less abandon me. When we first could talk privately on this visit, she merely asked, "How can I help you, Jim?" To this day, her Christ-like demeanor awes me.

From that time in 1981 until I finally again won my release on parole in 1995, Jean encouraged me, she wrote and visited me, and

she badgered others on my behalf. Jean became for me a beautiful role model of the person I yearned to become. She showed me I was on the right track in my efforts to live the philosophy set forth in *The Magnificent Obsession*. She not only saved my life, but by her example, she helped provide me a new way to live. I continue to regard Jean as one of God's few saints on this far-less-than-perfect earth.

While I was jailed in Indiana on the false charges, I suffered a heart attack that led to an ongoing heart condition. After I returned to Lewisburg in 1983, medical personnel sent me out of the prison for a cardiac evaluation to a large medical facility, the Geisinger Medical Center, in nearby Danville. I appreciated the courtesy and comfort the personnel at Geisinger extended, especially considering I came to them in handcuffs, shackles, and chains. So when an appeal for the Geisinger Children's Hospital Center arrived in the mail in May 1984, I wanted to contribute. This began a three-year period during which I sent money to Geisinger regularly. I also persuaded some of my fellow inmates to do the same. I had no idea that I might someday reap any personal benefits from my actions, beyond the immediate satisfaction of doing some good.

But on March 2, 1987, when I was viciously assaulted and severely injured by another inmate, the authorities sent me to Geisinger. When I awoke from unconsciousness, I found myself in a private room, not the usual accommodation afforded a prisoner. Over the few days of my hospitalization at Geisinger, I was spoiled with royal treatment and kindness. Nurses told me that as a faithful contributor to the hospital, the staff wanted to give me the best care possible. I detected amazement and resentment on the part of prison staff assigned to guard me day and night. I returned to the prison hospital prematurely, considering my condition. I believe the authorities did not want me to receive the exceptional level of care and treatment that they themselves might not receive if they were Geisinger patients.

About six months after the Lewisburg assault, the authorities sent me to the U.S. Medical Center for Federal Prisoners in Springfield, Missouri, for rehabilitation. I had spent twelve years, from 1956 to 1968, at the Medical Center and felt ambivalent about returning

there. I knew that the facilities would be more helpful to me than would those of a maximum-security facility such as Terre Haute or Lewisburg. However, being in southwestern Missouri would place me far away from the support of Jean and others who had come into my life at Lewisburg.

All my property, including the legal papers that I had gathered and saved over the years, as well as my personal belongings, was taken from me in transit. Weeks went by at Springfield without my property being returned to me, although I knew it had arrived at the institution's Receiving and Discharge area. I felt very frustrated about this, so one day when I walked down a hallway and my companion told me that one of the Medical Center's higher officers was headed toward us, I decided to approach him directly about my problem. I went up to the man, introduced myself, and told him I had been at the Medical Center for several weeks without any of my personal belongings; I asked him if he would assist me to regain these. In a minute, he told me his name was Captain Brush, and he said, "Follow me." We went to a staff telephone nearby and he called the Receiving and Discharge room. "This is Captain Brush. I have Inmate James P. Taylor here and I want all his personal property given to him immediately. I'm sending him directly to you now, so have it ready." I felt incredibly grateful that an officer who did not even know me took up my cause so swiftly. I felt that at least I had one powerful advocate in this institution, which diminished my apprehensions immensely. When I arrived at the Receiving and Discharge area, all my property, neatly arranged, waited for me.

In the following two years of my stay at Springfield, I did not have occasion to ask Captain Brush for any more favors. But his presence reassured me. I ran into Brush again in 1992. We had both been transferred to Fort Worth, me as an inmate and he as Associate Warden. As my parole became more probable and the date drew nearer, I became the victim of repeated false reports on my behavior by staff who did not want me to gain my release. The staff's irritation was exacerbated as I continued my practice of filing grievances and bringing suits against the institution and individual employees. Their disciplinary reports put me in jeopardy of not only some short-term punishment but also the possibility of a delayed release date. When I was notified of the first

false accusation, I went to Associate Warden Brush. I do not know why he so willingly believed my denials then, or why he so quickly took up my cause earlier in Springfield. He said to me, "Don't worry about it, Jim, I'll take care of it. And if you have any more problems like this again, let me know." On the many subsequent occasions of staff writing shots on me, I appealed to Mr. Brush and the reports disappeared.

Since my release in 1995, I have made inquiries into the whereabouts of Mr. Brush, thinking he might by this time be a Warden of some institution. I was unable to locate him within the system, so I think he may have retired. I would like to thank him again for his trust and advocacy.

My move to the FCI in Phoenix was the first time the Bureau of Prisons assigned me to less than a maximum-security facility. I assume their decision took into consideration my serious disabilities and which put me at risk of further victimization if placed in a high-security prison.

Shortly after I arrived at Phoenix, I asked to be assigned to work. For the previous twenty-five years, I had been an Industrial Cost Accountant for Unicor. The Unicor people at Phoenix agreed to try me out in an accounting position. I worked very hard, but even using a magnifying glass and having previous familiarity with business machines, I failed to do the required work correctly. A new label, "Unassigned," accompanied my records, which meant an inmate did not work. I believe this was the first time I felt so wholly inadequate since my early adult years in Fort Lauderdale when I could not support my wife and child.

Shortly thereafter, an acquaintance who worked as an inmate clerk told me he had spoken to his boss, the institution's Safety Officer. The inmate said that Mr. Mark Freeman wanted to see me in his office, and so I went, a little nervous, to find out why. Mr. Freeman explained that his clerk told him about the assault while on a Unicor job at Lewisburg. He asked if I ever received any monetary compensation for the fact that my injuries resulted in an inability to continue working. I told him I had not received anything, nor was I aware that I might be entitled to any compensation. Mr. Freeman told me he would call Lewisburg to check whether the details I related to him were factual. He said, if true,

I was entitled to monies starting at the time of the injuries to the present and he would see to it that I received my due.

I was skeptical that I would receive any money from the system, as I had never heard of such a program before, yet I felt excited about the prospect of acquiring some funds that might help me exist a little more comfortably. But I forgot all about the possibility until a check for about five thousand dollars arrived in my mail. Immediately, I went to Mark Freeman's office and thanked him for his thoughtfulness and assistance. Others certainly knew about the existence of the Inmate Accident Compensation System applicable to me, but no one until Mr. Freeman bothered to act on my behalf.

A short while later, a young inmate told me that he was about to be released but he did not want to leave Phoenix for fear he might be killed on the streets of his Los Angeles neighborhood. Paul said he planned to ask the warden to please not release him, that he wanted to stay in custody. He felt safer at the correctional institution than in his hometown environment. I could not believe he would ask for an extended stay so I said I wanted to go along and witness the conversation. We went to the yard to find the warden. I listened as Paul walked up to and begged the warden to keep him there at Phoenix. The warden showed no understanding of Paul's dilemma and told him he had no choice—he would be released on the assigned date. The whole situation made me incredulous. I thought about it for days and then decided that the only helpful response I could make would be to share my good fortune and soften the blow for Paul. I told him I would send $1,500 to some reliable friends of his, to pass on to him when he got back home. I put no strings on this money, nor did I advise Paul how to use it. I just hoped that he would use the money to set himself up for some success. Paul had so few advantages in his life that he probably did not really believe there would be money waiting for him when he got home.

Not every story has a happy ending. I followed up and learned that Paul blew the $1,500 on drugs soon after his release, and eventually returned to prison.

After a year in Phoenix I was transferred to the Federal Correctional Institution at Ashland, Kentucky. At a point where I had

regained many of my functions, I was eager to pursue my primary goal of release. Here again a staff member took a special interest and offered to help me, another surprise blessing.

One day I conversed with a fellow inmate who worked in the chaplains' office at Ashland. I told him I needed help with my upcoming parole hearing. I had huge quantities of legal papers and several audiotapes of previous parole hearings that needed review, and considering my disabilities, handling all this by myself seemed overwhelming. The inmate told me that Father John Noe, the Catholic chaplain, was a good man who helped other inmates with similar tasks. I countered that I was not a Catholic and he said that didn't matter. So I decided I would pursue his recommendation, as I knew of no better alternative.

I went to Father Noe's office and introduced myself. Father Noe had a big, firm handshake and a receptive demeanor. He listened as I told him I needed help badly, that back in 1983, my parole was revoked relying on false information and violations of my rights. Father Noe said he needed time to review all the documentation I provided and whatever other prison records he could find. He said, "If I determine that you have misrepresented yourself and the facts, I won't help you. But if all you say is true, I'll come to your parole hearing and speak on your behalf. It will take me some time to go through all the material, so you'll have to wait."

I waited quite a few months for Father Noe's verdict. Finally, one day he summoned me to his office and said, "You were telling me the truth. I'm going to try to help you." Father Noe and a psychologist who worked at the institution both came to the parole hearing conducted at Ashland later that year, 1992. Father Noe told the Parole Commission, "I've reviewed all Mr. Taylor's records and I've discovered that there have been injustices in his case. Someone from the Commission needs to review all these records. Mr. Taylor should be released at this time and some reparations should be made to him."

The usual process occurred. The hearing examiner stepped out of the room, then returned to basically say nothing except that he would not, on his own, change anything about my status, but would refer all the documents I gave him to the National Parole Commission for their study and action. One usually receives the

Parole Commission's Notice of Action about a month or two after a hearing such as this. But before Father Noe, the psychologist or I received that notice, I was summarily transferred yet again, this time to the Federal Correctional Institution at Fort Worth, Texas.

I have already described how angry and frustrated I felt when I received notification that parole was denied me this time. The wholly false entry about the 1985 murder remained in my record despite my proper communication to prove its inaccuracy. Despite this horrible setback, I can still hold dear the kind and assertive advocacy given to me by Father John Noe of the Ashland FCI. He helped me when I truly needed help, and because of this, I attended the Catholic Mass he celebrated every week at the institution, as long as I was there. I thought this was the way I could best demonstrate to him my sincere gratitude.

I have mentioned how happy I was to find Mr. Brush as the Associate Warden at Fort Worth when I arrived. Mark Freeman had also transferred to Fort Worth into the Safety Officer job, an equally pleasant surprise. When I visited him he asked me if I had received any more compensation for my injuries beyond the one payment he helped me obtain. I said, "No," again surprised that I might be entitled to something further. He assured me I qualified to receive ongoing payments as compensation, and once again he made the necessary calls so that I received another back-payment, this time worth about $1,700, as well as an ongoing small monthly compensation payment. Miracles do happen.

Unable to work, I spent much time in the law library at Fort Worth. I could read somewhat at this point, though rather painstakingly, with a powerful magnifying glass. I became acquainted with a lovely, elderly lady by the name of Mildred Pollard, an employee in the inmate library. At first, she observed how much money I spent making copies on the library's copy machine. One day she asked me why I made so many copies. I explained to her that each court in which I filed my many cases demanded anywhere from four to twelve copies of documents and exhibits in order for the case to proceed. This meant I needed to prepare hundreds, maybe thousands, of duplicated pages. The compensation money disappeared quickly as I fought various battles in the courts and in the federal administrative and legislative offices.

Mildred Pollard was sympathetic and apparently decided to risk her job and reputation. She said, "Bring me all the things you need copied and I'll make them when I'm here." And she did this, insisting that I need not pay her for her assistance nor the library for the copies. Our friendship grew. I stayed in the library until closing hours most evenings, or I returned there at closing time, so I could walk Mrs. Pollard out to the front door and carry her heavy tote bag. She brought cookies, brownies, and even bananas into the institution for me when she learned that sweets and bananas were favorites of mine. We talked about her love of travel, especially cruises. She told me many stories about her relative, Jimmy Dean, the famous country-western musician. She was a beautiful soul.

One evening when I accompanied Mrs. Pollard to the front door, we were up the steps and almost at the door, when out of the darkness jumped my unit manager. This guy, whom I already knew to be quite punitive, yelled into my face, "Don't ever let me catch you around this door again with this lady, or I'll have you put in the hole." Mrs. Pollard gently took her tote bag from me and said good night. The next day, she and I talked about the unit manager's emphatic threat. We decided it was best if I walked her only to near the front door.

When I was finally given a parole date, I relayed the good news to Mrs. Pollard and she shared my joy. After I married, I called her one evening and told her about my good life in Minneapolis. She was cheerful as ever and pleased to hear from me. She talked a short while with Katherine during that phone call. In 1998, I attempted to reach her again but no one answered her phone the many times I called. I feared she might have become sick or even died, so I wrote a letter to her. Her daughter answered my letter with the news that Mrs. Pollard had suffered a stroke and could no longer live alone. The daughter moved her mother to southern Texas, far from Fort Worth, to keep her close. In 1999, the daughter again responded to my inquiries and let me know that my friend passed away in May of that year.

At Fort Worth I was assigned to a single room, a privilege usually conferred on inmates who did not present behavior problems. One day I came into my unit and other inmates warned me that I now had a roommate. They told me John Aslakson was "one of

those bikers." The minute I heard this, I was hot. "What the hell did they put this guy in my room for?" I said to myself. I went to the room and John tried to start a conversation, but I uttered only short responses. I left the room and the unit building and went out into the evening cool. I walked by myself to the recreation area some distance from the unit, using my heavy cane to offer some guidance and security. I walked around the quarter-mile running track many times, stewing with my irate feelings for some time. Then, as I began to calm down and assess what had happened, I recognized my own bad attitude and anti-social behavior toward the young man. I put the situation in another perspective for myself. I imagined that if John were my son, how would I, his father, want him to be treated? Then I felt ashamed for how I had acted toward him.

I made up my mind I would thereafter treat John Aslakson as a son. This proved difficult for me, because I had no particular liking for biker culture, and I could tell when we first met that John fit the stereotype of a typical biker. When I returned to our room, I immediately put into practice what I had determined to do. I think John was surprised by the sudden change in my attitude. As I acted more kindly, he let down his biker façade. He brought me some of his concerns and questions. I gave him advice. We developed a father-and-son type of relationship.

One evening I returned to the room and found the second bed and John Aslakson gone. I assumed he was transferred somewhere else. When I got into my own bed that night and lay my head on the pillow, I heard the rustling sound of paper near my ear. I found under the pillow an envelope labeled "Mr. Taylor." I found someone to read me the letter inside:

Jim,
I'm very happy to have met you and got to know you in the short stay here. Your a very interested and quite unique man.

At times when I felt life was unbearable, you made it bearable for me. Your presents in my life had made it worthwhile. You're an excellent bunkie. I could not have asked for any more respect than you had shown me.

To me your a joy to have had around. I imagine that you felt as I did we may have a problem in the beginning. The

age difference, lifestyle and need for privacy all could have been factors in this, yet we got along just fine. The comfort you gave with your very being and my being without my own father while here cannot be explained in words. I do thank you for your ability to care and show concern.

Please keep in touch. I'm interested in your legal outcome as well as knowing about your everyday life as it falls into place for you. Again, Jim, thank you for all you have done to assist me.

John

Someday I hope to touch a life the way you did mine.

This letter served as confirmation that I had come a long way from the Jim Taylor of earlier years. Acting kindly and generously benefited not only me with the satisfaction of accomplishment, but more importantly benefited another human being who now intended to "pass it on" when the occasion presented itself.

I also tried to help a man named Buddy Sheets, who served a short sentence at FCI–Fort Worth in 1992 for some relatively minor crime. One Sunday, I was out in the recreation area shooting baskets while visitors interacted with inmates in the adjacent visitors' picnic grounds. A crowd started to gather as I put one shot after another through the iron hoop. I counted as I made seventy-four consecutive free throws. As I finished that series, Buddy Sheets approached me. His parents and his wife had been visiting him. His father observed me shooting baskets and asked him what my name was. When Buddy told his father "Jim Taylor," his Dad sent him over to ask me if I had ever lived in Pennsylvania. I told Buddy I spent a few months in 1942 at a prep school called Kiski, near the small town of Saltsburg, east of Pittsburgh.

A few hours later, Buddy found me and told me that his father wanted to visit me when he came to Fort Worth again because his father thought he might know me from those days in 1942. When Don Sheets came to Fort Worth the next time, he introduced himself and told me he was originally from an area of Pennsylvania in close proximity to Saltsburg. Don said that as a young man, he used to watch some Kiski sports events and practices; he clearly remembered me as both a football player and as a guy who had

exceptional ability shooting a basketball. We were both amazed that fifty years later we would meet again in a federal penal institution in Texas.

Don and Ara Mae Sheets continued to visit their son, but usually Don spent the time with me while Ara Mae visited Buddy. This was the first time I received any visitors, other than attorneys, since Jean used to visit me at Lewisburg. These personal contacts gave me the friendly connection I craved. I grew more touched when both Don and Ara Mae continued to visit me after Buddy's release. They lived in Gatesville, about one hundred miles away, and so to visit me they used many hours of their time plus the expenses of travel. They always insisted on buying me treats from the institution vending machines. I liked Don and Ara Mae because they were unpretentious and generous folks. Recently, I asked them why they reached out so far for me. Ara Mae replied, "Because we knew you needed someone."

The Sheets became very interested in my efforts to gain freedom, and once we knew that I would attain parole status, they wanted to help me set up a parole plan. They offered to be my primary support system in the community, and obviously, with my disabilities, I would need considerable support. They extended themselves greatly. They purchased a motor home, put it on their property, and told the authorities that I could live there rent-free. We envisioned how I would help them by sorting, cataloging, and pricing the enormous accumulation of antiques and collectibles which they had amassed over decades and which, at this time, they wanted to sell to supplement their retirement income. We thought this was an excellent plan, but parole authorities rejected it because it might put me in close contact with Buddy Sheets. Parolees are forbidden from associating with anyone who has been convicted of a crime. I thought this might be my only opportunity to have the kind of support I felt I needed, so the rejection left me devastated.

When I finally had a definite date and place to begin my parole, I needed another favor. I had accumulated twenty-seven large cardboard boxes containing my legal, medical and institutional records and there was no way I could ship them to a halfway house. I needed a place where these very important papers could be stored until I could provide my own space for them. The

Sheets volunteered to store all these boxes for me. About eighteen months after my release, by then settled with Katherine in our Minneapolis home, Don and Ara Mae drove out of their way, on their yearly trip to visit Don's Pennsylvania relatives, to bring me the boxes of records.

All that Don and Ara Mae did, they did out of pure kindness. To this day I do not know if they consider themselves Christian, but their daily lives reflect the true meaning of Christianity. They came upon me like the Good Samaritan of the New Testament. I was a stranger for whom they had no formal responsibility, yet they treated me like a family member. We maintain a close relationship to this day.

love story

I N 1993, after Senator Edward Kennedy lent his support to my efforts to correct misinformation in my parole file, I began to actually believe that I might soon gain my freedom. I started to imagine the numerous possibilities of how I might live in normal society. I considered becoming self-employed, as I had been during my previous brief release in 1980–81. I had no thoughts of even attempting to develop any close personal relationships.

In 1992, I was transferred to the Federal Correctional Institution in Fort Worth, Texas. My continuing efforts toward freedom culminated in September 1994, with the authorities granting me a presumptive release date of March 29, 1995. By this time, I would be almost seventy years old. I had been in prison most of my life since 1950, was legally blind, and had no financial assets. I needed to develop a parole plan that would be acceptable to the U.S. Parole Commission. I formulated two different parole plans during the next few months utilizing the support of the Sheets family and another Texas friend I had met in confinement. Each plan, when presented to the Parole Commission, was summarily denied.

This left me in a quandary. I knew of no other potentially supportive people who would help me develop an acceptable plan.

I did not want Jean to take on this role because she had already done so once, and the outcome was disappointing. Now she was much older and I could not burden her again. The Government would never allow me to accept the help of any former inmates or their relatives. As the date for my release drew closer the authorities demanded that I contact my only sibling, my sister, Sally. I had totally lost contact with Sally for forty years until the early 1990s. Sally and her husband, Joe, lived in Florida, and we exchanged occasional stiffly written letters. Certainly our tentative relationship would not handle the pressure of an impaired parollee in need of a home. But the authorities made it sound as if I had to call upon her or I would not be released.

So in the presence of an institutional parole officer, I forced myself to make the necessary telephone call to Sally and her husband. I tried to explain to them that if I came to Florida, I would only live in their home for a brief period, and that I fully planned to find a way to support myself. Nonetheless, Sally and Joe were aghast with my appeal to them, and as I recall, one of them hung up on me. I felt humiliated receiving this rejection in front of the parole officer. He then advised me that if I could not develop an acceptable plan, the authorities would send me to Minnesota, the state where I committed the original offense, since by law that state was required to accept me. So it was to be Minnesota, or remain in prison.

I tried to imagine living in Minnesota. I knew absolutely no one in that state. At first I envisioned that the authorities might send me to Thief River Falls, where my serious offense occurred in November 1955. How would I be able to make it there? Memories of the crime probably lingered in the town. I could not imagine the shame of running into a member of the Lindberg family. Soon that fear passed, as I was informed that I would be sent to a halfway house in Minneapolis. This was still a bad dream. I could think of no possible way to obtain an income, housing, or a job. I had no adequate winter clothing. Would my face, which was partially paralyzed, freeze in the cold without my awareness? How would I, as a visually impaired person, navigate on icy walkways? An attorney in Dallas who assisted me in legal matters wrote to the federal authorities, questioning their decision to send me to Minnesota, describing their plan as "a design for failure."

Yet I was not a person to fall into depression anymore. When I realized that the authorities might truly want me to fail, I became determined that I would succeed, even though I had no idea how to achieve this. It was similar to those old days of playing competitive sports—I might not know anything about the opposition or the conditions of the playing field, but I always entered the competition with a positive attitude toward winning the game.

I now reconsidered my present challenge by recalling lessons learned. I remembered that over the years, I fortunately had encountered many good, decent, and loving people. In fact, as I looked back, there was almost always someone willing to help me. Some had faith and acted towards me in ways that put their very livelihoods at risk. I responded in kind. Just as it is risky for correctional staff to trust an inmate, it is also risky for an inmate to trust a staff person.

So when I came out into the free world, I held within me a paradox. I had no reason to believe that anyone would help me, much less be my friend; certainly I knew of no such person in Minnesota. And yet I believed there would be supportive people and a way for me to succeed, because I had always, somehow, been blessed by the presence of people who cared for me.

In the early morning hours of March 29, 1995, I entered free life. I could hardly believe this day had finally come. But away I went, traveling via airport taxi from the Federal Correctional Institution, a place I had learned to navigate, to the Dallas–Fort Worth airport, one of the world's largest. From the moment I walked out the gates of the FCI, I was on my own. I felt almost overwhelmed with fear, yet I forced myself to ask questions of people near me. People must have assumed me to be a regular elderly man. They gave help easily, and soon I was on a plane bound for Minneapolis. The flight attendants were particularly attentive to my needs and my anxiety lessened. Upon my arrival, airport personnel assisted in locating a taxi service to take me to the Volunteers of America Halfway House on East Lake Street in Minneapolis. I arrived safely but with virtually no money. The institutional authorities refused to allow me to withdraw any funds from my own small savings in my inmate account, saying they would send this money to me in a few months. Instead, they issued me fifty dollars. The transport service to the Dallas–Fort Worth airport cost me twen-

ty-one dollars. The taxi service to the halfway house in Minneapolis cost me another twenty-one dollars. So as I entered my new lodgings in Minneapolis, to begin my new life of relative freedom, I carried in my pocket a grand total of eight dollars.

The conditions of my parole stated that I could stay in the Volunteers of America halfway house four months. After that, failure to find independent accommodation could result in my return to prison. I was not concerned about that yet. I could only focus on my freedom. I cannot describe the relief. This is why I had worked so long and so hard. I left the halfway house and ambled outside. What a thrill to have a life outside of walls! I was able to grope my way down a city street and smell the cold March air. I had nowhere to go, but to be outside was enough of a destination.

On the first or second day of my residency, I met Lance Woodruff, my counselor. Lance was a large man, quite imposing, but I soon discovered he had sympathy for troubled people. Lance approached his tasks on my behalf full of optimism. He knew the community resources, and what he did not know he willingly researched. He provided me with names and phone numbers of agencies that might be able to help. I made the phone calls, and soon my calendar filled up with appointments. At first, Lance drove me to State Services for the Blind, Hennepin County Economic Assistance, and the Veterans Administration Medical Center. I learned about Metro Mobility, a transportation service for disabled people in the Minneapolis–St. Paul area, but eligibility for this service took weeks to establish. I met with local doctors to start a medical history and treatment program. I also met with attorneys, primarily to discuss the wisdom of accepting the government's offer of worker's compensation for the serious injuries I had incurred on my assigned job while in federal custody in exchange for a promise not to sue.

Lance was the first of many people who helped me become a Minnesotan, as he extended a welcome, connected me to others, and saw me on my way to independence. He also looked the other way as I compulsively gathered furniture and household supplies in preparation for the move to my own apartment. My room at the halfway house became packed with these things, way beyond what the rules for an orderly bedroom permitted. Not only was my room crammed to the gills, but other residents also stored my things in their rooms.

Lance showed me a great deal of respect, more than I could have expected. One day as he drove me somewhere in his car, we happened upon a young resident of the halfway house who was not authorized to be outside the facility. Lance pulled his car over and told him he'd better get back to where he belonged. The young man grimaced and turned back toward the halfway house. We continued on our way and I said, "Lance, I know this young man violated the rules. I know you're well within your rights to see that his parole is revoked. Please don't do this. He knows you've seen him and if he goes back to the house, he'll be showing you that he's trying to correct his error. Let him learn from this experience." Lance accepted my suggestion and that young man did not violate the rules again, at least while I was there to observe.

Things started falling into place. Old friends, many of whom I helped out of one jam or another in the past, sent me gifts of money. I started moving around the city independently to purchase needed items. However, the whole prospect of finding housing loomed large and forbidding. Lance advised me that I needed more help than he could give, considering his other duties. He suggested that I call the Hennepin County Social Services Department, to see if a social worker might be able to help me find housing and possibly address my many other needs. I made the suggested call and soon Kathleen Murphy, a Hennepin County social worker, came to the halfway house.

I usually introduce myself to professionals by offering a few official documents that speak to my accomplishments throughout incarceration. I guess I do this because I am acutely aware that to present myself as an ex-convict will likely result in a negative initial response. So when Kathy Murphy came for our first interview, I showed her some of these documents. She seemed interested in my history, as well as my present predicament, although she could not possibly assimilate all my history in one, or even a few, sessions. While we focused on the housing question, we discussed much of my past.

My own efforts trying to find a place to rent had resulted in outright refusals, obviously due to my lack of rental history and my criminal background. But Kathy knew about subsidized housing for seniors in the community, and these landlords at least accepted my application with some measure of openness.

By June, I still had no real prospects for housing. Lance made

it quite clear that August 1 was still my deadline. Even the managers of the special housing that Kathy Murphy had located, and to which I applied, had serious reservations. I understood all this, yet it was disheartening. But then one manager of a subsidized apartment building, The Maryland Apartments, indicated less hesitation. She impressed me as a forthright person who would independently evaluate my application. Then, in fact, at the end of June, this manager called and advised me of an apartment I could rent as of August 1. She wanted me to come to the Maryland to check it out for myself. The first-floor, one-bedroom apartment satisfied my needs. I was both grateful and enormously relieved to be able to tell Lance, and my parole officer, that I had a suitable place to live.

Kathy then told me of a reasonably priced moving service for the furniture and household supplies I had acquired for my new apartment. I left the Volunteers of America and my counselor, Lance Woodruff, on August 1, 1995. I did not sleep for the next twenty-four hours, as I was so pleased to be in my own place, arranging and settling my belongings without someone telling me how, when and where to do it. When Kathy arrived on the morning of August 2 to take me to an appointment with a health insurance expert, I was exhausted, but euphorically happy. Perturbed that I had been up all night, she rescheduled the appointment, feeling I was too tired to constructively engage in an information session. I think, however, that she understood my pride and excitement at finally having my own apartment.

Kathy and I discussed my need for ongoing assistance, such as help with cooking, cleaning, shopping, medication management, and orientation to my new neighborhood. She arranged housekeeping and personal care assistance. State Services for the Blind secured a mobility instructor, Gordon Oien, who instructed me in the use of a white cane. He also taught me to navigate my immediate neighborhood and how to use the metropolitan bus system. I should have learned to use a white cane while still in custody, but I had decided against this because I wanted other inmates to be uncertain about how little I could see. Fellow inmates knew I had lost some sight, but to carry a white cane would have telegraphed my vulnerability. In prison I had devised for myself a heavy cane, which I believed would offer more protection than a flimsy white cane ever could.

During one of my days at the VA Medical Center, a social worker gave me the idea that I might be eligible to receive a seeing-eye dog. This excited me—I have always loved dogs—and the prospect of having a seeing-eye dog presented notions of increased independence, functionality, and companionship. In prison, I believed I would lead quite a solitary existence once I got my freedom. I now began to recognize that I did not want to be completely alone. I think I recall correctly that the VA social worker provided me with a referral to a local Lions Club for their assistance in accessing a guide dog program. Soon I had an application in process to Leader Dogs for the Blind in Rochester, Michigan, a suburb of Detroit. I had no idea if my parole officer would allow me to go to Michigan to participate in such a program, yet I wanted to pursue this opportunity to the fullest.

I had made a promise to God that if I ever got out of confinement, I would attend some church service every week as long as I was physically able. So when I arrived at the Volunteers of America halfway house in March 1995, I needed to find a church. I asked Lance to recommend a church in the neighborhood and he told me that the Holy Trinity Lutheran Church was within a block. I investigated further and learned how to walk there and the times for the Sunday services. And so I began to fulfill my promise by attending this church, under the leadership of Pastor Ronald Johnson, every Sunday. From the beginning, the members of the congregation were incredibly friendly and welcoming.

Soon I personally met Pastor Johnson, who displayed the same attitude even when I told him I came to church from the nearby halfway house. He treated me like a normal human being. He visited and took me to lunch while I lived in the halfway house, and then he maintained his personal support by continuing our individual contacts after I moved into my own apartment in a different neighborhood. Pastor Johnson even put me on the waiting list for residency at the subsidized apartment building for seniors sponsored by his church and located adjacent to the church. This showed me that he did not view me as a risk to the many other seniors in that building. This confidence was a true gift.

Although I do not regularly attend the Holy Trinity Lutheran Church these days, I still go occasionally. Pastor Johnson and his flock continue to be very hospitable. Pastor Johnson wrote a letter of recommendation to the Parole Commission on my behalf

and he agreed to appear at any hearing where his input might be helpful.

From the beginning of my contact with Kathy Murphy, whom I called Katherine because I could never remember Kathy or Kathleen, she seemed more than an impersonal professional helper. She acted genuinely interested and concerned about my welfare, not just my housing needs. I perceived that she provided more than a routine level of social services. I began to think how fortunate I might be if she would become more a friend to me than a professional helper, and thus remain in my life for the long term. I tested this possibility by suggesting that we play some tennis, or that she come visit on the weekends. She very clearly stated that she could not and would not do this, as she was my social worker, and not a friend. I did not give up. But I also tried to find other ways to bring life into my little apartment home. The Maryland did not allow pets, except for fish or caged birds. I bought a cockatiel and named him Casey. I could not bear to keep him caged, as I knew what it felt like to be caged myself. I came to love that little bird, and he showed affection toward me by spending most of his time perched on my left shoulder.

My application for a seeing-eye dog was approved in October. I received a letter from Leader Dogs for the Blind about enrolling in classes to begin on November 1, and my parole officer agreed that I could go to Michigan for this training. The Lions Club paid my airfare. Mr. Vern Hartjes, a club officer, helped me enormously. He drove me to the Minneapolis airport, saw me onto the plane, and upon my return was there to drive me home with my new Leader Dog. Copper was a frisky, huggable golden retriever. Vern shared in the pleasure of Copper's entrance into my life. He came to see us from time to time, to observe how Copper and I worked together. When Vern saw that Copper and I had become a successful team, he asked me if I would speak at Lions Club meetings about the guide dog experience. At several Lions Club events, I gratefully spoke to members about how important their support was for the Leader Dog program.

In early October, Kathy Murphy informed me that because I had expressed so much interest in a personal relationship, her supervisor had determined that another social worker should take over my case. I felt apprehensive. I did not want to lose Katherine as my social worker because I trusted her, and I did not know

if she would continue to see me. She would not reveal how she would respond to my requests for friendship once she was no longer my social worker, telling me instead that I could ask only after she officially left my case.

I soon had a new social worker, but it took me a few days before I called Katherine again. When I did, she gave me her home telephone number and asked me to call her there from now on. I was delighted.

Katherine and I had just started to date when I left Minneapolis to participate in the training to receive my guide dog. Leader Dogs for the Blind is in Rochester, Michigan, only a few miles from Birmingham, the town where I grew up. Being in Rochester did not trigger any memories for me, but one day the trainers took us, with our new dogs, to practice in the neighboring town. My instructor described for me a route around a city block that I was expected to walk with my dog. "Do you think you can manage that?" he asked.

"Tell me the names of the streets," I answered. He did, to which I then responded, "I can walk around this block without a dog. On my right is the police station. Facing us is the park, and on my left is the community center where I learned to dance. I grew up in this town."

I passed this test, and went on to acquire many other new skills in the next few weeks. When I returned from Michigan with Copper, Katherine awaited me. I told Copper he would love Katherine, and indeed he did. I trained Casey and Copper to appreciate each other. My little family and social circle were developing.

As a Christmas present that year, I dared to present Katherine with an engagement ring. This was my way of sounding out the prospects for our relationship. I knew that it was quite early in our relationship to bring up the subject of marriage, yet I had the feeling that time might not be on my side. I was seventy years old, and I had serious disabilities, including a heart condition. The fact that I even considered marriage might appear overly optimistic in view of my well-learned hesitation to trust people, my lack of financial assets, and my physical self-consciousness. Katherine graciously accepted the ring, but told me that she was not ready to wear it. She said she needed more time to ponder whether she could commit herself to a long-term, marital relationship with me.

But she did appreciate my belief that my time might be limited. I asked her to listen carefully to the words of "September Song" (by Maxwell Anderson and Kurt Weill) and to think of me.

Oh, it's a long, long while from May to December,
But the days grow short when you reach September.
When the autumn weather turns the leaves to flame,
One hasn't got time for the waiting game.
Oh, the days dwindle down to a precious few. September, November!
And these few precious days, I'll spend with you.
These precious days, I'll spend with you.

To my pleasure, within two months Katherine accepted my proposal, and we took our life-time vows on May 4th, 1996, at St. Stephen's Catholic Church, with Father Patrick Griffin officiating. We told virtually no one about our plans, so the announcements we later made to others, in person and in writing, were greeted with some surprise. I began to view myself as a family man. Our family included Katherine and me, plus Copper and Casey. Unfortunately, soon thereafter our family of four became a family of three. Casey was perched on my shoulder one day as I walked out of the apartment to escort a friend to her car. A bus roared by, and Casey, apparently startled, flew off my shoulder. I walked many hours in the nearby park and Katherine helped me put up "Lost Bird" signs, but we never received any word of Casey. Even today, thinking about the loss of this small friend saddens me.

As time passes, Katherine and I grow closer and our relationship matures. There is no way I can adequately describe what I truly feel for this woman, Katherine Murphy. I continue to call her Katherine, because in history there was another Katherine called "The Great." My Katherine is Katherine the Great in my mind and my heart. I have my faults. I am sure Katherine knows that she also has faults. But I think we have each experienced enough life to play past the faults and look to the virtues in one another. I believe that we will continue to enjoy our good marriage, which is built on accentuating the positive.

From the beginning, what I appreciated about Katherine was her willingness to get to know me as an individual, not as a cat-

egory or a special case. She told me fairly early in our relationship that she had checked out some details I had relayed about my criminal history. Katherine verified information I shared with her about the background and friendships of the U.S. Attorney who prosecuted my capital case. Soon after she became my social worker, she brought me a copy of the obituary of George MacKinnon as it appeared in the Minneapolis newspaper in May 1995. She later told me that she pored through Minneapolis Public Library microfilm records for local newspaper accounts of my case, which filled the papers during late 1955 and the first half of 1956. The fact that she took the time to develop her own sense of my honesty and trustworthiness was uplifting. So many people find it possible to make their judgments without much valid information. I appreciated becoming known to her as who I really am.

After we married, I set about expanding Katherine's knowledge of my past. I thought it would be helpful if we could together visit places and people of importance to me, mostly those from the good and happy times of my life. These people and places had taken on extraordinary significance during my long years of prison confinement. We decided to take our first trip in the fall of 1996. Our first stop was in Saltsburg, Pennsylvania, a very small town a short distance east of Pittsburgh, the site of an equally small boarding school, Kiskimenitas (Kiski) Preparatory School, which I attended at age seventeen. We traveled next to Maryland, where I introduced Katherine to Jean, my long-time partner in my struggle for release. It was a true pleasure to introduce Katherine and Jean.

Katherine and I then traveled to Connecticut so I could show her my paternal grandmother's home in Quaker Hill, built in 1736, where my family spent most of the summers during my youth. I pointed out the places where I spent time during those most pleasurable summers, including my aunt and uncle's large home in nearby New London, overlooking Long Island Sound. On the way back from Connecticut we stopped for a couple of days in Birmingham, Michigan, to see my boyhood home, schools, and a couple of old friends.

The pieces of the past that I had wanted to share with Katherine were located in states other than Minnesota. But one day it occurred to me that I had met a helpful man in Minneapo-

lis during my stay in the Hennepin County Jail in 1956. Leo Vet-vick was the Protestant chaplain who advocated on my behalf. He could still be in Minneapolis, so I took my magnifying glass to the phone book, found his name, and called him. It must have been thirty years since we had last spoken or written, but he lived in a retirement community not far away. Leo agreed to come visit me. Again, I was able to present to Katherine a person who had known me long ago, and who had a sympathetic attitude toward me. Leo and his wife visited with Katherine and me a few more times before his death in 2003.

In the spring of 1997, Katherine and I flew to Florida to spend a week. My primary goal was to meet my sister, Sally, for the first

time in over forty years. I also wanted to travel to Fort Lauderdale so I could show Katherine some of my old haunts. Sally had not actually invited Katherine and me to spend more than a lunch and afternoon with her and her husband, Joe. Because of this, and because I had no definite plans to visit specific people in Fort Lauderdale, we arranged to stay near the ocean beaches for several days, just vacationing by ourselves. We visited Sally and Joe in their home for a few hours, but it appeared to us that Sally was quite uncomfortable in my presence. She and Joe were gracious, however. Sally mentioned how difficult a father we had, and how his abusive behavior focused on me. I was surprised to learn that our father had once struck even Sally some time after I no longer lived in the family home. These words from Sally confirmed to Katherine many of the things I had told her about my family.

When we arrived in Fort Lauderdale in our rented car, I directed Katherine throughout the city to view the homes I had lived in, and other places where I had spent time with my friends. Also, while we were in Fort Lauderdale, Katherine and I used Sally's directions to find the city cemetery where my parents and my aunts and uncles are buried. We placed flowers on their graves while I thought of how much I would have liked more opportunities to reconcile with my parents before they passed on.

In September 1998, we took a road trip with some friends to the hills of western North Carolina. Before we left Minnesota, I phoned Father John Noe, the Catholic chaplain at the Federal Correctional Institution in Ashland, Kentucky, and he agreed to meet us as we traveled through the area. Father Noe rendered me tremendous support and assistance in 1991 and 1992, and I was eager for Katherine to meet him. We enjoyed a pleasant breakfast together, and Father Noe related how he had reviewed my extensive records and advocated for me before the U.S. Parole Commission.

While in North Carolina, we were pleased to visit with my old friends who live in Texas, Don and Ara Mae Sheets, who happened to be traveling through on their yearly trip to Don's boyhood home in Pennsylvania.

On our way back from North Carolina, we spent a most enjoyable evening with C.M. and Evelyn Newton in Lexington, Kentucky. C.M., who is a few years younger than me, followed me around like a little brother when I was an older teenager playing

football and basketball in Fort Lauderdale. I lived a very short time with C.M.'s family after I left my parents' home at age eighteen. C.M. went on to become a noted college basketball coach and administrator; he finished his career as Athletic Director at the University of Kentucky.

These trips were extremely meaningful to me, as they brought back many good memories, and they allowed me to reconnect with some of the places and people I recalled so fondly. I also experienced a tremendous sense of loss for all of the people we could not meet because they had died. Also, many of the places themselves had changed dramatically over the years. Perhaps more important was what I could share with my love, Katherine. Not only could she see for herself some of what I had described, but also, I believe she was able to verify many facets of my complicated and improbable life experiences. These trips brought us closer together in understanding and trust. In the year 2000, we again traveled to Florida. We visited Sally and Joe, and again our visit accomplished much less than I had hoped for in terms of Sally accepting me as a changed person.

During all of the years of my imprisonment, I worked to maintain excellent physical condition. Were it not for the disabilities that resulted from the assault I suffered in 1987, I would likely today be one of those senior citizens who compete successfully in tennis tournaments or run marathons. Before Copper died in 2005 (one of my hardest losses), I continued my ability to walk a good distance so that, almost every day, we circled the three-mile path around Lake of the Isles, only two blocks from where we live. I played in the Twin Cities Senior Tennis League for several years and enjoyed the competition and companionship of other senior tennis players.

My wife Katherine is a golfer and she encouraged me to learn this sport. Until recently I played in the Sister Kenny Disabled Golfers program. Playing golf is much more difficult for me than tennis, because it was not a game I played often as a young man. Now I depend on someone else to first advise me from the tee about the length and direction of the fairway, and then advise me about my alignment in relation to the flag. In addition, I depend on someone to watch where my golf ball lands and take me to it.

Then this entire process is repeated over and over throughout the round. Considerable patience is required to play golf with me, but the many disabled golfers and their companions in the League were all patient and encouraging.

Although the level of my play is greatly diminished from what it was in my youth and from what it might have been in my senior years, I still thrill at the freedom I now have to pursue these activities. To walk around the lake, to play tennis and golf, and to try to ski, with people whom I choose, in places where I need not watch my back—these things are worth so much.

My Katherine has gone swimming with me in the Atlantic Ocean and in lakes and pools. On each occasion, I felt disoriented and deathly afraid of losing my way or drowning. Thoughts of having a heart attack while in the water also trouble me. Whatever happened to the young man who loved to swim in the roughest surf of the Atlantic Ocean, and who was a lifeguard on the Fort Lauderdale beaches in the 1940s?

One of my favorite activities back then was diving on the reefs off the Fort Lauderdale beaches. I usually went out early in the mornings, using a facemask, swim-fins, a knife, and a three-pronged spear on a long shaft. The end of the spear shaft had a long stout cord attached, so if I directed the spear toward or into a fish or lobster, or even into a coral reef, I retrieved it by merely hauling in the cord attached to my wrist. I sold many of my captured lobster tails to hotels and restaurants along the beachfront for twenty-five cents apiece. I seldom speared fish because they could bleed or discharge body fluids, which would attract barracuda and sharks.

In addition to those dangerous creatures, Green Moray eels hid in the coral reefs. These six feet long eels are poisonous. A Green Moray eel could seize a person under water and hold him until he drowned. I always carried a sharp knife in a sheath on my right hip so that, if necessary, I could quickly grasp it and cut off the eel's head. Many times Moray eels struck out at me, but thankfully they grabbed only my steel spear. When that happened, I hastily vacated the area, retrieving my spear with the attached cord only when at a safe distance.

Living as I do today with my loving wife in a condominium in Minneapolis, Minnesota, I am no longer in an ocean full of animal

predators, nor in a prison containing many human predators. My termination from parole supervision in September 2000 released me from my last fear of being channeled back into prison by some false accusation or re-interpretation of the law. I feel safe for the first time in fifty years.

reunion

URING THE FORTY-SOME YEARS of my penal confinement, I devoted little attention to events of the past. My concerns centered on my day-to-day survival. I learned about the need for constant vigilance in my first, one-year incarceration in that hellhole called Goochland State Farm in the State of Virginia.

In subsequent institutions, it was only during solitary confinement, or when locked in a private room that I allowed myself to ponder memories of times past. I especially liked to recall the pleasant things of the past, for these brought some light and brightness to an otherwise hard and dark existence. The only other occasions when I indulged myself with memories were during the Christmas season, when even prisoners become a bit more kind toward each other and thus I could let my guard down a bit. Then I would come close to tears as I recalled the warmth and smells of Christmases in my childhood family home. Otherwise, I deliberately set aside all thoughts of family and old friends in Michigan, Connecticut and Florida. Ironically, and perhaps understandably, my family and friends made virtually no effort to contact me in prison over the years.

I did not think often about my love and my life with Mary Bea, the girl I married when I was about nineteen, or about our daugh-

ter, Jackie, born in late 1944. I left them for the last time in Fort Lauderdale, Florida, about 1947, and I heard a few years later that Mary Bea remarried and started a new life.

However, shortly after my release from confinement on March 29, 1995, I felt able to think more about matters of the past. Among the worst of my regrets was the desertion of my wife and child during the mid-1940s. It seemed to me that I should go to Florida and make it known to my former wife and my daughter exactly why I left, and how and why I eventually ended up in prison for most of my life thereafter.

In April 1997, when Katherine and I traveled to Florida, we looked up my old friend, Roland Hodges. Roland and I attended Fort Lauderdale High School at the same time, and we played football and basketball together on the high school teams during the 1943–44 school year. When Katherine and I met and visited with Roland, I learned that my former wife, Mary Bea, had died about a month before this visit. I felt sad to learn that she had suffered from cancer, and disappointment that I had missed a possible opportunity to meet her again, to apologize for the hurts I caused both her and our daughter fifty years earlier. Roland also confirmed what I thought I remembered, that Mary Bea had married a Mr. Thomson, a well-to-do man several years her senior, while she was still a young woman, and that the marriage apparently had been successful.

Because time ran out for us on this trip, I could not seek out my daughter. When we got home, I began to wonder more about Jackie. Where was she now, how was her childhood, and what sort of adult life did she have? I often wondered whether or not I made the right decision for Mary Bea, Jackie and myself when I left them. I wanted to find some answers, and now, with Mary Bea no longer alive, finding Jackie became even more important to me. Once during 1998, and then a few times during 1999, I telephoned Roland in Fort Lauderdale. I asked him if he would help me find Jackie. Katherine and I planned another trip to Florida in February 2000, and hoped we might be able to meet Jackie while there. He agreed to look into the matter. After a time, Roland provided me the information that Jackie lived in the St. Petersburg area, and that she had a business interest in some restaurants. Roland would not or could not tell me a definitive surname for Jackie, or

an address or phone number, but he remembered that one of the restaurants that Jackie owned or managed was called Trumpeter's Swan.

Shortly after Roland told me this, and without first talking it over with Katherine, I telephoned the Trumpeter's Swan Restaurant and asked for Jackie. She was unavailable, but I left my name and phone number. That evening, when I told Katherine of my attempt to reach Jackie, she became quite upset with me for making the call without any preliminary or mediatory communication. She felt that Jackie might be disturbed to hear from her long-lost biological father in this manner, and that this might result in an outcome the exact opposite of my hope; that is, I would perhaps receive no response. However, just as we finished our breakfast the next morning, a Saturday, the phone rang. I answered, and a woman identified herself as the sister of Jackie Thomson and asked, "Why, after all these years, did you call Jackie?" The voice was strongly questioning, even challenging.

I thought, "Uh-oh, I don't want to blow this!" So I replied, "Here, I'd like you to talk with my wife. She's a social worker."

Katherine reluctantly took the phone receiver and later told me that she thought I was handing off a telemarketer to her. Katherine also told me that the woman—Deirdre by name, Jackie's younger half-sister—started the conversation expressing indignation that I had called. She said that the message I left, which included describing myself as Jackie's father, had disturbed Jackie—in fact, that Jackie felt threatened by this. Katherine assured Deirdre that my only intent was to establish contact that might possibly lead to a meeting, and that there was absolutely no threat intended. Deirdre told Katherine that Jackie was happy without me, that she had a full life, and in short, had no interest in a meeting. Deirdre also told Katherine that my abandonment of her mother and sister had caused a great deal of sorrow and shame, especially to Mary Bea, as she was forced to move back into her parents' home with Jackie when I left. During the conversation it became apparent that Deirdre knew I had been in prison for many years. She expressed skepticism when Katherine explained that I had undergone a spiritual transformation. Katherine told Deirdre that I was a unique person, and very intelligent. Deirdre responded that Jackie, also, was unique and highly intelli-

gent. Apparently softening a bit during the conversation, she said that Jackie would at most be interested in my medical or genetic history, as this could be useful to her. Katherine told her as much as we know. Deirdre ended the conversation, promising to talk all this over with Jackie.

After that phone conversation, Katherine suggested that I should not get my hopes up. We both started to think that a letter to Jackie from me, explaining something about my current situation and why I hoped to meet her, would be a good idea at this time. It might provide her with more information to consider than what she had at her disposal so far—the message of a call, out of the blue, from a long-absent biological father, and a report of a conversation between her sister and Jim Taylor's wife. So, on January 27, 2000, I mailed a letter to Jackie, in care of the restaurant address, the only address for her I had. The letter began, "Without a waste of words, let me begin by first emphasizing that I do not wish to bring any further problems into your life." I went on to explain how I wanted most of all to make myself available to her, to answer her perhaps many questions about why I left her mother and her. I wanted to tell her everything I knew about my motivations at that time. I wrote how I had loved her and her mother very much, and that I was truly sorry for the hurt and the shame I brought into their lives. The time was short for her to reply to my letter, since we planned to leave for Florida on February 16.

On February 13, a Sunday, we were entertaining in honor of Katherine's mother's ninety-fourth birthday. Besides my mother-in-law, Katherine's niece from California and three friends visited our home that evening. We just finished our dinner when the phone rang. Katherine answered, and quickly disappeared with the cordless phone into the bedroom. She was gone for twenty minutes or so, and the guests began to make conversation about their need to be on their way. Katherine emerged, hung up the phone, and proceeded to assist those leaving. It took her some time to bundle up her mother in winter clothing for the ride home. During this process, Katherine whispered to me that she had been talking with Jackie. She said that Jackie had agreed to continue the conversation after Katherine returned from driving her mother home, but she also said that Jackie did not think she wanted to meet with us when we came to Florida.

When Katherine returned, she called Jackie, and the conversation proceeded. Very soon I was asked to pick up the extension phone, and I heard my daughter's adult voice for the first time. Her voice had a raspy edge, and I could not imagine the woman attached to it. She wanted me to know that her mother and her aunts had frequently told her that her biological father had many positive attributes, including intelligence and creativity, and that I was an excellent athlete. She said that they had never denigrated me, but rather had been more concerned and confused as they received information that I was descending into criminal activity.

I asked Jackie about herself, and she reported a basically happy childhood, with a kind and loving mother and adoptive father. She described her own current lifestyle as "very unconventional," which she explained included living in a large home on the Gulf of Mexico with her six business partners. She told me about her caring relationship with her parents until their deaths, and with her half-sister, Deirdre. She also said she had maintained closeness with several of her maternal aunts and their children, her cousins, many of whom had migrated to the St. Petersburg area.

She shocked both Katherine and me when she mentioned that she knew some things about my current life and our travel plans from discussion with my sister, Sally. Sally and her husband lived in Fort Lauderdale all of their adult lives until they retired to the Orlando area a few years ago. In our one visit, and in the several letters and the phone conversations we had had to that point, Sally never mentioned that she maintained contact with my daughter. Jackie shocked me further by telling me that her mother had been the matron of honor at Sally's wedding, and that Mary Bea and Sally continued a friendship throughout the years until Mary Bea's death in 1997.

After recovering somewhat from this startling information, I told Jackie how happy I was for her that she had so many positive things in her life, and I urged her to consider meeting Katherine and me during our upcoming trip to Florida. She agreed to this, and suggested we call her when we arrived in Orlando. She had somehow thought, probably from discussion with Sally, that we were traveling the next day, a misconception that we corrected, but which indicated to me that Jackie had waited until the last possible moment to contact us before we began our trip to her part of the country. When we called Jackie from our Orlando

motel, she suggested that we come to her home in St. Petersburg the following day.

Imagine my excitement. I would meet my daughter tomorrow! I hoped that we would come to know each other enough so that we might start to build a meaningful relationship. I did, however, have one concern. The day before Katherine and I were to fly to Florida, I acquired an addition to my countenance that I feared would project a stereotypical image of an ex-convict. I had gone on a few errands in our Minneapolis neighborhood, and returning with my hands full with a briefcase, a bag of bananas, my white cane and the leash of my guide dog, Copper, I slipped and fell. The left side of my head and face hit the icy sidewalk. I righted myself and then groggily walked into the lobby of our apartment building. The people in the lobby gasped at the sight of blood on my face and insisted on calling an ambulance. Before I knew it, Copper and I were at University Hospital Emergency Room, and I received nine stitches under my left eye. By the time we arrived in Florida, I had a magnificent shiner.

Katherine and I drove to St. Petersburg on February 17. The directions from Jackie led us to a gulf-front compound, composed of several buildings surrounding a private tennis court. Jackie, Deirdre, and a few of Jackie's business and residence partners met us in the driveway and introduced themselves. Through my slightly improved eyesight, I saw a solid woman with light hair. Jackie seemed quite friendly and relaxed. She and the others led us into the main house, and the others drifted away, leaving Jackie with Katherine and me. We sat and conversed for an hour or two, while several of Jackie's housemates occasionally came into the main house, sometimes joining the conversation. Jackie brought out an old photo of her mother and me wearing 1940s-style bathing suits, as well as my old diploma from Miami Technical High School. Katherine described the fine details of these things to me. Jackie told me about her mother's death and about how, on her deathbed, Mary Bea had given Jackie an old, but carefully-preserved, linen embroidered envelope which had within it a professionally-photographed picture of me, taken at about age seventeen. When I heard this story and touched the envelope and picture, I felt almost overwhelmed with emotion, knowing that Mary Bea had loved me, that she had kept me in her heart all these years, and that she wanted to share that with our daughter.

After talking and touring the compound, Jackie brought us into a dining room. A light lunch was set out. All of the house-mates and Deirdre joined us. I had a difficult time comprehending the scene, since I did not know how many people were present and exactly who they were. I could not distinguish one voice from another and so sometimes I had difficulty following the conversation. When the large group was first assembled, I think I said something about wanting to explain some things about my criminal activity, how and why I first got into it, and why it continued.

But before I was able to start, a not-unfriendly male questioner, one of Jackie's partners, pulled me from my intended storyline by asking, "Why were you arrested in Indiana [in 1981] wearing women's clothing?" He and the others, who said they had learned about this arrest by pulling reports off the Internet from Indiana newspapers, answered their own question by saying that they assumed this was a disguise I wore in preparation to commit a crime. The truth, which I told them, was probably more startling and unsettling to them; that no crime at all had been planned or executed. I told them I wore female attire as part of my preparation for undergoing a transgender operation. Katherine tells me that no one seemed to bat an eye at this revelation, and we proceeded to talk about my short but serious past criminal involvement. At one point, Jackie asked all the others to leave her and Deirdre alone with Katherine and me. We continued to talk about ourselves. Jackie and I discovered we share some striking similarities—we each like to play singles tennis, not doubles; neither of us likes mangoes; and we each have a bad right knee. With her permission, Katherine took some photographs of Jackie's home, and one picture of Jackie and me together.

When it became apparent that Jackie and Deirdre were ready to bring the evening to a close, Katherine and I rose to leave. Jackie and Deirdre walked us to our car. We hugged one another and said our good-byes without any specific plan for the future. As Katherine backed the car out of the driveway, Judy, one of the housemates, ran out of the dark. While Jackie remained in the shadow close to the house, Judy said they wanted us to stop for dinner at Trumpeter's, their nearby restaurant. We were certainly hungry at that point, since it was about 8:30 P.M. We took them up on their offer and enjoyed a very nice dinner at one of the three restaurants owned by my daughter and six other people. Kather-

ine told me later how amazed she was at observing all the physical similarities between Jackie and me. She said that, like me, Jackie is blue-eyed and blond, with refined facial features — we both look quite characteristically Anglo-Saxon.

I was pleased to discover my daughter so apparently happy and successful. It confirmed for me that I had made the best decision possible at that long-ago time when I left Mary Bea and Jackie, one of the few good decisions I made during that period of my life. I wanted to explain to Jackie the circumstances under which this happened, but the constraints of our limited time defeated my purpose. It was extremely important to me that my daughter hear the whole story directly from me as to why I left them, and why I then became involved in many irresponsible and illegal activities during the next decade of my life. I am extremely disappointed and saddened over my failures of the past, but more so my failure to accomplish my goals in our first visit. There have been no more visits, only Christmas cards, since February 2000.

I think that Jackie and my sister Sally have lived fully without me. I am in a much different mental place; deprived of family and friends for decades, I kept a space for them within myself. When I could afford to I nurtured my memories of my loved ones there. But my sister and daughter do not need the close relationship I desire. They have each allowed me to visit, but there has not been any strong indication from either of them that they want to spend more quality time together. Each seems to maintain a barrier of reluctance and mistrust between us. Jackie and Sally no doubt wonder, "Is this 'good guy' for real? Or is he still a con? If I trust him, will I and those I love be hurt again?" I fully understand their fears, and this is to my own great and continuing sorrow.

a new self

BEGINNING WITH MY BIRTH to an unprepared, unbalanced young woman and continuing through my childhood, adolescence and young adult life, many negative forces shaped my personality and character. Over the years as I learned to introspect, I came to an understanding that these formative influences were the reasons I evolved into a criminal offender. But reasons are not excuses. I knew from the moment I walked into that bank in Thief River Falls, Minnesota, that I was wrong, and that whatever happened was my responsibility. Coming to terms with myself meant that I began to care. I not only accepted responsibility for the consequences of my actions, but I let the full impact of those consequences sink deeply into my entire being. At that point I began to feel revulsion for the person I had become, sadness for my many victims, and remorse for it all.

With the help of one or two dedicated prison psychiatrists who worked diligently with me during the first several years of my life sentence, I thought about my adoptive family and my past ways of relating and reacting, primarily to my father. I came to appreciate many of my father's positive characteristics. He was a good employer to the men who worked for him. In some ways he was a good husband and provider to my mother. He repaid the good will and financial backing he received from my mother's parents

when he wanted to go into business for himself. He financially assisted the higher education of my mother's two brothers, my Uncles Joe and Curly, who both became osteopathic physicians. He was also a generous person in the community, and self-assured enough to befriend our town's only Italian man, only Jewish man, and an obviously gay man. The community responded by voting him into a Justice of the Peace position, for which he never campaigned. The position did not provide large financial rewards, but it brought him substantial respect.

The more I thought about my father in relation to myself, the more I realized that he was not a self-assured parent. I believe he felt threatened by me, even when I was a small boy. As long as he had the physical ability, he bullied me. As I gained in age, stature and athletic prowess, his fear, resentment and hostility toward me grew. I cannot explain the sexual abuse, or his seeming lack of awareness about the sexual exploitation I incurred from the young man who taught me to drive. I suspect that his own relationship with the gay man in Birmingham may have been sexual, but I do not know for certain. I do know that my father's abuse tore the fabric of my childhood and that was the condition of my Self (in Freud's terms) as I entered manhood.

I have thought recently about my father as a product of his own upbringing and realize that I know next to nothing about my grandfather, Peter Taylor, Grandma Taylor's husband. What my father told me as I grew up made it appear that Grandfather Taylor died when my father was still a boy, and that he had to work to support his family during high school. However, when I visited the Taylor family gravesite near Quaker Hill in 1996, I saw that Peter Taylor died in 1919, when my father was thirty-two years old. I was not born yet in 1919, but in all the family conversations I heard during those many summers with the Connecticut Taylors, I never heard one single word about Peter Taylor. I believe he could be the key to understanding his first-born son, James Walter Taylor.

No matter how conflicted the relationship between us, as I thought about my father, particularly after his death in 1959, I regretted my own extreme hostility toward him. I often fantasized about how, if ever I had the chance to be in his presence again, I would hug him and say, "Let's forget the past and start all

over again." But I am not naïve enough to believe my father would respond lovingly. Just because I have changed, there is little likelihood that James Walter Taylor would have a different attitude toward me, even in the hereafter.

I remember my mother, Esther Norton Taylor, only with love. She was a warm person, and she often tried to protect me, usually unsuccessfully, from my father. She did not command the respect from my father that Grandma Taylor did, perhaps because she pleaded with him to stop his abuse, rather than demanded it. She did not have the same natural strength of character as did Grandma Taylor, and yet my mother was a very dear person. I have no understanding of my mother's participation in the nude family swim event that I so hated, nor of her awareness of what my father was doing with me sexually in their bed.

My mother made peace with my father despite his faults. She was a woman of her times, and those times called for wives to be economically dependent and subservient in marriage. She enjoyed the life my father provided her. Yet I know she suffered immensely as she watched my father berate and abuse me, unable to stop it. I am sure she never considered divorce, as divorce was regarded as a disgrace in those days.

Eventually, I left the family home in order to protect my mother from the anger that my father displaced onto her when he could no longer physically handle me. I deeply appreciate my mother's efforts to shield me from my father, and I am ashamed of the sorrow and embarrassment I caused her with my irresponsible, and later criminal, behavior. She deserved better from me.

The series of failures I experienced, as a young family man and as a collegiate and professional athlete, damaged my self-confidence and left me disillusioned about my life's prospects. I hated the thought of conforming to society's prescription for success: to achieve, in sequence, education, career, marriage, family, old age and finally, death. That route turned me off, probably because it was too close to the course my father endorsed. I knew what I did not want, but I had no clear idea of what I did, except for fame and fortune. And I wanted both of them immediately, so that I might flash them in my father's face, but not because I thought this would gain his approval. No, by this time, I wanted to hurl

my successes at him in order to retaliate, to exceed all his accomplishments, and to prove him wrong for all his assertions of my inadequacies.

My emotions propelled me. Although I did not understand until a long time later that I was the victim of sexual abuse by my father, by my driving instructor, and by the Naval petty officer, I was deeply affected and confused by those experiences. Further, I believe that the many head injuries I incurred on the athletic fields of my youth contributed to my impulsiveness and irrational behavior. My first arrest and criminal charge resulted from an act I never even dreamed was a crime. I merely went along with a friend's story about our being FBI agents so that we could keep our dates out late. Then I was thrown in among the wolves at Goochland State Farm for post-dating some checks. My punishment included being raped innumerable times. I traveled on a very slippery slope, and could not perceive a way off the incline. Next I knowingly engaged in some indisputably criminal behavior, by participating in a stolen car ring. When I was sent to the federal penitentiary at Terre Haute, I knew I was a psychological mess. I repeatedly pleaded for psychological treatment, but the authorities chose to ignore this request. Shortly thereafter, I was sentenced for my most serious, deadly offenses. Psychiatrists diagnosed me with schizophrenia, which internally I rejected, not believing that I had ever suffered the break with reality, delusions or hallucinations, nor dementia, which characterize this condition. Outwardly, however, I consented to the diagnosis, and then explored whether this might reduce the sentence I had received. Today I would say that I suffered from a personality disorder characterized by narcissistic, antisocial, and even paranoid thinking and activity. My history of head injuries added another layer of distortion to my thinking. Further, I had totally lost contact with any sense of God or my spiritual self, as these ideas were never a strong part of my upbringing.

I hardly recognized the person I had become on that cold November night in 1955. I never intended to kill anyone, certainly not a cordial stranger, yet I had. But I was not ready, until some time later, to take responsibility for my actions. So when I had the clear intuition that my arrest was imminent, I planned to not be taken alive, and to take out any arresting officers with

me. That is why I put the loaded guns around me when I went to sleep that night. And yet, if I had really wanted to die, and to kill more, the logical thing to do was to stay awake, ready to defend myself in that bedroom. On some level, obviously, I wanted to be caught alive, face the consequences of my behavior, and be prevented from any further destruction.

I became a respectable person in my own eyes only after I opened myself to faith in God, the goodness of love, and the satisfaction of helping others. Focusing on these, I could put the losses I faced into proper perspective. I have come to a place of forgiveness, balance and peace. The competitive athlete in me, who spent countless hours perfecting his shots at the free throw line, believes we must strive for perfection in all the day-to-day areas of our lives. But I also believe that we will not become perfect and whole until we are reunited with God after death.

It sounds like a strange thing to say, but I now believe that a long-term prison sentence was my salvation. I thank God for my confinement because it gave me time to change. I also thank God for bringing into my life some very special people who believed in me. By His grace, I was able, over time, to glean from these miserable places called prisons the lessons I never learned as a child, youth, and young adult. Perhaps I was enabled to do this precisely because at the funeral of my victim, Kenneth Lindberg, the pastor prayed for me, and may have, by his example, encouraged the mourning family and community to do likewise. I like to think that those prayers were powerful enough to have had a significant impact on my life. Kenneth Lindberg's funeral took place before I was arrested, and I did not have occasion to read about the funeral in the newspapers; Reverend Vetvick mentioned it when he counseled me in jail as I awaited my fate. I know I was heartened and very moved by reading that Mrs. Lindberg, despite her grief, publicly asked that I not receive the death penalty.

During the psychotherapy I received at the Medical Center, I never trusted any psychiatrist enough to talk about the sexual abuse from my childhood and adolescence, nor about the sexual exploitation I endured at Goochland. My conscious reason was a concern that I would be labeled homosexual and assigned to live in the unit designated for them. Having briefly experienced that unit after the authorities discovered my stash of women's

clothing, I knew the hazards of rampant promiscuity and subsequent violence. As I look back, I see that the shame I felt as a sex abuse victim might also have deterred me from confiding in the psychiatrists. After I left the Medical Center in 1968, there was never again an opportunity within the prison system to engage in psychotherapy. So I came to some understanding of what constitutes sexual abuse in the same way the general public came to understand the subject—by reading about this issue in the popular press. I know now that I was not responsible for the acts of the significantly older males who abused me.

When I began my sexual relationships in prison, I was not the victim I had been in my youth. Yet, my decision to act as a female was not freely chosen, but a means of survival. It also offered a way for me to avoid hurting other people. As a young man who sought sexual pleasures, I hurt many women and their families, and I did not want to hurt people any more. As time went by, the female role became familiar, and even comfortable, to the point that I believed it to be a manifestation of my true nature. Seemingly it became a logical next-step for me to seek surgery to become as biologically female as possible. I was not able to gain a balanced perspective on these matters until after my release from the prison system.

When people now say to me, "What a shame," or "What a waste," referring to the major part of my life spent in prison, I reply, "No, not at all. I had some rare experiences that few other people have in this life, and through these experiences I learned exactly what I needed to learn." I decided I wanted to be an accountant. That I studied accounting was ironic, because I so resisted my dad's urgings that I become a proficient mathematician while I was in school. I also learned a lot about the law and became a better-than-average jailhouse lawyer. I lost many of these skills and specific knowledge in these fields when I was assaulted and suffered the traumatic brain injury in 1987. These days I often wonder how my life might have differed had I retained my full intelligence, memory and professional skills.

Most importantly, in prison I learned about human beings. There were educated and sophisticated staff and inmates, as well as buffoons and disturbed people in both groups. I carefully studied the people I encountered, because I wanted to understand

their motivations and their philosophies of living. I gathered this knowledge to use in my own quest for self-improvement. Also, because a penal community has more than its share of the emotionally, mentally and physically needy, I had many opportunities to share what knowledge I acquired and to help others if I could.

From the beginning of my confinement in federal custody, I had the sense to not make my situation any worse than it already was. From those early years to the later ones, I had many chances to escape. Over and over, I declined invitations to accompany others in their escape plans, maintaining in my mind, that with enough diligence on my part, someone in authority would listen, hear, and then act on my behalf so that the system itself would someday set me free.

Over the decades, I came to understand and to accept responsibility for the harm I had done to so many people. I became sincerely remorseful, yet cognizant that, though I may wish to, I could never fully compensate those I had harmed. All I could do was to turn myself around, to transform my own Self into the kind of man I could respect. That is what my mission became—to be the best person I could be within my environment.

I started the process of coming to terms with myself, and I saw a self-centered, irresponsible, resentful, confused, depressed and immature person. When Larry Nelson reached out to me, he continued the work that Reverend Leo Vetvick began. From Larry, I felt real love, and I absorbed his caring like a man parched with thirst. When Larry told me to go ahead and use my knife against a guard if I was so determined, he also told me he did not want me to do this, and I put the knife down out of love for Larry. That incident was momentous in my realization that I could change, that there were desirable ways to live my life, even in confinement, and that love was powerful in the process of change. I wanted to become a better person, and Larry was an excellent model of the kind of man I wanted to be.

It was during those years of my association with Larry Nelson that I read *The Magnificent Obsession*. Many people, I have learned, find inspiration for turning around their lives through religious faith. I found that to be true for myself, also, but only later, after I had other transformative experiences. I experimented with the methods I read about in *The Magnificent Obsession*, reach-

ing out to others in need, helping them without any expectation of reciprocal help or expressed gratitude, and to my surprise, I experienced considerable satisfaction, and even happiness. Paradoxically, though I did not expect it, I was rewarded with many blessings. Other people helped me when I most needed help, and some offered themselves in friendship. I had friends like I never had before, and true friends are invaluable in prison. I discovered that in focusing my attention on the problems of others, instead of considering only my own suffering and predicament, most of my own personal problems resolved themselves.

My faith developed in God, the Source of Goodness. Once God was real to me, I begged Him for forgiveness and mercy. I prayed intently and eventually felt that God forgave me. I was then able to forgive myself, and I felt peace within for the first time in my life. I could only then forgive others for wrongs done to me. I forgave my father because he never understood that the kindness and encouragement he demonstrated in the outside community would have been the most effective techniques to gain harmony within our home. I forgave the lieutenant at Springfield who destroyed all the family photos and letters I owned. I even forgave the federal prosecutor who did his best to secure the death penalty for me as a means of advancing his career.

I did not forge a new sexual Self until the last several years, and not while I was imprisoned. It was meeting, loving, and being loved by Katherine that impelled me to re-evaluate my sexual Self. Since Katherine loved me as a man, I wanted to be a complete man for her. Yet, the female persona offered me a comfortable space, a space I felt I still needed if I was to be alone in this world. As much as I wanted to trust that Katherine's love was enduring, and she would be my lifelong companion, I was not immediately certain. Over a period of time, I developed the necessary trust, and Katherine became my new comfortable space. I now regard my attempts to be a woman as an escape maneuver from the miserable life I was forced to live for so long. It afforded me a way to leave my own body and mind, and to take on another Self. To come to trust Katherine completely has allowed me to more fully integrate the feminine side into the masculine side of my Self, and thus reclaim my true male identity.

Like the mythological Tiresias, I gained a unique perspective from my experience in the female role. I am not nearly so im-

pressed with the power of money, authority, and physical strength as I used to be. I developed sensitivity to my own and others' emotions and feelings, and I discovered a nurturing, caring side of myself. These characteristics are now a part of my persona, and give me balance.

When I lost most of my vision, my friend Jean told me that this was an opportunity for me to grow. After initially reacting with anger to that idea, I realized Jean was right. I developed the senses of sound and touch more fully to compensate for my loss of sight, taste and smell. Before, I always counted on reading others' body language accurately. When I could no longer see those bodies clearly, I put greater reliance on my intuition, thus honing it into a keener tool. I became much more able and willing to engage with those who had mental or physical disabilities, as I came to realize that disabilities do not define the person.

Since I have been so involved in the criminal "justice" system in this country, I developed some strong opinions on the subject. I fiercely oppose capital punishment, primarily because I accept the teachings of Jesus Christ, who advised us to do good to those who hate us and to always act with love. I fully realize that some people are so anti-social and dangerous they should not be allowed into free society. We do not yet have the knowledge and skill to successfully treat such social pathology. But unfortunately, Americans neither have the will nor the wisdom to regard and treat criminals as the psychologically disturbed people they are. In my opinion, many criminals are the resultant "mistakes" when families, neighborhoods, and larger communities do not adequately nurture all children. Instead of trying to correct our mistakes, Americans prefer to bury them, in prisons or in the ground—out of sight, out of mind. We react to these people with fear, anger, and disgust, and often leave our intellects out of our calculations. We treat such human beings like spent coffee grounds. And then we wonder why parolees re-offend.

We are able to bury people who commit horrendous and violent crimes because we define them as unlike ourselves, as an "other." The "other" becomes worthless, a disposable object. Then sometimes the "other" is one of us—our brother, our father, our friend. We may then finally realize that revenge, punishment, and the death penalty are not answers. Why do we have such diffi-

culty understanding what Jesus taught through his life—that violence is never the right answer to violence, and that only love and forgiveness are acceptable?

I observed hundreds, perhaps thousands, of men who have broken the law, and I do not believe that punishment alone ever changed one of them in a positive direction. I did, however, see men become more resentful as they were punished, and then leave prison as prime candidates for committing even worse crimes than their original offenses. Make no mistake; I am not arguing that all serious offenders need is love and forgiveness. Nor am I saying that punishment is totally counterproductive. My argument is, that while punishment is necessary and often therapeutic for the serious offender, it is not enough. We should study people who commit violent crimes with an eye toward both helping them change toward the good and preventing young people from developing into the same kind of disordered adults.

For as long as I can remember I have questioned and even resented most of the authority figures I have known. I believe, over the course of my life, I tempered that resentment to a socially appropriate degree of cynicism. Related to that idea is my own aversion to having authority over anyone else. I refuse to allow myself to be in that position. There, people so often attempt to impose their own beliefs, opinions, and will on others, which I do not believe anyone has the right to do.

My spirituality is God-centered, not concerned with specific doctrines or specific religions. I believe that all religions have a share of the truth, but not all of it, and a share of the blame for evil in the world. Thus, religions have no right to my allegiance or to claim that others need to be within their particular fold in order to gain favor with God. I worship in any of God's houses, with any of His people, and I believe all people are God's people.

I believe in the ultimate value of doing the best with whatever we are given, whether that seems to be good or bad. In my view, every situation we find ourselves in can be regarded for its potential good. To worry about things is useless, and negativity is worthless. After all, I survived when death came so close, so often; there must be a reason for me to be alive. Coming to these insights before I was assaulted in 1987, it was easier for me to hearken to the words of my friend and mentor, Jean, when she told

me that the loss of my vision could benefit me by giving me the opportunity to be more understanding of others with disabilities. The challenge in that remark pushed me further in my philosophy of positive living. A "why me?" attitude is indicative of weakness and lack of faith. I prefer to find strength in the face of difficulty, to have faith that everything on this earth can be put to some good purpose.

My own experiences taught me the ripple effect of positive thinking and good deeds. Not only did the ripples come back to me with countless blessings, I know that people I helped were then energized to give to others in need, to "pass it on." Being negative and causing harm set off just as many ripple effects on humanity and the world. So it comes down to making a choice with the one life we are given—to contribute to the good or to the evil in this world.

Within *The Magnificent Obsession*, I found not only the concept of giving what I had, but also of giving what I had not. In other words, I gave money to people when some authorities advised me to save my money for my own necessities in the event that I might someday be released from prison. I did not give away money because I thought I would not need it in the future. I gave it away because someone else needed it then, and in the faith that somehow, when I needed help, there would be someone to help me. When I finally was released in 1995 with only fifty dollars, forty-two of which had to be spent for transportation to my assigned halfway house, I lapsed into some anger and resentment at the system. But I also maintained my faith that in some way I could not foresee, I would not only survive, but I would be blessed with enough.

My wife introduced me to one of her heroines, Dorothy Day, who lived her Catholic faith radically, serving the poor and the dispossessed while fighting militarism in every way she could. What Dorothy Day taught parallels the lesson about giving in *The Magnificent Obsession*: "Suppose you want to go to California and it costs one hundred dollars. You have fifteen dollars. It is not enough. So give it away, give it to the poor. Then you suddenly have twenty-five dollars, and that is not enough, and the only thing to do is to give it away, too. Even seventy-five dollars. That is not enough. Tell God you want more. Throw it away reck-

lessly. You will get back your hundred-fold. You will get what you need. Maybe it will come in graces. Maybe it will cover your spiritual needs, not just your physical. But sow, sow! As ye sow, so shall ye reap."

The one word for my philosophy of living is "hope." Love is the action that flows from hope, and love is the greatest power and force for change in the world. I feel great sorrow for my actions that flowed from hate; but I have hope, and I have done my best to balance out the evil I have done with acts of love.

My greatest apology and greatest debt belong to the Lindberg family, whose husband and father I stole from their world. From the community of Thief River Falls I took one of its upstanding citizens. If nothing else, the years I suffered in prison for my crime demonstrated the horror of what I had done. No act of mine can ever replace the life I destroyed. Those who knew Lindberg are much older now, and many have probably passed. I know my apology is too late. But, at my own advanced age, it is all I have left to offer.

termination of parole

I MAGINE YOURSELF caught in a fierce thunderstorm or hurricane, unable to find shelter from the pelting rain and violent wind—for days, months, years, decades. This book attempts to describe the reality of spending fifty years in such a maelstrom. I was first arrested at age twenty-five and remained under the jurisdiction of state or federal correctional authorities every moment until September 2000, when I was seventy-five years old. I survived only as a willow tree survives in a storm. The storm to which I was exposed was fierce and as violent as a tropical hurricane. I resisted, but not as a strong tall oak would. I bent, I yielded, and like a willow in a storm, I was not broken.

I sought termination of my parole in 1998, three years after my release into the community. After the usual delay one comes to expect when interacting with the government, the U.S. Parole Commission denied my request, citing their need to continue monitoring my "stability." I wrote the Commission and asked, "What kind of stability—behavioral, mental, physical, financial?" There was no response to my inquiry.

I waited until the year 2000. Federal policies state that after five years on parole, the parolee "shall" (which in legal parlance means "must") be terminated from parole, unless the government shows at a formal hearing that the parolee is likely to present a

danger to society. I prepared for this hearing by hiring an attorney from Larry Leventhal and Associates in Minneapolis. No parole hearing was ever scheduled, though the five-year mark occurred in April 2000. As the summer waned and I remained on parole, David Garelick, my attorney, made telephone calls and wrote a strongly worded letter to the U.S. Parole Commission. On September 25, I heard the good news that my parole was finally terminated, effective September 18, 2000. On September 26, my parole officer, then a Ms. Betsy Callahan, came to my home with an official document entitled, "Certification of Early Termination." It stated, "You are hereby discharged from parole."

How to react, after such a long wait? I sensed that people expected me to act exuberantly. While I felt both happy and relieved, I was not ecstatic. The reason for this measured response is that I do not require another human being or an organization to certify that I deserve freedom. I knew that a long time ago, in the 1970s, after I had served about twenty years. I already recognized many of the serious flaws in my own character, which led to my wrong choices in the late 1940s and early 1950s, and I had begun long ago a process of making restitution to humanity for the wrongs I had done it. I earned the parole granted in 1980, and every minute I was incarcerated after being arrested in April 1981 was an injustice of monumental proportions. The so-called "Certification of *Early* Termination," dated September 2000, was not early at all—indeed, it was very, very late.

The parole termination document also states, "You are commended for having responded positively to supervision." Supervision, I tolerated. What I responded positively to were the many people who reached out to me with interest, tangible assistance, true compassion, and sometimes even love. This is what changes people and what changed me, not supervision according to a bureaucratic protocol. This is not to say that officers employed by the government could not be agents of change if they interacted with a parolee such as me with sincere interest, as an individual human being worthy of concern.

I hold no malice toward any of those, primarily members of the U.S. Parole Commission, who were responsible for my incarceration well beyond the requirements of justice. So many of these people are unable to see or act upon unmistakable signs of refor-

mation, probably because they are trained well to expect the negative and to protect themselves from criticism for being "soft." I feel real sorrow for these people, who spend years and years in the correctional field, yet cannot realize when the object of their correction has already been corrected. They are blinder than I.

To enter the penal system as a serious offender with a long sentence, a man needs to learn very quickly the ways to survive, or he will not. He needs to learn that it is never safe to report any problems to authorities, even threats of violence. He must figure out how to solve problems on his own. On a few occasions, I made an example of my willingness to physically defend myself, but mostly I created an image of myself as a person who could defend himself and could not be pushed beyond some undefined point. I also defended myself by being a person whom others wanted to protect.

Looking back, I appreciate the decompression experiences extended to me as I passed from the Lewisburg maximum-security penitentiary, through the federal prison at Terre Haute, Indiana, the U. S. Medical Center at Springfield, Missouri, and then three Federal Correctional Institutions, before my final release in 1995. I had to assess these different environments to ascertain exactly what was required to survive in each setting. This was not easy, since by this time I was visually and otherwise impaired. Gradually, the threats to my survival lessened, as the security measures around me decreased. The storm became less tempestuous. I could relax a little and begin to discard some of the survival habits I had acquired.

In very recent years, the federal system has eliminated parole. This means that a federal "lifer" such as myself will not ever have an opportunity for release; he is truly in prison until he dies. For those with lesser federal sentences, the entire sentence is now served in an institution before release to the community without any supervision. I do not believe I needed parole supervision in order to succeed in the community. I am, however, grateful for it. It was the parole system that required me to live in Minnesota, against my will and rational judgment. Yet here I have found happiness in the security and love of my Katherine, and other new friends.

My last parole officer, Betsy Callahan, told me that I could vote, which I did for the first time in my life in November 2000.

No longer do I need to submit a monthly written report to a parole officer regarding my activities and finances. It is unnecessary to request a parole officer's permission for any overnights I want to spend outside my home. Never again will I need to carry a written document that indicates my conviction as a murderer, nor must I report my physical presence to a United States Probation Office if and when I travel to places around the country. In 2003, I even traveled outside the continental United States, to Ireland, as an ordinary citizen with just a passport. I can associate with whomever I please, without avoiding like the plague anyone who has been convicted of a crime. Realizing all this, I believe the storm has finally passed.

My freedom is, however, not complete because of the emotional and mental shackles which are still so much a part of me. Nightmares of being the victim of impending or actual violence have lessened in the last few years and I hope they will leave me entirely in the future. My habit of awaking at five o'clock in the morning, a necessary precaution while in high-security prisons because that is when cell doors are unlocked and one is vulnerable if asleep, has also diminished over time. I always lock our apartment doors, and I lock our fourth-floor balcony door on hot summer nights when Katherine prefers it open. Perhaps I will develop enough belief in my own security that I will shed these habits and other such acquired survival techniques, along with my fear that any police siren I hear is a personal warning. Within me there is a certain degree of stress, which is not the norm among people having more typical life experiences. I hope this will substantially decrease, and that I am not too old to learn how to live in the sunshine of love and freedom.

timeline

1925

June 13: Born to teenage mother, Detroit

1928

January: Placement in Taylor home, Birmingham, MI

1929

Adopted sister Sally arrives

1935

Uncle Louis Markow dies

1936

Grandma Taylor dies

1938

Driving lessons with Bob

1941–2

Cranbrook Preparatory School Bloomfield Hills, MI

Spring: Injured playing baseball—concussion

1942

Fall: Kiskimenitas Springs Preparatory School, Saltsburg, PA

1943

March: 8-day coma due to concussion playing baseball

May 6: Enlists in U.S. Navy

July: Head injury in boxing incident

August 12: Honorable discharge from U.S. Navy

September: Fort Lauderdale High School

1944

April: Mary Bea pregnant

Marries Mary Bea

December: Jackie born

1945

Spring: University of Miami

Fall: University of Nevada–Reno

Breaks ribs playing football

1946

May–July: Nautilus VA Hospital, Miami Beach, FL

Summer: Traveling sales job with Southern Ribbon and Carbon Company, Birmingham, AL

Fall: East Carolina Teachers College, Greenville, NC

1947

Summer: Counselor at YMCA camp, Charlotte, NC

Fall: Sales Job, Lincoln National Life insurance Co., Charlotte, NC

Plays semi-professional football for Charlotte Clippers

Coaches football, University of NC–Charlotte

Coaches football, Charlotte Central High School

1948

Teaches at Conway High School, NC

Summer: moves to Murfreesboro, NC

Late summer: Employed at hotel in Virginia Beach, VA

Impregnates Barbara

Plays District Fast-Pitch Softball Tournament

Moves to Richmond, VA, for National Regional Fast-Pitch Softball Tournament

Works at Morton Jewelry Store

Plays professional football for Richmond Rebels

Breaks collarbone playing football

1949

June: Bay Pines VA Hospital, FL

Bone-graft surgery and long-term rehabilitation

Divorced by Mary Bea

1950

March: Released from Bay Pines, VA, Hospital

Kicks morphine/Demerol addiction

Moves to Phillipsburg, NJ, with Helen

Moves to Abdington, PA

Moves to Buies Creek, NC

Marries Mary Lou

Employed as an insurance agent, Elizabeth City, NC

September 9: Arrested for impersonating FBI agent

Promotion to insurance office manager, Lynchburg, VA

1951

February: Mary Lou gives birth to daughter

Deserts Mary Lou for Charlotte

Marries Charlotte in SC (bigamy)

February 21: Arrested for bad checks

Jailed in Lynchburg, VA

June: Sentenced to Goochland State Farm, VA

1952

February 26: Released from Goochland State Farm

Taken to federal court in Raleigh, NC

Pleads nolo contendre to impersonation charge

Sentenced to 18 months in Federal Reformatory for Men, Petersburg, VA

1953

April 20: Released from Federal Reformatory for Men in Petersburg

July 31: Arrested for involvement in stolen car ring

1954

April 12: Pleads guilty, sentenced to 2 years at the U.S. Penitentiary, Terre Haute, IN

1955

October 29: Released from USP Terre Haute, IN

November 12: Robs bank in Thief River Falls, MN, and kills Kenneth Lindberg

December 8: Arrested in Joplin, MS, and transferred to Hennepin County Jail, Minneapolis, MN, and charged in federal court

Meets Rev. Leo Vetvick

1956

April: Confesses to FBI

July 5: Sentenced to two 10-year terms, plus life term, to be served consecutively in the US Bureau of Prisons

July 12: First suicide attempt, arrives at U.S. Penitentiary in Leavenworth, KS

Attempts suicide again

Transferred to the U.S. Medical Center for Federal Prisoners, Springfield, MO

1957

October 28–29: Forensic Psychiatry Seminar, meets Dr. Karl Menninger

1959

January: Father dies

Meets Larry Nelson

Works in Education Department of the Medical Center

1960

Reads *The Magnificent Obsession* by Lloyd Douglas

1961

Review hearing in federal court, Minneapolis, MN

1964

February: Mother dies

1968

April: Transferred to U.S. Penitentiary in Leavenworth, KS

May: Transferred back to Hennepin County Jail, Minneapolis, MN, to wait for review hearing

1969

November: Brief review hearing federal court

November: Returned to USP Leavenworth, KS

1972

Begins correspondence with Jean T.

1975

Stabbed at USP Leavenworth, KS

Transferred to USP Lewisburg, PA

1978

Transferred to U.S. Penitentiary in Atlanta, GA

April: Jean's presentation to parole commission

Transferred back to Lewisburg, PA

1980

January 28: Released from USP Lewisburg on parole

Lives in halfway house, Anderson, IN

Sells voice-stress analysis equipment and Amway products

Attends Anderson College

Counseled to wear female clothing

May: Moves to own apartment

Rents house with Patsy and her children in Alexandria, IN

December: Marries Patsy

1981

April 25: Arrested and charged with armed robbery, held in Madison County (IN) Jail

Suffers heart attack

Charges reduced to conspiracy to commit armed robbery

1983

March 14: Judge Sauce suppresses wiretaps and dismisses charges, without prejudice

March 16: Taken into federal custody and transported to USP Terre Haute, IN

April 4: Preliminary Parole Revocation Hearing; no witnesses allowed; probable cause found to hold for final hearing

July 21: Final parole hearing held ahead of schedule, sentenced to 72 months (6 years)

July 22: Returned to USP Lewisburg, PA

August: Charges reinstated in Indiana

August: US Parole reaffirms the July decision of Hearing Examiner except more than doubles the sentence to 168 months (14 years)

1985

March 8: Transported to IN to stand trial on reinstated charges

August 15: Judge Sauce dismisses charges with prejudice

August 16: Returned to USP Lewisburg, PA

1986

February 19: Interim parole hearing, 1983 decision reaffirmed

1987

March 2: Assaulted with lead pipe during Unicor job

May 19: Transferred to USP Terre Haute, IN

September 25: Transferred to U.S. Medical Center for Prisoners, Springfield, MO

1988

March 30: Interim parole hearing, 1983 decision reaffirmed, false information found on record

Assumes correction of the erroneous record

May 11: U.S. Parole Board affirms March decision of Hearing Examiner and supports the affirmation based on false record

Writes U.S. Parole Board with documentation that their records regarding the murder in 1985 are erroneous and asks for the correction of record

1989

October 2: Transferred to FCI Phoenix, AZ

1990

November 5: Transferred to FCI Ashland, KY

1992

Interim parole hearing, 1983 decision reaffirmed

March 13: Transferred to FCI Fort Worth, TX

April 12: U.S. Parole Board affirms Hearing Examiner's decision and supports affirmation based on false record of a 1985 murder

Writes letters to all member of the U.S. Senate Judiciary Committee

1993

May: Records corrected

1994

May: Informed that records corrected

1995

March 29: Parole granted; flies from Fort Worth to Minneapolis

Lives in halfway house

Meets social worker Kathleen Murphy

August 1: Moves into own apartment

November: Attends Guide Dog training in MI, receives Copper

December 25: Gives Kathy engagement ring

1996

May 4: Marries Kathy

September: Travels to MD, PA, MI and CT to see relatives, friends and old haunts

1997

April: Reunites with sister Sally, FL

2000

February: Meets daughter Jackie, FL

September 18: Parole terminated

2005

April: Copper dies

the confession

Hennepin County Jail
Minneapolis, Minnesota
April 9, 1956 9:25 a.m.

I, JAMES PETER TAYLOR, make the following free
and voluntary statement entirely of my own
volition to Special Agents Harry D. Berglund and
Richard M. Pranke, both of whom have identified
themselves to me as Special Agents of the Federal
Bureau of Investigation. No threats, promises,
or inducements have been made to me to make this
statement and I have been advised any statements
I make can be used against me in court. I have
also been advised of my right to counsel. In view
of this, my counsel, Irving Nemerov and Walter
Riordan, are both present representing me while I
give this entirely free and voluntary statement
to Special Agents Richard M. Pranke and Harry D.
Berglund.

My name is JAMES PETER TAYLOR. I was born June
13, 1925, at Detroit, Michigan.

During the whole of my incarceration at the
federal penitentiary at Terre Haute, Indiana, I
sat in on many sessions which were composed wholly

of different inmates, ideas, or schemes to pull off the perfect crime, etc. Often I would sit and interject a comment, other times possibly ridicule. On one occasion a group of us got talking about the advisability of trying. Each man was going to do a crime or commit a crime, something that was big from a monetary standpoint. Many of the men present made comments about the different ways they would rob a bank.

Several times, on later occasions after this one particular session, I talked to smaller groups concerning the same thing. After many of these sessions, I went to a Mr. Ben Bakken, an inmate in the penitentiary with me. We discussed very thoroughly the different ways in which a bank could be robbed. Since I had never been an advocate of violence, I told Bakken that I would rather work out something if I was going to rob a bank, where no violence would have to be used: that is, a weapon or gun, or anything like that. I saw Bakken on two or three different occasions by himself, after the rest of the inmates had gone to institution movies. We sat on his bunk and discussed at length bank procedure. I asked him whether he knew of any bank that would have a substantial amount that he could thoroughly case for me. Mr. Bakken told me then that there was a chain of five banks in northern Minnesota. I think Mr. Bakken mentioned that his bank was one of this chain of five, but I am not positive. When I professed interest in one of these five banks he had mentioned, he definitely steered me away from the bank where he had been employed, and went on to state that there was a bank at Thief River Falls which was the main bank.

Mr. Bakken stated that the Thief River Falls bank was the hub or parent bank of this group.

He then went on to describe in minute detail
the interior of the bank itself and the two main
employees of said bank: these employees being a
Mr. George Werstlein and a Mr. Kenneth Lindbergh. « 1
He then stated that Mr. Werstlein had been a
very sick man for a number of years and spent
little time at the Thief River bank, delegating
most of the responsibility to Mr. Lindbergh. He
further stated that Mr. Werstlein, because of his
insurance business, was seldom present for any
long periods of time at the bank.

I asked Mr. Bakken what kind of a man Mr.
Lindbergh was. He described Mr. Lindbergh in
every way, his character, habits, his weaknesses,
in such a way that I felt I knew the man before
I even met him. Along with this description, he
informed me that Mr. Lindbergh would be anxious
for new business to come into the bank and that on
this score he would be very gullible.

I went on to ask Bakken what would be the best
way if one were going to try to get all of the
funds from the Thief River Falls bank and to do so
without using force or violence. He said at that
time to give him a few days to think the matter
over and to see him the next time the inmates went
to the movies. On the next occasion Mr. Bakken
said he had thought the whole matter over and he
came up with the following idea:

He stated that if a business man were to make
an appointment to deposit a rather large sum of
money in the Thief River bank after hours, that
he believed the vault would be left open. I asked
Mr. Bakken how he had come to this conclusion.
He said that that would be his practice and that
he knew Kenneth Lindbergh personally, and that he
felt sure that he would handle this matter in the
same way. I then asked Bakken what amount should

1. This spelling is how it appears in the original FBI confession.

be used when calling, stating that this deposit
was to be made. When no answer was immediately
forthcoming, I mentioned $40,000. Bakken told
me that this was too much: that $25,000 would
be a better figure and would not arouse as much
suspicion.

After having this last talk with Bakken, I
talked to several other inmates; one being Roy
V. Moore, the other being Lloyd Kern. Moore was
interested and said that he would meet me at Terre
Haute upon my release. In the meantime he would
contact my parents and do some things for me.
When he did not contact my parents I then talked
further with Kern, who decided that he would go
into this Thief River thing with me. I then went
back and talked to Bakken once more. We discussed
how many men it would be advisable to use in such
a crime. Bakken then asked me, "What will I get
out of it?" I then asked him what he wanted. He
said just as long as he got a few thousand dollars
he would be satisfied. He then told me "Please
do not do anything as long as I am still in the
penitentiary." I told Bakken it would be better
if it was done while he was in the penitentiary,
since once he was out he might well be a prime
suspect.

Upon my release October 29th (1955) from Terre
Haute, I went first to Brazil, Indiana, where my
foster parents had sent some clothing for me
to pick up. While in Brazil I made three long
distance phone calls; one to Mr. And Mrs. Emil
Keller at Detroit, Michigan, asking them to send
me some money as I had a deal cooking in Missouri
that would mean a few thousand dollars to me; that
upon the conclusion of this deal I would see them
in Detroit.

2 »

2. Perhaps I was trying to distance myself from my (adoptive) parents by
 referring to them in 1956 as "foster parents." Or maybe I was trying to
 garner sympathy by implying that I had grown up in foster homes, without
 the permanency of birth or adoption. Whatever my motivation, I am refer-
 ring to Esther and James W. Taylor, the only parents I ever knew.

At this point I would like to interject the
following:

While at the federal penitentiary, a Mr. Paul
Courtwright, an inmate, informed me that he had
between five and six thousand dollars hidden in
a mine shaft in Missouri. He described in great
detail where this particular money was. He asked
me to please locate the money, find a lawyer, and
get him started to work on getting him removed to
a federal hospital: that the balance of the money
would be mine.

After phoning the Kellers in Brazil, Indiana,
I telephoned a Russell Scott in Tennessee, who is
the brother of a Mr. Jack Scott, who is an inmate
at Terre Haute. The inmate Jack Scott had told
me that he would help me out when I first got out
of the penitentiary and had directed his brother
to send me $100.00 upon request. I then phoned
to Indianapolis making a hotel registration for
that night. I went to Indianapolis, then checked
in at a hotel, and went to Western Union. I went
to Western Union and received $200.00 which the
Kellers in Detroit had sent me. I then contacted
Mr. Scott in Tennessee by phone (I had missed him
on the first call from Brazil, hadn't been able to
locate him). Mr. Scott in turn sent me $100.00
which I picked up at the Western Union Office later
that evening.

That same night I called my ex-wife, Mrs. Alice
M. Cote. Around midnight I got on board a plane « 3
and traveled to Louisville, Kentucky, where I
immediately located Lloyd Kern. We then talked
at length about the Thief River junket which we
had discussed while in prison. I informed Kern at
this time that my plans had changed: that I had
some other things I was going to do in Missouri.
I stayed several days with Kern and then went by

3. I am not sure I was ever legally married to this woman, but perhaps I was.

plane to Joplin, Missouri. I arrived on a Sunday around noon time. I checked into the Conners Hotel, changed into some old clothes, and went directly out to the area where the lead and zinc mines are located. Most of these mines have been abandoned for years. I arrived at the old mine field and tramped over most of the area without being able to find the exact mine I was looking for. I returned to the hotel.

The next day I returned to the mines with a taxicab driver who I had hired to lower me into the mine shaft. (He drove taxicabs at night). The cab driver by the name of Haley and I then purchased some rope, constructed a "Bosun" seat on which he would lower me into these mine shafts. Some of those shafts were two or three hundred feet deep. I searched most of this week. Finally when I had narrowed the search down and was almost certain that I had found the right mine, I found that this mine had caved in a month or two previous to my arrival. I tried to get down this mine regardless, but could not, and gave up my attempt to find the money allegedly hidden in the mine.

On the night that Roy V. Moore was supposed to have met me in Terre Haute at the Terre Haute House in Terre Haute, Indiana, being discouraged in my efforts in Missouri, I called the Terre Haute House and had Moore paged. He was not there. It was then that the Thief River project came back to mind. By this time I had already wired the Kellers in Detroit for another hundred dollars which they had sent me, just when I was about to run out of money.

I had done everything that I could to try and help Paul Courtwright, including calling his brother in Denver, Colorado, on several occasions,

(which were lengthy conversations). I called
another brother in Kansas City. I contacted his
people in Oronogo, Missouri. Now almost without
funds I realized I had to do something, or I felt
I had to do something. I then, since my arrival,
had been using the name FREDERICK ISIDORE, and had
met a young lady who worked in the Travel Service
Office in the Conners Hotel. I had no identification
of any kind but through this young woman was able
to cash a $500.00 personal check on a non-existent
bank account in Birmingham, Michigan. Using the
money gained from this check, I left Joplin and
traveled to Louisville, Kentucky, where I again
contacted Lloyd Kern. The original plan, as we
once again went over in regards to the Thief
River Falls bank, was to go to Thief River Falls
using two automobiles. I had accumulated a fairly
sizeable amount of Nembutals with which to put
Mr. Lindbergh asleep with. We were also to have
bought planned and elaborate disguises in Chicago,
Illinois.

At this point I would like to add that Mr.
Bakken had exaggerated greatly the amount of money
that was actually kept in the Thief River Falls
bank.

Kern and I talked this whole thing over again
but his wife was very reluctant to let him use
her car. I had been introduced to Kern's wife as
an old service buddy by the name of Jim Rogers.
I proposed to his wife that she allow him to use
the car to go to Detroit: that I had friends there
who would get him a job. I might add that Kern was
out of work at the time and on parole from Terre
Haute.

While in Louisville I went to a bank and got
a $5.00 cashier's check which I then forwarded
to the bank in Michigan on which I had written

the $500.00 check in Missouri. With this check
I enclosed a note stating that this was to open
a new account with $5.00: that more would be
forthcoming as soon as other financial arrangements
and a transferal of funds was made.

Kern's family was in very bad shape financially.
His wife's automobile too was in very poor
condition. Before we left Louisville I had Kern's
car fixed up. I left his wife with enough money to
tide them over for a week and helped Kern pay some
of his bills at the time.

It was decided that Kern would first leave going
to Chicago driving his wife's car; that I would
wait until several hours had elapsed and would
then go to Chicago by plane. This we did. However,
just before I left to go to the airport an old
boyfriend of Mrs. Kern's, who had been courting
her during Kern's imprisonment, dropped in.

Kern and I had prearranged our meeting at a
certain hotel, I don't remember the name of it,
in Chicago. I arrived first and checked in at this
hotel, went to bed and awaited Kern's arrival. It
was the original plan to go into Thief River Falls
in a stolen automobile leaving Kern's car parked
somewhere. Just before Kern had left for Chicago
I gave him the greater part of the money we had
left, so that if he had any car trouble, or any
emergencies came up, he would be able to take care
of them.

When Kern first arrived at the hotel and came up
to my hotel room, I mentioned his wife's visitor.
Kern at the time did not seem to be too disturbed
over this but a very short while later, left the
room, stating he had to do some errand of which
I have now forgotten. He said he would be back
within half an hour. This was about 8:00 in the
morning. I waited for several hours and Kern did

not reappear. I later learned that he had returned directly to Louisville.

 Time 10:25 a.m. (Intermission)
 to 10:32 a.m.

 I waited around the hotel lobby, walked around in front of the hotel, still thinking he might return. Finally I returned to the hotel room, whereupon counting what was left of the money I had, I realized I could little more than get to Thief River Falls by plane. I had checked the schedule by phone in my room. I called from a telephone booth, checked the schedules, and had found out that after arriving in Thief River Falls, I would have a total of a little over $4.00 if I were to even attempt what we had started by myself. I don't know why I even started after this. It seemed like I was caught up in something that I had just gone so far and was bound to go the rest of the way regardless. I didn't even have enough money to procure the disguises, since Kern had the bulk of the money, nor did I have a weapon in the event that some trouble arose. I went to a hardware store which carried sporting goods, thinking possibly I could buy an old second hand gun. This store did not carry any firearms at all but suggested that I go to another place which they named. This was quite some distance away and would have consumed hours of time. I saw a hatchet lying upon the counter and asked the man how much it was. I bought this hatchet which was a typical boy scouts hatchet. I didn't have any idea of what I wanted to use the hatchet for, other than I felt at least I had some kind of a weapon. « 4
 I left Chicago that evening by plane and flew to Minneapolis. When I arrived at the airport

4. I decided to eliminate from my confession any mention of the fox-hole digger I used in the brutal fight with Lindberg, and instead say that the killing weapon was a small hatchet I bought earlier and later disposed of in the Mississippi River. I embellished the story with details of my purchase of the hatchet and of how I carried it into the crime scene. Sure enough, I heard and read about the long hours divers spent in the dead of that

I asked a young lady at the cigar counter about
the hotels. She mentioned the Nicollet. I went to
the Nicollet Hotel and registered and went to my
room under the name of Herbert F. Johnson. While
in Terre Haute Penitentiary I had picked this
name from a man who lived in Racine, when they
got to discussing different eminent people in his
locality, where they lived and how they lived,
etc. He, during this conversation, told me Herbert
F. Johnson's name and gave me his address. This
man was Anton Urbush.

I then went downstairs, went to the Jolly
Miller and had several Scotch and Sodas, then
returned to my room. This was Friday, November
11th, about 1:00 o'clock in the morning that I
returned to my room. I sat pondering over what
to do. I wanted at this time again to forget the
whole thing but for some reason pushed on. I had a
bottle of whiskey in my bag and had several more
drinks before I went to sleep.

The next morning I went to the Leamington
Hotel where I called the Thief River Falls bank
from the telephone booth in the lobby of this
hotel. I asked for Mr. Kenneth Lindbergh. I
told him when I was on the wire that my name
was Herbert F. Johnson; that I was coming up to
Thief River, and had some rather large business
transactions to make while in that area. I told
him that I would be arriving around three o'clock,
Saturday afternoon, that same afternoon, and
that I realized that this would inconvenience
him, but would appreciate all the help that he
could give me with this particular transaction.
That since I was not acquainted too well with
that area, that he could fill me in with much
pertinent information. I then asked him if he
would be so kind as to have dinner with me that

Minnesota winter, searching for the hatchet in the frigid waters of the Mis-
sissippi. They may have even seen the fox-hole digger in their dives, but
would have ignored it as irrelevant. After many tries, the divers reported
that they could not find the hatchet. I felt some smug satisfaction.

night; that during dinner we could discuss much
of the information which would be so valuable to
me in the forthcoming deal. Mr. Lindbergh then
stated that he was to go, I believe, with his wife
and children to some school event that evening,
but that he would be glad to accommodate me and
make other arrangements with his family so that
he could accompany me to dinner. I hung up the
phone and then the thought occurred to me that I
had forgotten to mention that this was strictly
confidential. I went out to the cigar girl in the
Leamington lobby and got some more change, went
back to the phone booth, and again was connected
with Mr. Lindbergh. I informed him that I was
sorry that I had neglected to add a few minutes
before, that I would appreciate his keeping this
business confidential. That I would be bringing my
secretary, a Miss Hadley, along with me. Would
he be so kind as to make a reservation for us in
a Thief River hotel (two separate rooms)? I then
hung up the phone and went to the airport where I
caught a plane to Thief River Falls.

At this point I would like to interject the
following:

At the time of my arrest, the Nembutals and
other forms of mild narcotics were found in my
possession. I had a doctor's prescription for
these for myself but had gotten them with the
object of using them on Mr. Lindbergh. I left
these by mistake in the hotel room in the medicine
cabinet.

I arrived at the Thief River Falls Airport
at approximately 3:15. I went into the airport
restaurant and ordered a cup of coffee and a roll
or sandwich. I had been drinking again early that
morning to fortify myself for what laid ahead;
just what, I did not know. One man finally offered

to drive me into Thief River Falls, since there were no taxis available. I could not have afforded a taxi now as I had only $.60. I was carrying a small, brown overnight bag, empty except for a shirt, pair of slacks, and the weapon which I had bought at the hardware store.

The man who drove me into Thief River Falls dropped me in front of a hotel stating that this would probably be the hotel where I would stay. I entered this hotel and asked the man in attendance whether he had a reservation for a Herbert F. Johnson. He stated that he did not but that in all likelihood it would be at the other hotel in town to which he directed me. I then walked around the block and entered the other hotel, asking whether they had a reservation for a Herbert F. Johnson. A woman informed me that she did have this reservation and one for a Miss Hadley. I then was quite nervous and came very close to turning back again; however, I didn't, since I could not pay for my way out of Thief River Falls. I stood in this lobby and, though it is not my custom to smoke cigarettes, smoked three or four. I told the woman that I would be back to register later on, picked up the bag, and after asking her directions to the bank, walked over to the bank. I knocked on the bank door. A very genial and smiling man answered my knock, opened the door and introduced himself as Kenneth Lindbergh. We shook hands during which time I introduced myself as Herbert F. Johnson. We walked into the main part of the bank. Mr. Lindbergh called a Mr. George Werstlein over to him and introduced us.

I noticed that a janitor was sweeping the floors in the bank. This was quite a shock as Bakken had informed me that I would not have to worry about anyone else being in the bank at that hour.

Mr. Lindbergh then took me into his office, helped me off with my coat and hat, and we sat down in two chairs facing one another. Mr. Werstlein retired behind a semi-closed partition within six feet from us. I knew that I could not disclose the nature of my business while all of these people were in the bank, but would have to stall off as best I could until they left. I led Mr. Lindbergh to believe that I was the Herbert F. Johnson of the Johnson Wax Company; that we were going to buy a large tract of land in that area to build a new plant; that to date we had kept all of our intentions very confidential and were still in only the planning stages of this new enterprise.

Lindbergh then asked me as to the labor situation. I then went on at great length to discuss how we wanted to use local people as much as possible. We then talked at great length about the number of high school seniors, about working conditions and employment conditions in that area. I t was about this time that Mr. Werstlein re-entered Mr. Lindbergh's office, stating that he was going to leave for home, and before he left, was there anything that he could help with. Lindbergh told Mr. Westlein that "ThanK You, no", he needed no help.

After Mr. Werstein's departure, Lindbergh and I sat and talked about hunting, fishing and athletics. I didn't know whether or not the janitor was still there, I hadn't seen him leave, and I didn't know if Mr. Werstlein would be coming back, or calling back. Shortly thereafter the telephone rang. Mr. Lindbergh answered the phone and affirmed the fact that everything was all right to Mr. Werstlein. He then returned and we talked for some while again. I had cold feet and still wanted to back out but I had no money to leave. I

had sixty cents. I knew I couldn't even get out
of town. Then there was the matter of, I knew Mr.
Lindbergh would ask me about putting the money
away if I tried to leave, this money which I could
not produce.

To stall further I mentioned the fact to Mr.
Lindbergh that he certainly had a nice, modern
looking bank. He then took me on a tour of the
whole bank, explaining the uses of all machines
and systems the bank used. I wanted to do this
myself to ascertain whether or not the janitor
was still in the bank. When we came back to Mr.
Lindbergh's office I opened the subject on hunting
and fishing once more. Finally, Mr. Lindbergh
mentioned, would I want a cashier's check for the
money. Trying a last desperate shot at hoping to
avoid the whole thing, I asked Mr. Lindbergh if
he would like to place the whole bag as it was in
the vault; that a check would not be necessary.
Mr. Lindbergh said he would feel better about it,
and he felt it would be the only way to handle
the matter, would be to give me a cashier's check
for the money. I then asked Mr. Lindbergh whether
or not he wanted to put the bag in as it was
since the money in the bag was in a lot of small
denominations. He said then that he thought it
best if he counted it before locking it up.

I then told Mr. Lindbergh to prepare himself
for a shock. I realized that Mr. Lindbergh was
a large man and that I did not want any kind of
a rumpus. Therefore, I gave Mr. Lindbergh the
following story:

I told him that I was with a large syndicate;
that his bank was being robbed. Mr. Lindbergh very
nearly passed out. I told him to please stay calm;
that no one would be hurt so long as everyone
cooperated. At this time Mr. Lindbergh, as I have

before stated, was visibly shaken, was very pale
and trembling. I felt that he might have a heart
attack. He asked if it would be all right if he
got a drink. I said most certainly and went with
Mr. Lindbergh to the lavatory in the back of the
bank where Mr. Lindbergh had a paper cupful of
water. He seemed to get ahold of himself a little
bit and we returned to his office. I believe it was
around 9:30 or 10:00 o'clock at this time.

Mr. Lindbergh asked me a couple of questions in
regards to why and how his bank was being robbed.
All I said in explanation was that there were
other members of the syndicate in town, some near
his home in the event that he did not cooperate.
Mr. Lindbergh then said, "It is funny thing but I
just mentioned to my wife today that I had never
been robbed." He then said, "Well, we might as
well get what you want."

This is another interjection: During the
conversation that evening in the bank, an alarm
had sounded at the bank. Mr. Lindbergh had gotten
up and gone back near the vault. The alarm ceased
during the time that he was gone. I then picked
up the bag and walked with Mr. Lindbergh to the
vault. He told me that he could not open the
safe where all the currency was since, I can't
remember but I believe that either Mr. Werstlein
had closed the safe with all the money in it just
before he left, or that he had closed it when
that alarm rang. He was able, however, to open up
another safe which contained silver and travelers
cheques. Mr. Lindbergh started to put the contents
of this safe into the bag while I was holding the
bag open. He spilled one box of silver and I then
began to help him as he had become very nervous
again. I asked Mr. Lindbergh, "Are you sure that
you can not open the other safe?" He manipulated

the dials and repeatedly said, "It is impossible;
that it will not open until Monday morning." Much
of this is in contradiction to the information
that I had received from Bakken.

We then walked out of the vault, which Mr.
Lindbergh closed behind us, and left the bag
containing the travelers cheques and silver by
the side door of the bank. During this time I
had been doing a lot of thinking in regards to
what I was going to do now with Mr. Lindbergh. I
couldn't just let him walk out of the bank and I
had forgotten all the sleeping potions which I had
intended to bring. The hatchet remained in the bag
all during this time. Mr. Lindbergh was completely
oblivious that I even had a hatchet. It was in the
bag and the clothes were on top.

In Lindbergh's office I decided that since by
the unusual turn of events, Mr. Werstein being in
town, the janitor being in the bank, and my being
so long delayed causing me to miss all possible
means of transportation out of Thief River, that
I would use Mr. Lindbergh's car to leave with. At
this point I thought of tying him up and leaving
him in the bank. Since I had nothing that I
felt suitable to tie Mr. Lindbergh with, and he
mentioned that Mr. Werstlein might drop in again
that evening, I decided to take Mr. Lindbergh with
me if he would come. I didn't know if he would
come or not. I don't know what I would have done
if he would have said no. I had it in my mind to
take Mr. Lindbergh back to Minneapolis now and
leave him drugged in the room which I was still
holding at the Nicollet Hotel. I wiped off all
the fingerprints in the locale of where I had been
sitting in Mr. Lindbergh's office and had done so
in the bank vault. We put on our coats and hats,
as I informed Mr. Lindbergh that I would be taking

him to Minneapolis, where he would be later set
free.

We walked together toward the rear of the bank
where Mr. Lindbergh turned off all the lights.
Mr. Lindbergh then picked up the bag containing
the travelers cheques and money and we walked out
of the door which Mr. Lindbergh swung shut with
his free hand. I asked him whether it had locked
behind him and he said it had. He then walked to
his car (showing me where it was) and where we
deposited the money in the bag on the floor of the
back seat. We then closed the car up and walked
to the corner in front of the bank. We stood and
talked on the corner for a few seconds. We then
returned to Lindbergh's car. I started to get in
on the right hand side and let Lindbergh drive;
however, he stated he was too nervous. I told
him I would drive but he would have to direct me
out of Thief River Falls. We drove at a fairly
good rate of speed directly to Detroit Lakes. Mr.
Lindbergh played the radio and we talked about
hunting and fishing during this drive. He asked me
several times whether I would please leave his car
where he could find it in Minneapolis, since he
took exceptionally good care of it, and would hate
to see it damaged in any way. I told him that I
was not concerned with taking his automobile, only
in getting out of Minnesota as fast as possible.

After going this far and then realizing only
the travelers cheques and silver, I was quite
disappointed. I knew that I could not carry
all that silver on a plane; that I would have
difficulty in even lifting the bag with all that
silver. When we arrived in Detroit Lakes we drove
past the city itself and on Highway No. 10, on the
southern outskirts of Detroit Lakes, we stopped
for gas. I had driven past this gas station first

and approached it from the south heading north. I
didn't have any money in my pockets still and the
money to pay for this gas came from money that Mr.
Lindbergh handed me. We then drove back into the
center of Detroit Lakes to the Greystone Hotel.
Mr. Lindbergh had stated that he had better call
his wife since she would be worried about him. I
told him I certainly could understand that and
would be glad to give him this opportunity.

I walked into the Greystone Hotel with Mr.
Lindbergh. We both walked directly to the men's
room. After coming back from the men's room, Mr.
Lindbergh stopped in a little hallway to use a pay
phone to call his wife. I stood within six feet of
Mr. Lindbergh every moment he was on that phone.
When Mr. Lindbergh had finished his conversation I
did not have the bag with me. The bag was out in
the car. I think Mr. Lindbergh went along with me
on this primarily because he was afraid that the
syndicate might harm his family.

Mr. Lindbergh and I then walked to the front
door of the hotel. We had just gotten through the
door when Mr. Lindbergh remembered that he needed
cigarettes. I told him that I would get them. He
went over and sat on the arm of a davenport or
chair, with his arms folded, waiting while I got
his cigarettes. I left him and I recrossed the
lobby, went to the woman who was at the hotel
desk, and bought the cigarettes for Mr. Lindbergh.
I then returned to Mr. Lindbergh, who was still
waiting for me near the door, and we walked out of
the hotel together. I handed him the cigarettes at
this time. We got back into Mr. Lindbergh's car
and started toward Minneapolis.

Mr. Lindbergh by this time had grown very
apprehensive and exceedingly nervous. I knew,
since I had already checked train and plane

schedules out of Minneapolis, that I had to follow
a very fast schedule from here on in. I knew that
I could not carry all of that silver around with
me. Twice I turned off the main Highway No. 10
and started down roads looking for an appropriate
place to ditch all the silver. On the second or
third time I found the road that turned out to be
Fiereck's farm road. I stopped the car, Lindbergh
and I each got out. He asked me what I was going
to do. I told him that I was going to bury the
silver. I took the bag out of the back sear and
with Mr. Lindbergh's help transferred it to the
trunk where I emptied the bag of its contents.
(Mr. Lindbergh did not see the hatchet. We just
emptied the money here.) The boxes of silver
dollars were very, very heavy. I decided that we
would try to find a place on the other side of a
barbed wire fence in which to bury the silver. The
only digging tool that I had at this time or could
use as such was the hatchet. At the time that Mr.
Lindbergh reached into the trunk of the car and
got one box of silver dollars in each hand and
turned toward the fence, which we were going to
cross, I picked up one box of silver dollars and
the hatchet with which to use to make some kind of
an entrenchment.

I held the wires open on the fence, the barbed
wire fence, while Mr. Lindbergh crawled through.
He then held the wires open for me. Mr. Lindbergh
and I then began walking down an incline toward
what looked like a little patch or thicket. We
waked almost to the bottom of this incline and
saw no place to bury the silver. We worked our
way up and down looking for a suitable spot. As
we started to go down the incline once more and
were about half way down, I noticed what looked or
felt like a slight depression (it was pitch dark

out). I slipped and stumbled toward Lindbergh. Lindbergh, with the box of silver dollars in his hand, apparently thinking I was attacking him, hit me on the side of the head with the box of silver dollars which he had in his hand. We then commenced a struggle of which I remember very little. I do remember, how much later I don't know, trying to find my hat. I found it and put it on my head only to find it was Lindbergh's. I then, on my hands and knees, searched the area to find my own hat. I found my own hat, picked up some of the silver dollars, returned them to the trunk of the car, leaving all of the silver and the hatchet, which I laid on some papers, in the trunk of the car.

5 »

It all happened so fast that I don't recall incidents. I know that after he hit me I knew that I was fighting for my life and I think Mr. Lindbergh felt the same way. The first conscious thing that I can remember after the struggle with Mr. Lindbergh was the fact of what a horrible thing I had done and what to do now. I took the hatchet and put it in the trunk of the car and laid it upon some newspapers. I then got into the car and at very high speeds drove directly to Minneapolis.

During the struggle with Mr. Lindbergh I had been given a slight nose bleed, had a bruise on the side of my face and head, which I used talcum powder on for several days. My head was full of some kind of thorns, badly scratched, and from the thorns I had a slight infection. I drove to within a half block of the Nicollet Hotel and parked Mr. Lindbergh's automobile.

On the way in from Crescent Lake when I first got to the outskirts of town, I saw a bridge (I got lost at first). I drove out partially upon

5. Substitute "foxhole digger" for hatchet.

this bridge, when I was sure no cars were in the
vicinity, suddenly stopped the car, took the
papers which the hatchet had rested on, and the
hatchet, and threw them into the river. I then
asked several cab drivers directions as to how to
get to the Nicollet Hotel. I parked the car within
a half block of the Nicollet Hotel, picked up the
bag with the travelers cheques, the silver was
still in the trunk, and walked into the Nicollet
Hotel. I was almost in a state of shock myself, so
much so that muddy and bloody as I was, I can not
remember being apprehensive about someone seeing
me. I went directly to my room, took a shower,
changed my clothes, and while doing so, called for
the bell boy to bring me some ice. I used this
ice to make me stiff drinks. The realization of
what I had done had still not completely dawned on
me. If it had I would have used the silver in the
automobile to leave town. I then, after changing
clothes, went back to Lindbergh's car. I changed
the gray flannel suit for a light gray gaberdine
suit. My top coat was so soiled that I had put
it in the bag and was not wearing it. I took
Lindbergh's car to north Minneapolis and parked it
on the first dark and deserted street I saw. Just
as I started to get out of the car some man came
out of the house and walked to his car parked just
a little ways up the street on the opposite side.
I therefore got back into Lindbergh's car and
waited until this man had driven off.

I then walked about a block and a half to two
blocks to an all-night eating place where there
were a great many milkmen having coffee, etc.,
early in the morning. This must have been about
5:45 a.m.

All I took out of Lindbergh's car were the
car keys and the registration which was on the

steering wheel. I got rid of them in Chicago.
Threw them away. I then ordered a cup of coffee
at this all-night eatery. I phoned for a cab to
pick me up at this address. Shortly thereafter
a cab came. I got in the cab, still without an
overcoat and traveled directly to the Nicollet
Hotel. I told the cab driver to wait as I would
be out in a few moments as soon as I had checked
out. I went inside the hotel, went upstairs, and
had another quick, stiff drink. I think I called
for some coffee. I then checked out of the hotel,
called for the bell boy, room service, and went
down to the desk. Up to this time, since arriving
in Thief River Falls, I had used the balance of
the money that Mr. Lindbergh had given me to pay
for the gas. I now was pushed into using the
first travelers cheque which I did. I cashed four
$50.00 travelers cheques with the woman clerk.
This woman did not ask me for, nor was she shown,
any identification whatsoever. The cab driver then
drove me to the airport where I caught a plane at
approximately 7:15 in the morning for Chicago.

Time: 12:14 p.m.
to 1:37 p.m. Adjourned for Lunch

This was the morning of November 13th. Then
I caught a cab from the Midway Airport after
arriving in Chicago and went directly to a hotel
in downtown Chicago. I cashed a small amount of
cheques at this hotel and in Chicago at various
places. I also disposed of the car keys and
registration blank which had belonged to Mr.
Lindbergh. I tore the registration up so that it
wouldn't be readable and ditched them in a trash
can.
That evening I took a plane to Detroit,

Michigan, and from the Willow Run Airport outside
of Detroit I went to a friend's home where I had
been invited to attend a birthday party.

I might add at this point that although several
people have claimed that I had an overcoat on
after I arrived in Minneapolis, and at the time I
arrived in Detroit, this is completely erroneous.
I had thrown some extra clothes over my arm which
might have conveyed the impression I had an
overcoat with me.

After leaving this friend's home at the party's
conclusion, I went to the home of Mr. And Mrs.
Emil Keller in Detroit, Michigan. Mr. Keller was « 6
an old friend. Monday morning I went into Detroit
and went to Kearn's Department Store where I
bought an overcoat. I registered at a hotel right
across the street from a bank in Detroit. I had
first put some travelers cheques in the hotel
safety deposit box. When I asked to withdraw a
portion of these cheques, I believe that I was
informed that I would have to withdraw all of
them. I withdrew all of them and went across
the street to the bank where I began endorsing
the travelers cheques and opening a deposit or
account under the name of Kenwell. After signing
or endorsing the bulk of those cheques, which was
quite a job in itself, I decided to call it a
day and returned later. I believe it was almost,
if not after, the closing hours of the bank. The
man whom I was dealing with at the bank informed
me that before I would be able to withdraw from
this account that I would have to provide him with
identification. I said that my identification was in
the hotel; that I would return, when I returned
the next day to finish signing the cheques,
bringing my identification with me at that time.

I thought that I had taken every cheque into

6. "Emil Keller" is the given name of Bill Keller.

the bank with me. The reason for this being that
when first arriving in Detroit I had rented an
automobile. These cheques had slid down behind the
back seat of the automobile when I had taken the
others out. The American Express cheques were the
ones that had fallen behind the back seat.

After leaving the bank I went to Hudson's
Department Store and bought two pieces of luggage,
giving a check written on this new account. This
check, I was told, would not be cleared until the
next day. I now decided, the devil with the whole
doggone thing. Forget the money.

One day I lifted up the back seat of the car
before I returned it to an agency and discovered
the balance of those cheques. I decided to cash
them. I stayed with the Kellers, I believe, until
the 19th, when Miss Richards arrived from Joplin.
During that week, in this rented car I believe
it was, I drove to Louisville, got Kern up in
the middle of the night, and told him what had
happened as best I could remember it. He then
accompanied me in going to Indianapolis where he
helped me pass these cheques. He was not actually
cashing them but he knew what I was doing and
what had happened. I registered in several hotels
with a piece or more of luggage in each hotel, I
believe, leading the people to believe I was a
doctor; that I was in town for a very short time,
passing through, awaiting an emergency call to
fly out of town. I then waited in the vicinity
of these hotels while Kern would make telephone
calls informing them that the plane was ready
for doctor so and so. At one department store,
where it seemed I might have difficulty in passing
some of these cheques, Kern walked up to me, this
was pre-arranged, and started addressing me as
doctor, and thanking me for what I had done for

his wife during her recent operation. (We thought
this was the end of all the travelers cheques.)
Kern then drove the car which I had rented to
Detroit and I caught a plane back to Detroit. Kern
had automobile trouble on the way to Detroit.
I had lent him the identification I had procured
since I had been in Detroit in the event of an
emergency or road trouble on the way to Detroit
from Indianapolis. When he did not show up on time
I was very much worried. Finally I received a wire
from him stating he was at a motel somewhere near
Fort Wayne.

Kern drove back and I flew back to Detroit.
Kern sent me a wire in Detroit telling me where
I could locate him and to call at once. I had a
very difficult time in locating Kern, since he was
traveling under an alias. When I did locate him
I told him to use my AAA card and get the car
repaired, then come on as soon as possible to
Detroit. Kern arrived in Detroit with the rented
car.

On the night of November 18th I took Kern
to the airport and saw him off, back home to
Louisville. A few moments later I met the plane
bringing Miss Richards from Missouri to Detroit.
She had a reservation at the Detroit Leland Hotel.
The next day Mr. and Mrs. Keller, Miss Richards,
and myself attended a football game at Ann Arbor,
Michigan. Saturday night we all went to Windsor,
Canada, to a supper club. Most of that Sunday
Miss Richards and I drove around Birmingham and
Detroit, Michigan. I believe it was Sunday night
that I saw Miss Richards off at Willow Run Airport
when she left to return to Joplin, Missouri.

I went out to Birmingham, saw one or two old
acquaintances, and later, I don't know the date,
played basketball for a man by the name of Roger

Reynolds in Detroit, with the Industrial Team or
some city league. I had planned to go to Joplin,
Missouri, for the Christmas holidays, as I was
invited to do so by the Richards. However, Miss
Richards seemed to want me to come before the
holidays and I made plans to do so. Mr. Keller, to
save me money, said that I could use his car to
drive to Missouri and he would use the rental car;
thus saving all the mileage.

It was at this time that I discovered, when
turning in one car and getting another, the
American Express cheques underneath the back seat.
I kept these cheques locked in a brief case. I
then decided that before I went to Missouri I
would get rid of the balance of the travelers
cheques I had just come upon. Knowing full well
all that had happened and that everyone would be
watching for these cheques, I can not say why I
did this.

I took a plane to Miami, Florida. When arriving
rented an automobile, registered at many different
hotels, cashing these cheques as fast as I could.
Upon completion of cashing the last cheque, or
what I thought was the last cheque, before leaving
Florida I visited my parents and got all of my
clothes and personal belongings which they had
been keeping in storage for me. My parents were
very cold; however, my mother drove with me down
into the city of Fort Lauderdale where I bought
a steamer trunk with which to put some of the
many things they had been keeping for me. I also
at this time bought a machete and a canteen. The
purpose of buying this machete was for a hunting
trip to clear the underbrush.

When I returned to my parent's house I parked
the rented automobile in the driveway and began
packing all of these boxes, that had been in

storage, into the steamer trunk and other bags of
mine. My father had to leave for a few moments and
when leaving, locked the doors so that I would be
sure not to get into the house. After completing
this packing, I said goodbye to my parents,
returned to Miami, and there in Miami shipped a
great bulk of my boxes through Air Express and
Railroad Express to Joplin, Missouri. I then
returned, via plane, to Detroit, Michigan.

While in Florida I had bought a 30.06 deer
rifle and a .22 caliber target pistol on a thirty-
eight frame. The pistol was for purposes of
"plinking" only. It was my intention at this
time to go hunting when I returned to Michigan,
which circumstances prevented. I then returned
to Detroit and to the Kellers' home. Mr. Keller
met me at the airport at Willow Run and took me
to their home. I then drove Mr. Keller's car to
Joplin, Missouri.

When I had first arrived in Detroit I took the
soiled top coat that I had at the time I was in
Thief River Falls, plus all the papers and folders
which the travelers cheques had come in, out to
an isolated area which I knew near Birmingham,
Michigan, bought a can of gasoline and burned
them.

About the 23rd I had at first intended to go
to New York City to cash the travelers cheques
and had booked a plane reservation to New York
City. The day before I was to leave I went to
a dentist in regards to a tooth that had been
giving me a lot of trouble. This dentist pulled my
tooth. That night I hemorrhaged a good deal from
my mouth. Either that night or the next night I
played basketball. My mouth had been hemorrhaging
on that day. I saw two other dentists in regards
to my mouth in order to stop the bleeding. One

advised me he thought it would be better, when I
told him I was going to New York, to cancel my
plane reservation and go by train, since even in
a pressurized airplane cabin my mouth might start
bleeding again. I played one game of basketball
before I left.

The night I left for New York Mr. and Mrs.
Keller saw me off at the train station. I fell
asleep in the roomette and awoke sometime in the
early morning feeling as if I were strangling. I
turned on the lights in the roomette and found
that I was covered with blood and was bleeding
severely. I tried to stop the bleeding as best
I could. When this proved unsuccessful I rang
for the porter. The porter brought me ice which
I used to try to stop the flow of blood. When
everything we tried was unsuccessful, the train
was stopped at Orrville, Ohio, where a Dr. Pye and
some policemen helped me from the train and took
me to the hospital. I was rushed right into the
operating room where Dr. Pye worked on my mouth.
Later that night Dr. Pye stopped the bleeding.

I was released from this hospital on
Thanksgiving Day and boarded a train bound for
Cleveland. I had now changed my plans and decided
to go to Florida instead of New York. In arriving
at the train station in Cleveland, I attempted
to pick up my luggage, when no redcaps were in
sight, and just this exertion caused my mouth to
start hemorrhaging again. I got into a cab. A few
minutes after riding in the cab my mouth seemed to
cease bleeding to some extent and so I decided to
go to a hotel instead of a hospital. I checked in
at a hotel. No sooner had I checked in and taken a
shower and my mouth started to hemorrhage again.
So I checked out of the hotel, caught a cab and
went directly to the emergency room at a Cleveland

Hospital. I had already made a plane reservation to leave Cleveland.

My mouth was treated at the hospital with vaseline packs, although by the time I had finally gotten to the hospital, it had almost ceased to bleed. I left this hospital and went directly to the airport where I made the trip to Florida. I have already related how I spent the duration of my time in Florida.

After borrowing Mr. Keller's car in Detroit I drove directly to Joplin, Missouri, where I went to Miss Richards' home as I had been invited to stay there. While in Joplin I picked up the articles which I had sent via express from Florida, including the two guns.

The night before I was arrested I played basketball in the town of Anderson, Missouri, for a Joplin team. When the game was over Miss Richards and I returned to Joplin where we had dinner and went to a couple of supper clubs. We returned early in the morning to her home. I went to my room. During the night I had called Mr. Keller in Detroit, telling him that I would be there awhile, and asking him what I owed him so I could send it through Western Union. When we arrived at the Richards' home I went to the bedroom where I had been staying and was awakened just a few hours later by a cordon of Federal Bureau of Investigation agents, who had surrounded my bed with guns and search lights.

A day after I had arrived in Joplin on this last trip I was going through my luggage and I found another travelers cheque. I put it away in my luggage to be disposed of and forgot about it. I understand it was found in my belongings.

Kenneth Lindbergh had no knowledge whatsoever, or had anything at all to do, with this crime,

and previous to the crime I had only been once in the State of Minnesota, which was for a period of

7 »

three hours, when I dropped off some children.

Time: 2:42 p.m. Conclusion of Statement

Signed JAMES PETER TAYLOR (Copy)

Witnessed by:

RICHARD M. PRANKE, Special Agent
Federal Bureau of Investigation
U. S. Department of Justice
Room 412—WCCO Bldg.
625 Second Avenue South
Minneapolis, Minnesota

HARRY C. BERGLUND, Special Agent
Federal Bureau of Investigation
U. S. Department of Justice
Room 412—WCCO Bldg.
625 Second Avenue South
Minneapolis, Minnesota

7. These were Alice M. Cote's children.

acknowledgments

Our greatest gratitude for the completion of this project goes to Ian Graham Leask, our literary consultant who, from the first day we met in 1998, believed in Jim and the importance of his story. Ian quickly disabused us of the notion that Jim needed a ghost-writer; he promised to critique and teach, but he insisted that Jim must write his own story, in his words and style. Ian's faith in Jim and then in the emerging *Willow* sustained us through the years of slogging through all the material, searching for an agent and a publisher, and so many rejections.

At the beginning of our work we received encouragement from the monetary boosts of Susan Grumann, Mary Kohls and Arlis Bovy. Other friends such as Gordon Oien, Miriam Morgan, Patrick Griffin, Kate Kane, Eva Ondrus, Sylvia and Arne Aronson, and Bill Ronan read various versions of the manuscript and provided helpful feedback.

We also recognize the immense contributions of Wendy Kaufman, Jed Bonniwell, and Alexei Esikoff who each edited our work and made it much more readable. And within our partnership, Jim wishes to here say, for the world to know, that he could not have written this book, much less survived and thrived in free society, without his faithful and loving partner, Katherine.